MAIN STREET MILLIONAIRE

How Real People Build Real Wealth – and Keep It!

BY JORDAN D. MAIN

Printed in the United States of America

First Printing, 2025

Cover art by Jordan D. Main and Adam Freund.

Back cover and book layout by Magellan Financial.

TABLE OF CONTENTS

INTRODUCTION

Why Wall Street Jargon Doesn't
Have to Ruin Your Retirement

Imagine you're at a family barbecue in Milford, Michigan, and your cousin starts yapping about "asset allocation", "sector rotations", and "RMDs." Your eyes glaze over faster than a donut at a Tim Hortons, and you grab another burger just to escape. That's how most folks feel about financial planning, like it's a foreign language spoken by Wall Street suits on CNBC. But here's the kicker: you don't need to be a finance guru to build wealth and retire with confidence. You just need a translator who speaks plain English.

I'm Jordan D. Main, president of Main Financial Group in Michigan, and I've spent 20+ years translating that jargon for *real people*— doctors, engineers, teachers—who are rockstars in their fields but feel lost when it comes to money.

Take Dr. Patel, a surgeon from Milford who came to me with a portfolio that looked like a jigsaw puzzle thrown together by a toddler. He had $3.8 million scattered across mutual funds, stocks, and a variable annuity, with fees eating over $67,000 a year.

"Jordan," he said, "I save lives, but I don't know what 'risk tolerance' means."

I compared it to his surgeries: "You wouldn't operate without knowing the patient's history, right? Your portfolio's the same—know its risks, or you're cutting blind."

It clicked.

We rebalanced his investments—50 percent stocks for growth, 50 percent fixed-rates and fixed-income for safety—slashed fees to 0.20 percent, and saved him nearly $1 million in future taxes with a Roth conversion. Now he's on track to retire at 65 and is planning a trip to Italy with his wife. That's what this book is about: turning Wall Street's gobbledygook into stories and strategies you can use to build a secure retirement.

This book isn't a dusty financial manual with charts you'll never read. It's like sitting down with me over coffee at a Michigan coffee house, hearing stories from my career, and getting no-nonsense advice on investing for wealth, balancing risk, cutting taxes, planning income and legacy, beating inflation, and using Social Security as one tool—not the whole toolbox. We'll cover the RIPT framework—Risk, Income, Portfolio, Taxes—to guide you through the chaos. My parents, both schoolteachers, taught me that education is about empowering people, not showing off. When my dad passed, over 1,000 people showed up to his funeral—not for his bank account, but for the lives he touched. That's my mission here: to teach you, not sell you.

Why does this matter? Because the stakes are high. A 2024 BlackRock study found 69 percent of retirees worry about outliving their savings. Inflation, averaging 3.2 percent from 1920-2024, can cut your buying power in half over 20 years. Taxes are a silent leech—401(k) withdrawals are taxed up to 37 percent, and 85 percent of Social Security can be taxable. Long-term care costs $10,000 and up per month in the Detroit area for 70 percent of those over age 65.

But with the right plan, you can dodge these traps. I've seen clients do it—like the couple who boosted their income by $1,300 a month with smart Social Security timing or the widow who turned a $500,000 IRA into a $1.75 million tax-free legacy.

Each chapter uses stories and stats to break down a piece of the puzzle:

- *Chapter One:* Learn why knowing your plan beats trusting the pros, with Susan's $20,000 tax mess.
- *Chapter Two:* Build wealth with compound interest and low fees, like Mike and Lisa's $100,000 fee save.
- *Chapter Three:* Shift to retirement mode, avoiding sequence of returns risk, with Tom's red zone story.
- *Chapter Four:* Match investments to your risk tolerance, like Marjorie's 90-mph portfolio.
- *Chapter Five:* Outsmart taxes with Roth conversions, like Eleanor's $400,000 save.
- *Chapter Six*: Beat inflation with equities and TIPS, like Betty's 2022 struggle.
- *Chapter Seven:* Optimize Social Security like Hannah and John did to boost their monthly income.

- *Chapter Eight:* Plan a tax-free legacy, like Dorothy's $1.5 million gift.
- *Chapter Nine:* Get a second opinion to avoid slow financial leaks.
- *Chapter Ten:* Stress-test for longevity and more, with George's $2 million wake-up.
- *Chapter Eleven*: Choose the right investment tools, like Karen's annuity swap.
- *Chapter Twelve:* Be your own CFO, like Roger's marina reviews.
- *Bonus Chapter:* Avoid the top 10 mistakes, like FOMO-driven crypto losses.

By the end, you'll have a well-rounded plan to build wealth and retire with confidence. So, grab that coffee, pretend we're at a diner, and let's start. Your retirement's too important for guesswork.

THE TAKEAWAY:

Wall Street jargon doesn't have to ruin your retirement. Learn the RIPT framework, use stories and stats to plan, and take control of your financial future with confidence.

CHAPTER ONE

The Education Edge:
Why Knowing Your Plan Beats Trusting the Pros

Picture this: I'm in my early twenties, fresh out of Michigan State with a shiny accounting degree, hunched over a desk in a stuffy office, drowning in tax forms. My tie was crooked, my coffee was cold, and I was starting to wonder if this was the glamorous career I'd signed up for.

Then Susan walked in. A nurse from Livonia, Michigan, Susan carried more than her hospital shift exhaustion—she carried a $20,000 tax bill that had hit her like a freight train. Her broker, all slick pinstripes and easy confidence, had been trading her account like it was his personal casino. He racked up commissions, triggered taxable events she never saw coming, and left her holding the bag.

Her voice cracked when she said, *"He told me to trust him. I thought he was the expert."*

That moment changed me. I realized most people don't lose their retirement because they're careless. They lose it because they walk straight into three traps:

- **Fees** that quietly drain thousands every year, compounding into six figures over a career.
- **Taxes** that blindside retirees when withdrawals, Social Security, and Medicare all collide.
- **Scams** that prey on trust, urgency, and confusion—sometimes wiping out savings in a single phone call.

These aren't rare accidents. They're predictable pitfalls in a financial system that thrives on complexity. And they keep even the smartest people—surgeons, engineers, teachers, executives—one bad decision away from jeopardizing decades of hard work.

Take Tom, a manager from Dearborn. He had saved diligently, building a $2 million nest egg inside his 401(k). What he didn't realize was that his "modest" 1.5 percent annual fee was quietly bleeding away $30,000 every year.

Multiply that by 20 years, and it wasn't a rounding error—it was the price of a lake house, a college education for his grandkids, and the peace of mind he thought he'd earned. His plan wasn't being sabotaged by the market—it was being sabotaged by hidden fees he couldn't even see.

And then there's Emily, a retired schoolteacher. She thought she was helping her grandson when she wired $8,000 to someone claiming to be him, stranded in Mexico. The voice on the phone sounded real—thanks to AI, it was eerily close to her grandson's. It was a scam, and by the time she realized it, the money was gone. Her lifetime of savings wasn't erased, but her confidence was. She told me later, *"I never thought I'd fall for something like that."*

Fees. Taxes. Scams. They're the termites in the foundation of retirement. They don't knock loudly at the door—they sneak in quietly, eating away at everything you've built.

This book is about changing that. It's about giving you what I call the **education edge**: enough clarity and confidence to ask sharper questions, to spot traps before they spring, and to own a plan you actually understand. You don't need to become a Wall Street quantitative analyst. You don't need a PhD in finance. But you do need to know when someone is putting your future at risk—whether it's through hidden fees, tax landmines, or slick sales tactics dressed up as advice.

Because here's the truth: **you don't retire on a mystery, you retire on a plan you understand.**

FROM PENSIONS TO "YOU'RE ON YOUR OWN"

If you want to understand why education matters more than ever, look backwards for a minute.

My parents – I've said it before – they were schoolteachers here in Michigan. When they retired, the checks just showed up—pension every month, Social Security deposits right on schedule, maybe some savings on the side for extras. They didn't worry about whether the market was up or down that week. The risk lived with the employer and the pension fund, not with them. If the stock market coughed, it was somebody else's cold.

But then came the great handoff. In the 1980s and 90s, the 401(k) and 403(b) showed up like the new kid in class and stole the show. What started as a tax loophole for executives quickly became the retirement plan for everyone. Companies realized something: *"Why carry the liability for decades when we can shift it to employees?"*

And just like that, America traded certainty for optionality. Pensions faded away. Retirement shifted from guaranteed income for life to "here's an account balance—good luck managing it."

We swapped pensions for participant statements. We traded security for risk. And along the way, nobody handed out the playbook. Teachers retired with steady checks, but their students—people my age—were left to figure out an entirely new system with little more than a packet of forms and a website login.

That's why education matters more than ever. Today, I meet teachers with over $1 million in their 403(b), engineers with $2 million in their 401(k), physicians with $3 or $4 million spread across practice plans and brokerage accounts. These balances are impressive—built one paycheck at a time—but they come with an invisible weight: **the responsibility of managing risk, sequencing withdrawals, and avoiding common traps.**

Here's the danger: missteps scale. A "tiny" 1 percent mistake on $3 million isn't tiny—it's $30,000. Every year. For decades.

And it's not just fees. Withdraw the wrong dollars at the wrong time, and you can trigger surprise taxes, higher Medicare premiums, or see your Social Security benefits taxed. Put blind trust in the wrong advisor, and you may be walking into a scam or a product that benefits them far more than it benefits you.

This is the new retirement reality: **you're on your own—unless you educate yourself.**

WHY SMART PEOPLE STILL FALL FOR "TRUST ME"

Over the years, I've sat across the table from some of the brightest minds you can imagine. Surgeons who make life-and-death decisions every day. Engineers who design bridges that carry thousands of cars without fail. Executives who manage companies with hundreds of employees and complex budgets. Teachers who shape young minds with patience and precision.

And yet, when it comes to their money, many of them have confessed the same thing: *"Jordan, I just trusted him. I thought he was the expert."*

It's not because they're careless or naïve. It's because the financial industry has perfected the art of exploiting human psychology. Here's why even the sharpest people get tripped up:

- **Authority Bias** – We're wired to defer to people who appear confident and credible. Put someone in a tailored suit, hand them a glossy brochure, sprinkle in acronyms like ETF, REIT, or beta coefficient, and suddenly their recommendations sound like gospel. Clients think, *"Well, he must know what he's talking about."*
- **Decision Fatigue** – A surgeon might spend twelve hours in the operating room, making a hundred high-stakes calls. An engineer might spend weeks running simulations to ensure a bridge doesn't collapse under stress. By the time they sit down to talk finances, their brain is cooked. Saying *"You handle it"* to an advisor feels like relief.
- **Complexity as a Sales Tactic** – The more complicated a product is, the less likely you are to ask hard questions. Advisors know this. They dress up variable annuities, structured notes, or complex mutual funds in layers of jargon. If it sounds too difficult to understand, many clients assume it must be too advanced to question.
- **Incentives You Don't See** – Here's the dirty little secret: if someone only gets paid when you buy a certain product, you're going to hear a lot of reasons why that product is "perfect for you." The pitch often sounds objective, but the paycheck behind it is anything but.

The Surgeon's Blind Spot

I'll never forget a surgeon who came to me, frustrated and embarrassed. He leaned back in his chair and said, *"Jordan, I make life-and-death calls every day. How did I miss this?"*

He was earning over **a million dollars a year,** and he had built a substantial portfolio—more than $4 million saved between his 401(k), IRAs, and brokerage accounts. His advisor told him he was paying a "reasonable" 1 percent management fee. What he didn't realize was that once you layered in fund expenses, platform costs, and hidden trading charges, his true cost was closer to 1.8 percent.

That may not sound like much on paper. But here's the math: **1.8 percent on $4 million is $72,000 a year.** And because his income and savings were still growing, that number wasn't static—it climbed higher every year. Over the next 20 years, even assuming normal market growth, the difference between his high-cost portfolio and a low-cost alternative was in the millions. Not thousands. Not hundreds of thousands. **Millions of dollars silently siphoned away.**

Think about that. This was a man who worked twelve-hour days in the operating room, saving lives with steady hands and flawless judgment. Yet when it came to his money, he had unknowingly signed off on bleeding away the equivalent of a private college education every single year—sometimes two—just in fees.

The market wasn't his enemy. The trap was.

The Engineer's Precision Miss

Then there was Sterling, an engineer in Novi. If anyone was wired to spot flaws in a system, it was him. He brought spreadsheets to our meeting that would make a CPA blush. He analyzed every mutual fund holding like it was a bridge schematic, double-checking the math as if lives depended on it.

But what Sterling missed was the layer beneath the numbers. His advisor told him the fee was 1.25 percent. The real cost, once you included fund expenses, was closer to 1.9 percent. That extra 0.65 percent didn't sound like much until we did the math: on **$2.2 million, it was $41,800 a year.**

And just like the surgeon, Sterling's costs weren't fixed—they grew as his portfolio grew. Over 25 years, that "rounding error" ballooned into well over a million dollars in lost wealth. Money that could have funded a lake house, his grandchildren's education, or simply bought him peace of mind.

Sterling shook his head in disbelief. *"Jordan, we stress-test bridges to withstand any load. I never stress-tested my retirement plan. If I had, I would have caught this years ago."*

The Executive's Assumption

Then there was Rachel, an executive who managed a team of 400 people and oversaw a multimillion-dollar budget. She could sniff out waste in her company's expense reports in seconds, but when it came to her personal retirement, she admitted she never once questioned the line items her advisor provided.

"It all looked professional," she told me. "I assumed the fees were normal." By the time we reviewed her plan, she had been overpaying for years—not out of neglect, but out of misplaced trust in polished presentations.

The Physician's Tax Trap

And it's not just about fees. Taxes trip up even the best of us. I once sat with a physician who had carefully charted out her retirement income but hadn't realized that withdrawing from the wrong account first would push her into a higher bracket and trigger Medicare surcharges. She said, *"I diagnose complex cases every day. How did I miss this?"*

Her medical training gave her razor-sharp diagnostic skills, but the tax code wasn't written in a language she was trained to read. And that disconnect was about to cost her tens of thousands in extra taxes every year.

THE DANGER OF "TRUST ME"

That's the danger of "trust me." It feels safe—until you realize the safety net you thought you had is filled with holes.

The truth is, the financial industry is built on the fact that most people don't want to ask questions they don't understand. And that's where blind trust gets expensive.

This book isn't about turning you into an advisor. It's about giving you the filters and the confidence to separate good advice from good theater. I want you to be able to sit across the table from any advisor—including me—and ask the questions that strip away the gloss:

- *"What's my all-in cost, in dollars and percentages?"*
- *"What happens to my income if the market drops 20 percent?"*
- *"Are you recommending this because it's best for me, or because it pays you?"*

The people I've worked with aren't less intelligent than their advisors—in fact, they're often far more accomplished in their own fields. What they lacked wasn't intelligence. It was education. And that's what the financial industry counts on.

When you build your education edge, you stop outsourcing blind trust. You stop hoping someone else has your best interest at heart. Instead, you own a plan you can actually explain, defend, and believe in. That's the difference between being a passenger in your retirement and finally taking the wheel.

Susan's Tax Shock (and What It Teaches)

Back to Susan. She was in her late 50s, a nurse who had clocked long shifts for decades and saved diligently. Like many people, she trusted her employer plan but was convinced by a smooth-talking salesman that she could "do better" if she rolled a portion of her retirement savings into something "more flexible."

It sounded good on paper—words like *"protection," "growth," and "guarantees"* filled the glossy brochure. The contract was thick enough to bruise an ankle, which, in hindsight, should have been a red flag. But Susan signed, believing she was getting a safer, smarter deal.

Then life happened. A family emergency hit, and Susan needed $30,000 in a hurry. She did what most people would do: she called her advisor, explained the situation, and requested a withdrawal.

That's when the hammer fell.

The money she pulled out came from **pre-tax retirement dollars**—which meant every penny counted as ordinary income, not capital gains. Worse, because she was still under age **59½,** she got hit with the 10 percent early withdrawal penalty. By the time federal and state taxes were applied, plus the penalty, her "$30,000 solution" shrank by about **$20,000 in taxes and penalties.**

In other words, the very "flexibility" she thought she was buying turned into rigidity at the worst possible time. She needed liquidity, but she had bought a product designed to lock money away. No one had explained the trade-offs, and when the crisis came, she was blindsided.

And that wasn't all. Hidden inside the product were **ongoing internal expenses**—administrative charges, rider costs, and investment sub-account fees—that quietly ate away at her balance year after year.

Those didn't show up in bold print on her statements; they were tucked into disclosures most people never read, or couldn't decipher if they did.

The result: Susan didn't break the law, and neither did her advisor. But the plan failed her because it was opaque. She was sold a product, not given an education.

When Susan and I finally sat down, the first thing I did wasn't to recommend another shiny product. It was to draw a map. We laid out her buckets of money:

- **Emergency cash** — money she could access at any time without penalties or surprises.
- **Protected income** — dollars earmarked for essentials like groceries, utilities, and insurance.
- **Long-term growth** — investments designed to beat inflation over the decades.
- **Tax-smart withdrawals** — a sequence that respected IRS rules, reduced future tax traps, and kept her income predictable.

It wasn't glamorous, but it was clear. For the first time, she had a plan she could explain back to me in her own words. She didn't walk out with a "hot pick" or a "can't-miss product." She walked out with confidence.

That's the real lesson of Susan's story: the costliest mistakes aren't usually made in the stock market. They're made in the fine print, in the tax code, and in the moments when life collides with money and no one has given you the rules of the game.

SCALE THE STAKES: TEACHERS, ENGINEERS, PHYSICIANS

Susan's $20,000 tax shock was painful, but it wasn't unusual. What made her case so important was this: she only had a portion of her nest egg exposed, and the mistake was still survivable.

But what happens when the numbers are bigger? What happens when the stakes aren't tens of thousands, but hundreds of thousands—or even millions?

That's where I often meet the next wave of clients.

The Teachers

I'll often meet a couple who both taught for 30 years. Between two

403(b) accounts, a 457 plan, and a small pension, they'll walk into my office with $1.2 to $1.6 million saved. And they almost always start the same way: *"We're simple. We don't need anything fancy."*

They're right. They don't need fancy—they need clarity. What they rarely realize is that even "plain vanilla" retirement plans are filled with decision points that carry tax consequences. When should they draw from pre-tax vs. Roth accounts? How will their withdrawals affect their Social Security taxation? If they sell in a down year, which dollars should go first? And how do they carve out enough "protected income" so a bad market doesn't turn into skipped grocery bills?

These aren't theoretical questions. They're the real-world mechanics that separate a stress-free retirement from one filled with sleepless nights.

The Engineer

Then there's someone like Sterling, the Novi engineer. You met him earlier, buried in spreadsheets. His $2.2 million rollover IRA looked well-managed on the surface—until we pulled back the curtain on fees. His advisor told him 1.25 percent. His real cost? Closer to 1.9 percent.

That "small" gap of 0.65 percent equaled **$41,800 a year**. And because fees scale with portfolio size, his costs were set to rise every year. Over 25 years, that "rounding error" would quietly strip away well over **a million dollars** of potential wealth.

Sterling could calculate torque and load-bearing stress in his sleep, but he'd never been taught to stress-test his retirement plan. Once we reframed the numbers in terms of opportunity cost—a lake house, college for the grandkids, financial peace—it clicked. What looked like a fee became a lifetime tax on his family's future.

The Physician

And then there are physicians. I recently worked with Dr. Priya, who had accumulated $3.1 million across her practice plan and multiple IRAs. Her portfolio looked solid. Her returns were fine. But when I asked her about her tax plan for Required Minimum Distributions (RMDs) in her 70s, she admitted she didn't have one.

Her first RMDs were projected to be so large they would push her into a higher bracket, increase the taxation of her Social Security, and trigger higher Medicare premiums. In other words, she was on track to hand an unnecessary six-figure gift to the IRS over the course of her retirement. We didn't sell her a miracle. Instead, we built a five-year Roth conversion ladder in her early 60s, deliberately filling tax brackets while her income was lower. We layered in a slice of principal-protected income for her essential expenses, so market dips wouldn't dictate her lifestyle. By the second meeting, she leaned back in her chair and said, *"For the first time, I know why we're doing what we're doing."*

That's the sound of education working.

THE COST OF "SMALL" FEES: THE MILLION-DOLLAR DRIP

People often shrug when they hear numbers like 1 or 1.5 percent. *"That doesn't sound so bad,"* they say. And if you're looking at a dinner bill, maybe it isn't. But in retirement planning, percentages don't stay small. They compound—year after year, decade after decade—until they quietly hollow out what could have been a fortune.

Let's run a simple thought experiment: Imagine two investors, each starting with **$2 million**, earning the exact same market returns over 25 years.

- **Investor A** pays **1.5 percent** all-in costs (advisory fees, fund expenses, trading costs).
- **Investor B** pays **0.25 percent** all-in costs (low-cost ETFs, transparent advisory fee).

At first, the gap looks trivial. After one year, it's "only" about **$25,000.** But by year five, the difference has compounded to six figures. By year 25, Investor B is ahead by **well over a million dollars.**

Same returns. Same markets. The only difference? Cost.

That's why I call fees the **invisible tax**. Unlike the IRS, which at least sends you a bill, fees come quietly. They don't show up as a line item on your 1040. They show up as a smaller balance than you should have had, a future lifestyle quietly downgraded without warning.

And the higher your balance, the worse the drip becomes:
- On $500,000, a 1 percent fee is $5,000 a year.
- On $1.5 million, it's $15,000 a year.

- On $3 million, it's $30,000 a year.

The math is merciless: what feels like a rounding error becomes a house, a college education, or a legacy—lost not because of bad markets, but because no one showed you the compounding drag.

I once had a client tell me, *"Jordan, my advisor says the returns cover the fees."* I smiled and said, *"That's like saying you're fine with a leaky roof because it only rains part of the time."* You don't ignore leaks; you fix them.

Here's the bottom line: you don't need to memorize formulas or run Monte Carlo simulations to protect yourself. You just need the reflex to ask one simple question: **"What's my total, all-in cost—expressed as both a percentage and in real dollars at my current balance?"**

If the answer isn't clear and straightforward, that's not an oversight. That's the red flag waving.

TAXES: WHERE GOOD PLANS GO TO DIE

Markets get all the headlines, but taxes quietly steal more retirements. I've seen families survive stock market crashes with patience and discipline—only to have their plans shredded by the IRS code.

Here's the uncomfortable truth: your 401(k), 403(b), and traditional IRA balances are not fully yours. You and Uncle Sam co-own that pile. Every dollar you withdraw is taxed as **ordinary income**, not capital gains. That means you'll pay at whatever marginal bracket you happen to be in at the time. The bigger your account, the bigger his slice.

Three places in particular blindside retirees:
1. **Sequencing Mistakes**
   Selling the wrong dollars at the wrong time is one of the fastest ways to inflate your tax bill. I've seen retirees liquidate pre-tax accounts early when they had after-tax cash available—or drain Roth money first when it should have been saved for later. The order matters. A single misstep can tilt your bracket for years.
2. **Required Minimum Distributions (RMDs)**
   You may not "need" the money in your 70s, but the IRS doesn't care. At age 73, they force you to begin pulling money from your pre-tax accounts whether you want to or not. The bigger your balance, the bigger the required withdrawal.

And those withdrawals don't happen in isolation. They can:
- Push your income into a higher tax bracket.
- Trigger taxation on up to 85 percent of your Social Security benefits.
- Increase your Medicare premiums through **IRMAA surcharges** (Income-Related Monthly Adjustment Amount). For high earners, that can mean an extra **$3,000–$5,000 a year** in premiums—money that could have been avoided with better planning.

3. **Inheritance Math**

   Under the SECURE Act, your kids can't stretch an inherited IRA over their lifetimes anymore. Instead, they have to drain the account within 10 years—and every withdrawal is taxed as ordinary income in *their* bracket. If they're in their peak earning years, that "inheritance" can come with a tax bill so large it feels like a penalty. I worked with one widow who wanted to leave her $500,000 IRA to her two sons. Both were engineers in high tax brackets. By the time we modeled out their mandatory withdrawals, nearly 40 percent of that IRA would end up with the IRS. The father had sweated for decades to build it, but the tax code was poised to take nearly half in just one decade.

WHAT EDUCATION LOOKS LIKE

The good news? Taxes aren't random. With the right strategy, they're predictable—and, to a degree, controllable.

- **Understand the order of operations.** Generally, it's cash first, then taxable brokerage, then pre-tax retirement accounts, and Roth last. But the exact mix depends on your bracket and your goals.
- **Use Roth conversions strategically.** The early retirement window—after work stops but before Social Security and RMDs begin—is often the golden opportunity. Converting during those years lets you fill lower brackets deliberately, shifting taxable money into tax-free Roth accounts for the future.
- **Leverage Qualified Charitable Distributions (QCDs).** If you're charitable, you can direct up to $100,000 per year from your IRA straight to charity once you're 70½. It satisfies your RMD, but it doesn't count as taxable income.

- **Coordinate across accounts.** Harvest gains in your taxable account in low-income years. Use losses to offset gains when markets dip. Don't just react—plan.

The goal isn't to pay zero tax—that's fantasy. The goal is to pay *the right tax, at the right time, in the right way.* When you get that right, you stop leaving surprise gifts to Uncle Sam.

RISK: DRIVE AT YOUR SPEED (NOT YOUR NEIGHBOR'S)

If fees are the invisible tax and Uncle Sam is the silent partner in your retirement, risk is the force that shows up front and center. Unlike fees or taxes, you feel it in your gut.

Risk isn't a moral virtue. It's not about being brave or timid. It's about alignment—matching the speed of your investments with the speed your life can handle.

I often tell clients: risk has two gears: **Risk Tolerance and Risk Capacity.**

Risk Tolerance: Your Emotions

This is your comfort level with swings in the market. Some people can see their portfolio drop 20 percent and sleep like a baby, confident it'll rebound. Others lose sleep if they're down 2 percent. Neither response is right or wrong—it's simply how your nervous system is wired.

Risk Capacity: Your Reality

This is your financial ability to withstand risk. It's math, not feelings. If your essential expenses are covered by Social Security, a pension, and a slice of protected income, you can afford to let your growth portfolio bounce around. But if you need to sell stocks each month just to buy groceries, your capacity for risk is far lower, no matter how tough you think you are.

WHEN THE GEARS DON'T MATCH

High tolerance but low capacity is like driving 90 miles an hour on bald tires—you're headed for a crash. Low tolerance but high capacity is like creeping along at 20 on the expressway—you'll arrive safely, but you'll waste years of potential growth along the way. Both mismatches sabotage the plan.

I once met with a couple who told me they were "comfortable with risk." Their risk number from Nitrogen scored them like they were driving 85 miles per hour. But when we stress-tested their plan, we saw that even a modest downturn would force them to liquidate investments to cover their mortgage and groceries. They weren't built for 85—they needed to slow down.

On the flip side, I worked with a retired teacher who had her essential expenses covered—pension, Social Security, and a modest annuity. She could have comfortably tolerated a more growth-oriented allocation. But because she hated seeing volatility, she kept everything in CDs earning barely 1 percent. The math was clear: she was losing purchasing power to inflation every single year. Her nerves were in the driver's seat, not her actual financial capacity.

How Fast Are You Driving into Retirement?

Source: Magellan Financial.

TOOLS THAT HELP

That's why we use www.mfgrisktest.com (free to use) to measure risk. They assign a score—think of it like a "speedometer" for your portfolio. The point isn't to label you conservative or aggressive. The point is to put your feelings and your finances on the same dashboard.

When those two align, surprises don't derail you. You know what to expect. And when you know what to expect, you can stop guessing and start living.

INCOME: YOU DON'T RETIRE ON A BALANCE, YOU RETIRE ON A PAYCHECK

When I ask people how much they've saved for retirement, they usually give me a number: *"We've got $1.5 million in our 401(k),"* or *"Between my IRA and brokerage, about $2 million."*

But here's the reality: you don't retire on a balance. You retire on a paycheck.

Think about it—your balance is just a number on a statement. What really matters is how reliably that number can be translated into monthly income that pays for your life: the groceries, the utilities, the insurance, the vacations, the grandkids' Christmas gifts. A big number with no strategy is like owning a farm but having no plan for harvesting the crops.

THE TWO BUDGETS

Every retiree has two budgets: the Math Budget and the Sleep Budget.

The Math Budget

The spreadsheets, Monte Carlo simulations, and projections. *This is the part that looks neat on paper.*

The Sleep Budget

How you feel when the market drops 18 percent and the news won't stop screaming about a recession. *This is the part that keeps you up at night—or lets you rest easy.*

A good income plan respects both.

LAYERED INCOME PLANNING

Here's how we design retirement paychecks:

- **Guaranteed Sources** – Social Security and any pensions. These are the foundation. You can't outlive them, and they arrive on time every month.
- **Protected Income for Essentials** – This is where we use principal-protected, fixed income strategies. Think of these as tools designed to underwrite the basics—groceries, insurance, property taxes—so your everyday life doesn't depend on the stock market's mood swings.
- **Growth Portfolio** – Equities and other risk assets built for long-term inflation fighting. This is where your money works to stay ahead of rising costs.
- **Cash Reserves** – Two to five years' worth of short-term expenses sitting in cash or high-quality fixed income, so you don't have to sell long-term investments in a downturn.

When your essentials are covered by steady, predictable sources, your growth portfolio can do what growth portfolios do—bounce around in the short term, but build wealth over time.

WHY IT MATTERS

I've seen retirees come into my office with $2 million saved but no paycheck strategy. They lived in constant fear of drawing down the wrong account at the wrong time, or worse—selling assets during a downturn just to pay their bills. That fear can be paralyzing.

By contrast, when we build a layered income plan, the conversation changes. Markets may still swing, but the retiree knows their "groceries and lights" money is safe. Suddenly, they can focus on enjoying life, not staring at CNBC with their stomach in knots.

HERE'S THE KEY TAKEAWAY:

Your retirement isn't about how big the pile is—it's about how steady the paychecks are.

THE RIPT FRAMEWORK: A DASHBOARD FOR DECISIONS

By now you've seen how retirement can go off the rails—fees that quietly erode balances, taxes that blindside you, risk that keeps you up at night, and income gaps that turn balances into anxiety. Each of these problems is dangerous on its own. Together, they can be devastating.

That's why I teach clients to think about their plan like a dashboard with four key gauges: **Risk, Income, Portfolio, and Taxes.**

If one gauge is cracked, the whole drive gets dicey. But when all four are working together, you can steer with confidence.

Risk – Know Your Speed

We already talked about tolerance (how you feel) and capacity (what you can actually handle). Your risk gauge measures both. If you're driving faster than your nerves or your finances can tolerate, you're courting disaster. If you're creeping along too slowly, you're leaving opportunity on the table.

Education here means knowing your number, setting guardrails, and aligning your investments with both your emotions and your math.

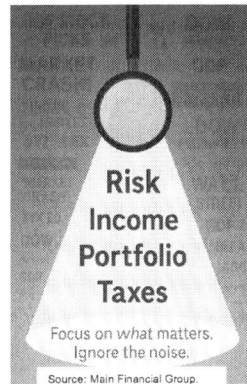

Risk
Income
Portfolio
Taxes

Focus on what matters.
Ignore the noise.

Source: Main Financial Group.

Income – Build Paychecks First

You don't retire on an account balance—you retire on predictable paychecks. The income gauge reminds you to start with essentials: Social Security, pensions, and principal-protected fixed income tools for the basics.

Growth investments and cash reserves come after. When this gauge is steady, your lifestyle doesn't rise and fall with the market ticker.

Portfolio – Own What You Can Explain

Your portfolio is the engine. It should be low-cost, broadly diversified, and positioned to give you growth without unnecessary complexity. If you can't explain in plain English what you own and why you own it, the portfolio gauge is flashing red.

Costs matter. Diversification matters. Tax location matters. But above all, clarity matters.

Taxes – Stay Ahead of the IRS

This is the gauge most people ignore until it's too late. A plan that doesn't account for Roth conversions, sequencing, RMDs, and inheritance rules isn't a plan—it's a time bomb.

Tax strategy isn't about eliminating taxes; it's about controlling when and how you pay them, so you keep more of what you earned and pass on more of what you built.

Why RIPT Works

The power of RIPT isn't in the letters themselves—it's in how they interact. Taxes change your portfolio decisions. Your portfolio changes your risk exposure. Your risk appetite changes your income strategy. And your income plan changes your tax picture.

It's not a checklist—it's a loop. A living system. That's why the most successful retirees don't treat planning as a one-time event. They review it annually, adjust for life changes, and make sure all four gauges are calibrated together.

When you see your plan through the RIPT framework, the complexity of retirement gets distilled into something simple, visual, and repeatable. It's like having a dashboard on a long drive—you can glance down, check the gauges, and know whether you're safe to keep going or need to pull over for a tune-up.

CASE LABS: WHAT EDUCATION CHANGES (THREE WALKTHROUGHS)

Frameworks are great, but they only matter if they hold up in real life. That's why I like to show clients what happens when we apply RIPT to their specific situations. Let's walk through three examples—an engineer, a physician, and a teacher couple.

Lab 1: The Novi Engineer (Fee Gravity)

<u>Before:</u> Sterling, the engineer from Novi, had a $2.2 million IRA. On paper, his advisor seemed to be doing a decent job. The reported management fee was 1.25 percent, which Sterling thought sounded reasonable.

But when we dug deeper, the real cost—once you included fund expenses and trading costs—was closer to 1.9 percent.

That meant **$41,800** a year quietly flowing out of his portfolio. And because the fee was a percentage of his balance, the "drip" only grew larger every year.

His portfolio was mostly active funds, rebalancing was sporadic, and there was no clear income or tax plan. The engine was running, but fuel was leaking everywhere.

<u>After:</u> We rebuilt his allocation around low-cost, broad-market ETFs and reduced his all-in cost to **0.35 percent**. That cut his annual expense to about $7,700. Year one savings alone: ~$34,000.

But the real win wasn't one year—it was the compounding of that difference over 20–25 years. Instead of watching fees siphon away a lake house's worth of wealth, Sterling could redirect that money to his family's future.

We also structured his accounts into buckets:
- Cash and short-term bonds for 3–5 years of expenses.
- A core equity growth sleeve for long-term inflation protection.
- A principal-protected fixed income layer to cover monthly essentials.
- A three-year Roth conversion ladder designed to deliberately fill tax brackets while rates were still favorable.

The math spoke for itself, but the look on Sterling's face when he realized his "retirement leaks" had been plugged—that was education turning into peace of mind.

Lab 2: The Ann Arbor Physician (RMD Avalanche Prevention)

<u>Before:</u> Dr. Priya, in her early 60s, had accumulated $3.1 million across her practice retirement plan and IRAs. Her portfolio looked solid and her returns were fine.

But no one had ever talked to her about tax sequencing. At age

73, when Required Minimum Distributions (RMDs) kicked in, her withdrawals would have been so large they'd push her into a higher tax bracket, increase the taxation of her Social Security, and trigger thousands in annual Medicare surcharges.

She wasn't in danger of running out of money. But she was on track to bleed six figures unnecessarily to the IRS over the course of her retirement.

After: We built a plan to wait one year—until her income dropped after winding down her practice—then start a five-year Roth conversion ladder. Each year, she filled up her lower tax brackets deliberately, shifting pre-tax dollars into Roth while tax rates were still favorable.

We mapped her income sources so that her essentials—mortgage, groceries, insurance—were covered by Social Security and a slice of principal-protected fixed income. That gave her growth portfolio freedom to ride out market swings without dictating her lifestyle.

When we finished, her projected RMDs had shrunk dramatically, her Medicare premium surprises were reduced, and she had more flexibility to leave tax-free assets to her children.

Her comment at the second meeting still makes me smile: *"For the first time, I know why we're doing what we're doing."*

Lab 3: The Teacher Couple (Sequence-of-Returns Defense)

Before: A couple walked in with $1.4 million spread across two 403(b)s, a 457, and a modest brokerage account. Their plan was simple: *"We'll just sell a little each month."* That works—*until it doesn't.*

A market downturn early in retirement can turn that strategy into a wealth drain, a trap known as **sequence-of-returns risk**.

If the market dropped 20 percent and they kept withdrawing at the same pace, they could lock in losses that permanently crippled their nest egg.

After: We restructured their accounts into time-segmented buckets:
- Two years of living expenses set aside in cash.
- Three years in short-term, high-quality bonds.
- Social Security plus a slice of fixed income product underwriting the essential bills.
- Growth investments set aside for long-term inflation protection.

Now, if markets dropped, they could pause withdrawals from the growth bucket and live off their cash and bonds. Their lifestyle stopped depending on the market's weather.

The change wasn't about chasing higher returns. It was about buying peace of mind.

Why These Labs Matter

What all three cases prove is simple: education changes the story. None of these clients walked out with a "hot pick." They walked out with a plan they could explain in plain English. And when you can explain your plan, you can own it.

THE RED-FLAG DECODER (AND GREEN FLAGS TO SEEK)

If retirement planning sometimes feels like trying to read invisible ink, that's because parts of the financial industry are designed to be opaque. But once you know the code, the traps aren't hard to spot.

Think of this section like your **decoder ring in a spy novel**—when you hear the wrong words, you know you're in danger. When you hear the right ones, you know you're on safer ground.

Red Flags (The Phrases That Should Make You Sweat)

- **"Don't worry about the fees. The returns will cover them."**
  Translation: You're paying more than you realize, and they don't want you to look under the hood. Fees never stay small when compounded.
- **"There's no risk here, and you can get stock-like returns."**
  Translation: They're overselling. If it sounds too good to be true, it is. Every investment has trade-offs.
- **"We'll figure out the taxes later."**
  Translation: They don't have a strategy—or worse, they don't want to admit they don't understand tax planning. Taxes are where good plans go to die.
- **"This is complicated; you don't need to understand it."**
  Translation: You should absolutely understand it, at least at a high level. Complexity is often camouflage for hidden costs.
- **Every problem has the same solution.**

Translation: You're not being advised—you're being sold. If every meeting ends with the same product pitch, you're not the priority.

Green Flags (The Phrases That Signal Clarity)
- **"Here's your total, all-in cost—advice, investments, and product—expressed as both a percentage and in real dollars at today's balance."**
  That's transparency.
- **"If the market drops 20 percent, here's how your paycheck continues without forced selling."**
  That's risk management.
- **"Before we invest a dollar, let's put every account into one of three tax buckets and sketch your withdrawal sequence."**
  That's tax strategy.
- **"If we do X, we give up Y. Here's why I'd still do X."**
  That's honesty about trade-offs, not fairy tales.
- **"We'll pressure-test this plan together every year. No autopilot."**
  That's accountability.

Why This Decoder Matters
Once you learn the code, you'll start hearing these phrases everywhere. Dinner seminars. Radio shows. Even glossy ads in your mailbox. The difference is, now you won't just hear them—you'll decode them.

Like a spy who suddenly sees the trapdoor in the floor, you'll know when someone is speaking in red flags. And just as importantly, you'll know the green flags that mark when you're on the right track.

This isn't about paranoia. It's about empowerment. Because when you hear the wrong phrases, you can stop the conversation, change advisors, or at least demand clarity. And when you hear the right ones, you know you're sitting across from someone who respects you enough to be transparent.

THE INVESTOR'S PLAYBOOK: FIVE HABITS OF THE EDUCATED

If the Red-Flag Decoder was your spy ring, the Playbook is your field guide. It's the manual you keep in your back pocket, the one you flip open when the noise gets too loud or the sales pitch feels too slick.

These are the **five habits that separate educated investors from everyone else:**

1. **Always Know the Score (Risk Number)**
   Don't drive without a speedometer. Your portfolio should have a risk score you can understand—one that matches both your emotional tolerance and financial capacity.

2. **Name Your Paycheck**
   Before you talk about chasing growth, you need to know: where is your retirement paycheck coming from? Will it arrive whether the market is up, down, or sideways?

3. **Sort the Buckets Before You Fill Them**
   Every dollar has a tax destiny. Pretax. Tax-free. Taxable. If you don't map those buckets now, the IRS will do it for you later—and they rarely choose the cheaper option.

4. **Decode Before You Decide**
   When you hear a product pitch, stop and translate it through your Decoder. Ask: *What's the fee? What's the trade-off? What's the worst-case scenario?*

5. **Rehearse the Crisis**
   Every year, sit down and walk through: What happens if the market drops 20 percent? What happens if I lose my spouse? What happens if taxes double? Good plans don't just imagine the sunny days; they prepare for the storms.

Why This Matters

Education without action is trivia. Habits are how education becomes protection. Follow the playbook, and you're no longer at the mercy of sales pitches or market swings. You've taken the wheel.

But what if you don't? What happens if you ignore the red flags, skip the buckets, and assume the good times will last forever?

That's when you get Amanda's story.

Amanda's Epilog: The Tax Shock That Could Have Been Avoided

Amanda wasn't uneducated. She was a schoolteacher. She understood hard work, discipline, and living within her means. What she didn't have was a decoder or a playbook.

For 35 years, she saved diligently into her 403(b). When she retired, she thought she was set. But no one had ever stopped to map her tax buckets, or to warn her what would happen when her Required Minimum Distributions (RMDs) collided with Social Security and a small pension.

The result? A tax bill that stunned her. The extra income pushed her into a higher bracket, triggered taxation on her Social Security, and even caused her Medicare premiums to spike. The nest egg that looked so solid on paper was suddenly leaking from multiple holes.

The worst part: it wasn't necessary. With Roth conversions during her lower-earning years, careful sequencing of withdrawals, and a proper plan, Amanda's shock could have been avoided.

Her story is the epilog of Chapter One for a reason. It's the proof that this isn't theory. This isn't about jargon or academic models. It's about the real-life consequences of leaving your future to chance—or to an advisor who tells you, "We'll figure out the taxes later."

CLOSING THE CHAPTER: FROM SHOCK TO STRATEGY

Amanda's story isn't unique. Every week, I meet people who've worked hard, saved diligently, and trusted that the system would reward their discipline—only to find that retirement is a minefield of traps. Higher-than-expected taxes. Portfolio risks they didn't see coming. Income that looked steady on paper but proved fragile in reality.

It's easy to dismiss Amanda's outcome as bad luck. But the truth is harsher: it was the result of **bad planning—or worse, no planning at all.** The red flags were there. The buckets could have been sorted. The conversions could have been staged. The income plan could have been drawn with taxes in mind. What she lacked wasn't discipline or effort; it was a **framework** to connect the pieces before it was too late.

That's where the rest of this book comes in. You now have the Decoder to spot trouble and the Playbook to build good habits. But tools without a strategy are just scattered pieces on a workbench.

What you need is a system—a way to bring Risk, Income, Portfolio, and Taxes together into a plan that protects you from the same fate Amanda faced.

This isn't about being a financial genius or having seven figures in the bank. It's about refusing to leave your future to chance or to advisors who avoid the hard conversations. You don't need to be told to "trust me." You need to be shown how every decision—when to claim Social Security, which accounts to draw from, whether to convert to Roth—fits into a coordinated strategy.

That's exactly what the chapters ahead will give you: **a clear framework, real stories, and the confidence to navigate retirement like the owner of your future—not a passenger in someone else's plan.**

So, take one last look at Amanda's tax shock. Let it be the warning you never have to live through yourself. Because the question isn't whether you'll face the same traps—it's whether you'll see them early enough to steer clear.

In Chapter Two, we begin assembling the framework piece by piece. We'll start with the first pillar: **Risk.** Not just the roller coaster of the stock market, but the deeper psychology of how much risk you can tolerate and how much you can truly afford to take.

Because once you know your speed, everything else in your retirement strategy starts to make sense.

CHAPTER TWO

Climbing the Money Mountain: Building Wealth in Your Working Years

Early in my career, when I started Main Financial Group, one of the very first couples who came to see me was Mike and Lisa, engineers from Livonia. On paper, they seemed to have everything lined up for a secure future. Between their positions at one of the Big Three automakers, they earned a combined $150,000 a year—solid, respectable money in 2006. They weren't extravagant spenders. They paid their bills, saved diligently in their workplace retirement plans, and even had a little tucked away for family vacations up north. Yet when they laid out their financial statements on my desk, the picture told a different story.

Their accounts were scattered: an old 401(k) from Mike's first employer, two more from Lisa's stints at Ford and GM, plus a smattering of small IRAs and bank CDs. It was like trying to manage half a dozen puzzle pieces with no box top to show the big picture. The problem wasn't that they weren't saving—it was that their savings weren't working together.

I'll never forget Mike's frustration as he sifted through the stack. "We've been doing everything we're supposed to do," he said, "but it feels like we're running in place." He compared it to hiking up a hill with a backpack full of rocks.

When I dug into the numbers, I discovered why: one of their old 401(k) accounts was charging 1.8 percent in annual fees. That might not sound like much, but stretched over decades it would quietly drain more than $100,000 from their nest egg.

We consolidated their accounts into a single IRA with low-cost, diversified ETFs, slashing fees down to a fraction of a percent. It wasn't exciting, but it was effective—like swapping out those rocks in their backpack for a good pair of climbing boots. Slowly but surely, their financial climb became easier.

Today, Mike and Lisa are on track not just for retirement at 62, but possibly for something even sweeter: that log cabin on Lake Huron they used to dream about on summer trips north.

But for every Mike and Lisa, there's a Todd and Brenda. Same age, same level of income, but a very different journey up the mountain. Todd left old retirement accounts scattered at every job change, never consolidating. Brenda couldn't resist following the "next big thing"— whether it was a hot mutual fund recommended by a co-worker or a tech stock hyped on TV.

They didn't watch fees, and they sold whenever the market dipped, convinced they were avoiding disaster. Over a decade, they worked just as hard as Mike and Lisa, but their retirement accounts barely grew. Their climb was filled with detours and slips, while Mike and Lisa kept moving steadily upward.

That contrast shows what this chapter is all about. Everyone faces the same mountain. The steepness of the trail doesn't change, but the choices you make determine whether you gain ground or keep sliding back. Some people are "drifters"—they leave their money scattered, never quite paying attention to where it's going. Others are "thrill-seekers"—they leap from trend to trend, hoping one lucky bet will rocket them to the summit.

But the most successful are the "steady climbers." They're not flashy, they're not chasing headlines, but step by step, they keep ascending until the summit is in sight.

Your working years are that climb. This isn't the time for waiting for the perfect moment. It's the *accumulation phase*—the years when steady, disciplined habits create momentum.

In this chapter, we'll explore the principles that help you gain altitude: starting early to harness the miracle of compound interest, avoiding the fee traps that sap your strength, steering clear of fear-driven decisions like market timing or chasing fads, and equipping yourself with the right mix of investments to withstand the climb.

Building wealth in your working years isn't about sprinting to the top or proving you're the smartest person on the trail. It's about having the endurance, discipline, and strategy to keep moving upward—even when the weather turns, the trail gets rocky, or other climbers are shouting about shortcuts. Because here's the truth: *shortcuts rarely work*. **The mountain rewards patience, preparation, and persistence.**

So, as we set out on this chapter together, imagine yourself standing at the base of that mountain. You've got years of work ahead of you, but every step counts. The right habits, the right tools, and the right guidance can turn what feels overwhelming into something achievable. Mike and Lisa's story proves it: with steady steps, a clear path, and a commitment to avoid unnecessary detours, the summit isn't just possible—it's waiting.

THE POWER OF STARTING EARLY: COMPOUND INTEREST IN ACTION

There's one force that separates those who reach the peak from those who run out of steam halfway up, it's compound interest. You've heard the phrase before—money making money on money—but until you see it in action, it's hard to appreciate its true power. It's the financial equivalent of planting a tree that grows into an entire orchard.

Albert Einstein supposedly called compound interest the eighth wonder of the world, and it's not hard to see why. When your investments generate returns, and those returns themselves generate returns, your wealth begins to grow at a pace that feels almost unfair. The only catch? *It takes time.* The earlier you start, the steeper and faster your mountain grows.

Take a simple example: a 25-year-old who saves $5,000 a year into a low-cost index fund earning an average 7 percent real return. After ten years, they stop contributing entirely. By 65, that account still grows to more than $1 million. Now imagine waiting until age 35 to start and contributing the same $5,000 a year for 30 straight years. You'd think more money in would mean a bigger balance—but no. At 65, that later starter has only about $500,000. The difference? Nothing more than ten extra years of compounding at the beginning.

This is what I tell younger clients all the time: you don't need to be perfect; you just need to start. Even small amounts matter. $100 a month invested at 25 grows to nearly $200,000 by 65. Delay until 40, and it's only $60,000. The math doesn't lie. Time is your most powerful ally, but it's also the one most people squander.

Mike and Lisa discovered this too late for their twenties, but not too late to make a difference. Once we consolidated their accounts and slashed their fees, their money finally had a chance to compound without leaks. In just 20 years, the fee savings alone added an extra

$80,000 to their nest egg. That's the difference between having a "leaky bucket" and a watertight one—every dollar stays in play, working harder for the future.

History provides some of the best examples of compounding at work. Benjamin Franklin, a man who understood patience as well as pennies, left two modest bequests of about £1,000 each (roughly $4,500 in today's terms) to the cities of Boston and Philadelphia in the late 1700s. The money was to be invested and left untouched for two centuries. By the time it was finally distributed, Franklin's gift had grown to more than $6.5 million. He didn't leave a fortune—he left time. And time did the rest.

One simple tool anyone can use to understand compounding is the "Rule of 72." Divide 72 by your rate of return, and you'll know roughly how many years it takes for your money to double. At 6 percent, it's 12 years. At 8 percent, it's 9 years. This isn't a trick; it's just the math of growth. Understanding it makes the invisible visible—you start to see how little decisions today turn into massive differences tomorrow.

So why do so many people put it off? It's not laziness—it's human nature. Behavioral economists call it "present bias": we value $100 today more than $100 in the future, even though the future version of that money could be worth much more. We tell ourselves we'll start next year, or when the kids are out of daycare, or when that raise comes through. But those delays are costly.

A client of mine, Melissa, an engineer in her thirties, came to me after ignoring her retirement account for nearly a decade. She had finally built up $60,000 in savings, but when we ran the numbers, she realized that if she'd started at 22, she'd already have close to $200,000. The look on her face said it all. It wasn't that she had done badly—it was that the invisible cost of waiting had stolen an opportunity from her.

Contrast that with another client, a teacher named Randy, who started saving just $100 a month straight out of college. He didn't think much of it—he just automated the transfer and forgot about it. Twenty years later, he had over $50,000, even though he never felt the pinch of missing that $100. By the time he was 65, that trickle had turned into hundreds of thousands of dollars. Randy didn't need a big income, just the discipline to start early and let compounding do the work.

The lesson here is simple: you don't have to wait until you're wealthy to start investing. In fact, the less you have, the more critical it is to start now. If you can scrape together $100 a month—the cost of one dinner out for a family of four—you can build a foundation that time will multiply. Think of it as giving your future self a raise.

The Benefits of Saving and Investing Early

		Save and Invest Early				Wait and Save	
Age	Year	Contribution	Portfolio Value	Age	Year	Contribution	Portfolio Value
23	1	$1,000.00	$1,100.00	23	1	$0.00	$0.00
24	2	$2,000.00	$3,210.00	24	2	$0.00	$0.00
25	3	$3,000.00	$6,531.00	25	3	$0.00	$0.00
26	4	$3,000.00	$10,184.10	26	4	$0.00	$0.00
27	5	$3,000.00	$14,202.51	27	5	$0.00	$0.00
28	6	$3,000.00	$18,622.76	28	6	$0.00	$0.00
29	7	$3,000.00	$23,485.04	29	7	$0.00	$0.00
30	8	$3,000.00	$28,833.54	30	8	$0.00	$0.00
31	9	$3,000.00	$34,716.89	31	9	$0.00	$0.00
32	10	$3,000.00	$41,188.58	32	10	$0.00	$0.00
33	11	$0.00	$45,307.44	33	11	$3,000.00	$3,300.00
34	12	$0.00	$49,838.19	34	12	$3,000.00	$6,630.00
35	13	$0.00	$54,822.01	35	13	$3,000.00	$10,293.00
36	14	$0.00	$60,304.21	36	14	$3,000.00	$14,322.30
37	15	$0.00	$66,334.63	37	15	$3,000.00	$18,754.53
38	16	$0.00	$72,968.09	38	16	$3,000.00	$23,629.98
39	17	$0.00	$80,264.90	39	17	$3,000.00	$28,992.98
40	18	$0.00	$88,291.39	40	18	$3,000.00	$34,892.28
41	19	$0.00	$97,120.53	41	19	$3,000.00	$41,381.51
42	20	$0.00	$106,832.58	42	20	$3,000.00	$48,519.66
43	21	$0.00	$117,515.84	43	21	$3,000.00	$56,371.62
44	22	$0.00	$129,267.42	44	22	$3,000.00	$65,008.79
45	23	$0.00	$142,194.16	45	23	$3,000.00	$74,509.66
46	24	$0.00	$156,413.58	46	24	$3,000.00	$84,960.63
47	25	$0.00	$172,054.94	47	25	$3,000.00	$96,456.69
48	26	$0.00	$189,260.43	48	26	$3,000.00	$109,102.36
49	27	$0.00	$208,186.48	49	27	$3,000.00	$123,012.60
50	28	$0.00	$229,005.12	50	28	$3,000.00	$138,313.86
51	29	$0.00	$251,905.64	51	29	$3,000.00	$155,145.25
52	30	$0.00	$277,096.20	52	30	$3,000.00	$173,659.77
53	31	$0.00	$304,805.82	53	31	$3,000.00	$194,025.75
54	32	$0.00	$335,286.40	54	32	$3,000.00	$216,428.32
55	33	$0.00	$368,815.04	55	33	$3,000.00	$241,071.16
56	34	$0.00	$405,696.55	56	34	$3,000.00	$268,178.27
57	35	$0.00	$446,266.20	57	35	$3,000.00	$297,996.10
58	36	$0.00	$490,892.82	58	36	$3,000.00	$330,795.71
59	37	$0.00	$539,982.10	59	37	$3,000.00	$366,875.28
60	38	$0.00	$593,980.31	60	38	$3,000.00	$406,562.81
61	39	$0.00	$653,378.34	61	39	$3,000.00	$450,219.09
62	40	$0.00	$718,716.18	62	40	$3,000.00	$498,241.00
63	41	$0.00	$790,587.80	63	41	$3,000.00	$551,065.10
64	42	$0.00	$869,646.58	64	42	$3,000.00	$609,171.61
65	43	$0.00	$956,611.23	65	43	$3,000.00	$673,088.77
66	44	$0.00	$1,052,272.36	66	44	$3,000.00	$743,397.64
67	45	$0.00	**$1,157,499.59**	67	45	$3,000.00	**$820,737.41**

Total Contribution: $27,000.00 $105,000.00

This illustration is based on a 10% annual return per year.

Source: Magellan Financial.

KEEPING FEES LOW:
THE HIDDEN DRAG ON YOUR CLIMB

If compound interest is the wind in your sails, fees are the barnacles on the hull. They don't seem threatening at first—just a small percentage here, a line item there—but over time they slow you down, sometimes enough to keep you from ever reaching the harbor.

In investing, a 1 percent fee doesn't just mean losing 1 percent a year. It means giving up a massive share of your potential growth. On a $100,000 portfolio growing at 7 percent annually, a 1 percent fee compounds against you to the tune of $108,000 over 30 years. That's the cost of a vacation home, a grandchild's college tuition, or five years of comfortable retirement spending.

Mike and Lisa learned this lesson firsthand. Their scattered 401(k)s charged fees ranging from 1.5 percent to 2 percent. Over the course of a decade, that meant $50,000 lost to nothing more than fine print. Once we rolled everything into a low-cost IRA built with ETFs—where the average expense ratio in 2024 was just 0.14 percent—we freed up thousands of dollars a year that now compound for them instead of a fund manager.

The damage these fees cause isn't always obvious because they're often buried. Mutual funds can charge 1 to 2 percent in expense ratios, plus hidden trading costs. Some annuities tack on mortality and expense fees, rider charges, and surrender penalties. Brokerage accounts may include transaction fees, commissions, or advisory fees stacked on top of fund costs. The math isn't complicated, but the industry counts on the fact that most people won't do it.

Take Karen, a small business owner from Rochester who came to me after buying a variable annuity at a "free dinner seminar." She thought she had found the perfect retirement solution, until we discovered the 3 percent annual fee buried in the prospectus. On her $300,000 portfolio, that meant $9,000 a year—enough to buy her family a Disney vacation every summer. Over ten years, it added up to nearly $100,000. We replaced it with a fixed-indexed annuity that eliminated the fees and gave her an additional $1,200 a month in guaranteed income for life. **Same dollars invested, radically different results.**

Or take Sarah, a teacher from Midland, whose pension carried hidden costs equal to nearly 3 percent annually. On her $1 million balance, she was losing about $30,000 a year to fees—money that could have funded her dream of helping pay for her grandkids' college tuition. When we moved her into a low-cost IRA built with ETFs, her savings jumped by $28,000 a year. Suddenly, that dream wasn't just possible, it was funded.

Fees also create what I call "phantom inflation." Just as rising prices silently erode your purchasing power, hidden costs quietly eat away at your returns. The SEC has estimated that over a 20-year horizon, high fees can consume nearly one-third of a portfolio's growth. Think of it as trying to climb a mountain with a hole in your oxygen tank. You might make progress, but you'll never reach the peak as strong as you could have.

Another client, Will, a small-business owner in Novi, came to me after years of working with a broker who charged him 1.5 percent annually for "management." On his $750,000 account, that was more than $11,000 a year—enough to cover an employee's salary or reinvest in his business. Worse, the funds themselves carried another 1 percent in expenses. All told, he was paying more than $20,000 a year in fees, without even realizing it. Once we transitioned him to a fiduciary model with ETFs, his costs dropped to under $2,000 annually. In just the first three years, the savings alone totaled more than $55,000—real money, put back to work for his future.

THE TAKEAWAY IS SIMPLE:

Every dollar you pay in fees is a dollar that can't compound for you. Unlike market performance, which no one can control, costs are one factor you can absolutely manage. Low-cost ETFs, fee transparency, and working with a fiduciary who is legally obligated to act in your best interest are your best protections.

In climbing terms, fees are like carrying unnecessary weight in your backpack. You might not notice at the start of the trail, but mile after mile, that extra burden grinds you down. Strip it away, and suddenly the climb feels lighter, faster, and more achievable.

AVOIDING THE FOMO TRAP: CHASING THRILLS THAT CRASH

If fees are the slow leak in your tire, fear of missing out, commonly referred to as FOMO, is the pothole that blows the whole wheel. Few traps derail investors faster than the urge to chase what's hot, what's hyped, or what everyone at the neighborhood barbecue seems to be talking about.

I'll never forget Joey, a 40-year-old IT manager and hipster from Royal Oak. In 2021, when Bitcoin was skyrocketing and everyone on social media seemed to be minting overnight millionaires, Joey poured half of his $200,000 savings into crypto. He wasn't reckless by nature—he was actually one of the most detail-oriented clients I'd met—but the headlines, the chatter at work, and the glowing stories on TV convinced him he'd miss the boat if he didn't get on. When crypto crashed 60 percent in 2022, he sold in a panic, locking in a $100,000 loss. That one decision erased years of disciplined saving.

And Joey isn't alone. I once worked with a surgeon in his early fifties who became enamored with biotech stocks after seeing a colleague double his money on one company's clinical-trial announcement. With a high income and a natural confidence in his ability to assess risk, he shifted nearly $400,000 into a handful of speculative biotech names. For a brief moment, it looked brilliant—his portfolio surged 20 percent in a matter of weeks. But when trial results came back negative and the stocks cratered, he was left with barely half of what he started with. The sting wasn't just financial. "I save lives for a living," he told me. "I thought I could outsmart the market, too." The truth was that his training in medicine didn't translate into immunity from herd behavior.

FOMO is dangerous because it disguises itself as opportunity. It whispers, "If everyone else is in, I should be too." Behavioral scientists tell us it's rooted in herd mentality—a survival instinct from our ancestors who stayed with the group to avoid predators. In today's markets, the "predators" are volatility and hype. Add in modern investing apps that deliver dopamine hits every time you trade, and it becomes less about building wealth and more about chasing a high.

A 2023 Morningstar study found that 70 percent of investors overestimated their tolerance for risk when markets were rising. Fueled by FOMO, they piled into trendy assets only to panic-sell at the first downturn. That cycle—buying high out of excitement, selling low out of fear—is the exact opposite of smart investing, yet it repeats itself every generation. The dot-com bubble in the late '90s, the housing boom of the mid-2000s, the crypto surge of 2021—different players, same game.

The antidote isn't to avoid investing altogether; it's to recognize the red flags before they lead you astray. I sometimes give clients what I call a **Red Flag Decoder.**

If you catch yourself saying things like:
- *"Everyone's doing it, I can't be left behind."*
- *"This time it's different."*
- *"It's only going up from here."*

…then you're not investing, you're gambling.

Joey learned this the hard way. When we rebuilt his portfolio, we shifted him into a diversified mix of ETFs across 11 sectors, using dollar-cost averaging so he added money steadily instead of in emotional bursts. His new strategy may not make cocktail-party headlines, but it's put him back on track with 8 percent annualized returns since 2022. The surgeon, too, eventually admitted he didn't need the thrill of speculation to fund his retirement. By rebalancing into a broader mix of stocks, bonds, and income products, he found peace of mind—something money can't buy directly, but good planning can provide.

The lesson is simple: chasing hype feels exciting in the moment, but it rarely leads you to the summit. The climb requires steadiness, not adrenaline.

THE MARKET TIMING MYTH: YOU'RE NOT A FORTUNE TELLER

Time in the Market vs. Timing the Market

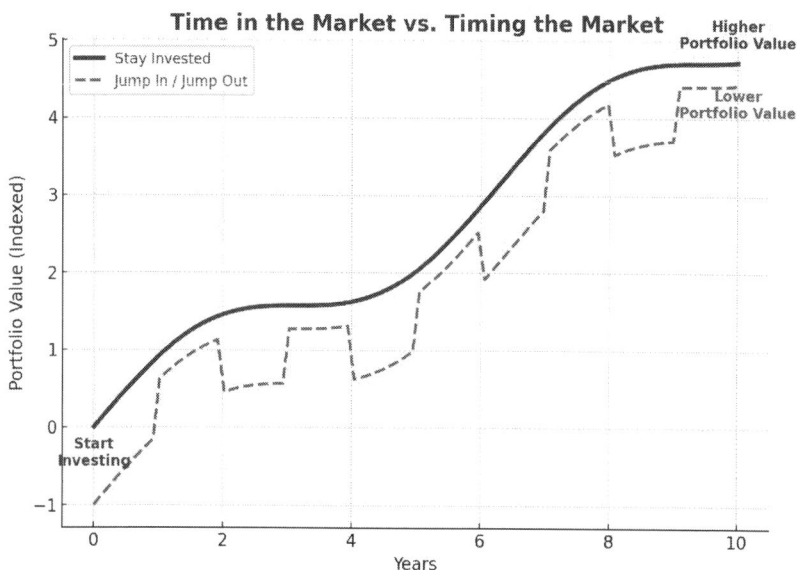

Source: Author's own calculations.

Of all the illusions that trip investors up, market timing may be the most seductive. The idea that you can sell before the market drops and buy back in just as it rises sounds logical, even empowering. But in practice it's more like trying to predict when the next Michigan snowstorm will arrive—you might get it right once or twice, but over time the odds catch up with you.

I think of Rosa, a 50-year-old nurse practitioner from White Lake who came into my office convinced she had cracked the code. "Jordan, I watch CNBC every morning," she told me. "Buy when it's low, sell when it's high—simple, right?" In 2022, when the S&P 500 fell 20 percent, Rosa sold her entire $600,000 portfolio, certain things would get worse. But when the market rebounded, she was left watching from the sidelines. By the time she bought back in, she had missed the rally, costing her $120,000. She didn't just lock in her losses—she also forfeited her chance to recover.

Greg, a salesman from Flint, fell into a similar trap in 2024. Worried about the election, he sold his $500,000 portfolio before "uncertainty" could hit. The market promptly rallied 12 percent. He had essentially paid $60,000 for peace of mind—a very expensive insurance policy against something that never happened.

History is full of these examples. During the dot-com crash in the early 2000s, many investors bailed out after the tech bubble burst, missing the rebound that began just two years later. In 2008, fear drove countless people out of the market when the S&P 500 plunged more than 50 percent. But those who stayed invested saw their portfolios recover and then grow more than threefold over the next decade. Missing just the first few months of those rebounds meant missing some of the best gains of a generation.

The data is damning. Fidelity has shown that missing the 10 best market days over a 20-year period can cut your returns in half—from 7 percent annually down to 3.5 percent. *And here's the kicker:* the best days almost always come right after the worst ones. That means if you jump out during volatility, you're almost guaranteed to miss the recovery. Vanguard's research confirms the same: market timers underperform buy-and-hold investors by 1.5 percent per year on average, simply because they sit on the sidelines during rebounds.

So why do smart people fall for it? Behavioral scientists call it the **illusion of control**. We see patterns, we watch the news, we scroll headlines on our phones, and we believe we can connect the dots. Add in **overconfidence bias**, the tendency to overrate our own abilities, and suddenly market timing feels not just possible but obvious. "I called the last downturn," someone will tell you. But even a broken clock is right twice a day. The real test isn't calling one move—it's doing it consistently, over decades, without missing. No one has pulled that off.

I once worked with a client named Alan, a retired auto executive. He timed the market perfectly in 2000, moving his portfolio to cash just before the tech bubble burst. For years, he told that story at dinner parties with pride. But in 2008, he tried it again—sold everything in October, certain the market would keep falling. It did for a while, and he felt vindicated. But when the rebound began in March 2009, he froze, waiting for "confirmation" that it was safe. By the time he re-entered, he had missed a 40 percent rebound. His single perfect call in 2000 was luck. His second call wiped out the benefit of the first. As Alan later admitted, "I confused luck with skill, and it cost me more than it ever saved me."

The truth is, market timing doesn't just cost money—it costs peace of mind. Investors who try it live in a constant state of hyper-vigilance, watching every headline, every market swing, as if their retirement depended on it. That stress alone is corrosive. And even when they're right, the anxiety of having to make the next call never ends.

The antidote isn't exciting, but it works: dollar-cost averaging. Invest a fixed amount every month, no matter what the headlines say. When prices fall, you buy more shares. When prices rise, you buy fewer. Over time, the highs and lows even out, and your average cost smooths the bumps. Rosa, after her costly experiment, adopted this discipline— investing $1,000 a month in a diversified ETF portfolio. No more guessing, no more panic. Since then, her portfolio has grown at 8 percent annually, not because she beat the market, but because she stopped trying.

Markets will always have ups and downs. The difference between reaching the summit and stalling halfway isn't predicting the next storm—it's staying on the trail regardless of the weather.

YOUR CLIMBING GEAR: BUILDING A SMART PORTFOLIO

Every climber needs the right gear before they set foot on the trail. Imagine heading up Mount Rainier with flip-flops and a bottle of water— you won't make it far. Building wealth is no different. You need a sturdy pack filled with essentials that will carry you through the climb. Over the years, I've found there are five pieces of "gear" that every investor needs to bring along.

1. Start Early and Harness Compound Interest

This is your climbing rope. It may not look like much at the start, but it holds you steady and gives you leverage as the trail gets steeper. Even small amounts, invested early, create momentum. I think of Randy, the teacher who started saving just $100 a month at age 22. He never thought of himself as wealthy, but by the time he hit his 50s, the quiet compounding of those dollars had already turned into six figures. His climb wasn't flashy—it was steady, dependable, and anchored by time.

2. Patch the Leaks: Keep Fees Low

This is your waterproof tent. Without it, even a small storm can drench you and ruin the trip. High fees are like holes in your shelter, letting the rain in year after year until you're soaked. Clients like Sarah, who lost $30,000 a year to hidden pension fees, didn't realize how exposed they were until we fixed it. Once the leaks were patched by moving her money into low-cost ETFs, she was finally protected from the financial storms that had been soaking her progress.

3. Pack Diversification

Diversification is your first-aid kit. You hope you won't need it, but when the trail gets rough, it can save you from disaster. Remember Joey, the IT manager who had bet too heavily on crypto? After rebuilding his portfolio into a diversified mix across 11 sectors—technology, health care, utilities, energy, and more—he no longer had to worry that one bad bet could knock him off the mountain. Broad exposure cushions the falls and helps you recover faster.

4. Avoid Dangerous Shortcuts: FOMO and Market Timing

This is your trail map. Without it, you risk wandering off-course when you see what looks like a quicker way to the top. But those shortcuts almost always lead to dead ends. Rosa's attempt to time the market in 2022 cost her $120,000. Joey's FOMO-driven crypto gamble lost him half his savings. Their mistakes weren't a lack of intelligence—it was the absence of a clear plan. With a disciplined route—dollar-cost averaging, diversification, and patience—the path might feel slower, but it gets you to the summit.

5. Bring a Guide: Work with a Fiduciary

Even the most experienced climbers hire guides on dangerous peaks. A fiduciary advisor is that guide—someone legally bound to put your interests first, helping you avoid traps and adjust when conditions change. Mike and Lisa's path to an early retirement wasn't about picking miracle investments; it was about steady, fiduciary-led choices that saved them $80,000 in fees and put them ahead of schedule. A good guide doesn't just carry your gear—they help you carry it wisely.

Finally, remember to **rebalance your pack**. Over time, your investments will drift—stocks may grow faster than bonds, or one sector may swell out of proportion. Rebalancing is the process of adjusting back to your original mix, selling a little of what's high and buying what's low. It's like repacking your bag at each rest stop, making sure the weight is balanced so you don't topple on the trail. This simple habit forces discipline—buying low, selling high—without emotion getting in the way.

The climb is never easy, but with the right gear, it becomes achievable. Too many people head up the mountain unprepared, weighed down by hidden costs, chasing shortcuts, or lugging unbalanced packs. But those who prepare—who bring the essentials and follow the map—find themselves reaching the summit with confidence, ready to enjoy the view.

CLOSING THE CHAPTER: THE VIEW FROM THE TOP

Mike and Lisa's story is proof of what's possible when you climb with the right gear and the right mindset. By consolidating their scattered 401(k)s, trimming their fees, and building a diversified portfolio, they turned a frustrating uphill slog into a steady ascent. They didn't need to chase fads or call the market—they just needed to keep walking. Today, their nest egg is not only on track for an early retirement, but also strong enough to fund the cabin on Lake Huron they once thought was just a dream.

That's the view from the top. It isn't just numbers on a statement—it's the peace of mind of knowing your climb has been worth it. It's the freedom to choose how you spend your days, whether that means traveling, spoiling your grandchildren, or finally taking up the hobbies you set aside during your working years. It's the confidence that comes from knowing you've prepared not just for the next five years, but for the decades ahead.

The journey up the mountain is about discipline: starting early, patching leaks, avoiding shortcuts, and following a steady map. But the summit isn't the end of the story. Once you reach the top, the real challenge begins—the descent into retirement. That phase requires just as much planning, because going down safely demands a different set of skills and strategies. In Chapter 3, we'll shift from accumulation to distribution, and from building wealth to preserving it. Because the last thing you want after years of climbing is to stumble on the way down.

So take a breath, enjoy the view, and get ready for the next leg of the journey. The mountain doesn't end at the peak—it simply changes. And with the right plan, the descent can be every bit as rewarding as the climb.

CHAPTER THREE

Getting Down Safely:
Shifting to Retirement Mode

Picture standing on the summit of a tall Michigan dune. You've climbed for what feels like forever, step after step, until your legs ache and the view finally opens before you: miles of water stretching across Lake Huron, the sky wide and endless. It's breathtaking. But then comes the sobering realization—the hardest part isn't getting up here. It's getting down safely.

Retirement works the same way. Most people spend their careers focused on the climb: saving into 401(k)s, building businesses, paying off mortgages, investing in the markets. Attorneys rack up decades in courtrooms, engineers design the products that keep industries running, doctors push through long nights at hospitals, CEOs and sales leaders chase growth quarter after quarter. After 30 or 40 years of work, they reach the summit with significant wealth—sometimes millions—accumulated. And yet, when it's time to retire, the question that weighs on them isn't *"Did I save enough?"* It's *"How do I use what I've built without watching it crumble beneath me?"*

That's the question Tom, a 62-year-old engineer from Sterling Heights, Michigan, brought into my office. After 35 years in the auto industry, he had saved just over $1.8 million, with a pension waiting to kick in at 65. On paper, he looked like someone who had done everything right. He and his wife had dreams of summers on Lake Huron and winters in Florida. Yet when he slid his portfolio statement across my desk, his hands shook ever so slightly. "I've climbed this money mountain," he said, "but now what? How do I get down without breaking my neck?"

Tom isn't alone. I've seen the same look on the faces of attorneys who've built multimillion-dollar practices, sales executives who thrived on high commissions, even business owners who sold companies for life-changing sums. They all discover the same truth: the climb and the descent are not the same journey. The rules change once you reach the peak.

During your working years, volatility can be a friend. A market downturn simply means you're buying at a discount, with plenty of time to recover. But in retirement, volatility becomes an enemy. You're no longer adding to your accounts—you're drawing from them. A steep market drop in the early years of retirement, coupled with withdrawals for living expenses, can erase decades of careful saving in a matter of months.

That is why I call the five to ten years before and after retirement the "red zone." Just like the final stretch of a football field where the pressure mounts and small mistakes carry outsized consequences, the red zone of retirement demands precision, discipline, and a new kind of playbook. It's the phase where even people with millions of dollars— people who look financially invincible on paper—can find themselves on shaky ground if they misstep.

This chapter is about navigating that red zone. It's about shifting from a lifetime of wealth-building into a season of wealth-protecting and income-designing. It's about creating a plan that transforms accumulated assets into reliable paychecks—paychecks you can count on whether the market soars or crashes. And most of all, it's about building the confidence to finally enjoy the view, whether that's a Lake Huron sunset, a Florida winter, or a long-delayed dream vacation, without constantly wondering if your money will last.

HOW WILL YOU GET DOWN THE MOUNTAIN?

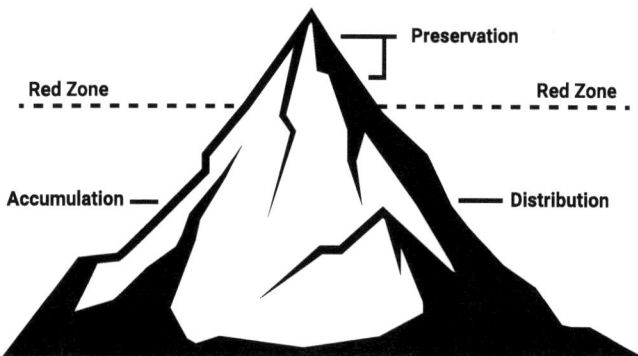

Source: Magellan Financial.

SECTION 1: THE RED ZONE: WHERE THE DESCENT GETS TRICKY

Every sport has a pressure zone. In football, it's the final twenty yards before the end zone—what coaches call the "red zone." The field shrinks, the defense tightens, and every decision carries more weight. Retirement planning has its own version of the red zone: the critical window from about five to ten years before retirement through the first decade after. It's here that your portfolio is at its peak value, but also its peak vulnerability.

Think of it this way: in your 40s and 50s, a market downturn is frustrating, but manageable. You're still earning, still contributing, and time is your ally. By the time you hit your early 60s, though, you've stopped adding fuel to the fire. From here on, every flame comes from the pile you've already built. And the moment you begin withdrawing from that pile—whether it's $5,000 a month to cover living expenses or $50,000 for a vacation home renovation—you've changed the math forever.

I saw this with Tom, our engineer from Sterling Heights. With nearly $2 million saved and a pension on the way, he looked bulletproof. But in 2022, when markets slid 20 percent, he did what many retirees do: he tested the waters by taking a few trial withdrawals to see how retirement might feel. What he didn't realize was that those withdrawals, taken while his account balance was down, locked in losses. A $40,000 withdrawal in the middle of a market dip is far costlier than the same withdrawal when markets are rising. It's like hiking down a steep, rocky trail—you need to be careful where you step, because one wrong move can have outsized consequences.

The red zone reality is that wealth alone doesn't guarantee security. I've had attorneys sit across from me with $3 million in IRAs, CEOs with $10 million windfalls from selling a business, and physicians with seven-figure taxable accounts.

On paper, their situations looked enviable. But when I stress-tested their plans, the same risks showed up: if a market downturn hit early, or if healthcare costs spiked, or if they overspent in the first few years, their seemingly massive nest eggs could erode faster than they ever imagined.

Why is the red zone so precarious? Three reasons:

1. **Sequence of returns risk.** The order of market returns matters more than the average return. Two retirees with identical portfolios can have wildly different outcomes depending on whether bad years come early or late.
2. **Longevity.** Today's retirees aren't planning for a 10- or 15-year retirements. They're planning for 25, 30, even 35 years. That means more years of withdrawals, more years of inflation, and more chances for the unexpected.
3. **Spending shifts.** Early retirement years often bring a burst of activity—travel, home projects, bucket-list goals—that raise spending above what many financial plans assume. Later years, healthcare and long-term care expenses can double or triple monthly costs.

Tom had a solid plan on paper, but the red zone exposed the cracks. Without a strategy to protect against early losses and to balance guaranteed income with market growth, even his $1.8 million could have been stretched thin. That's the sobering truth of the red zone: it isn't about whether you've climbed high enough. It's about whether you can descend safely without stumbling.

And here's the encouraging part—once you understand the terrain, you can prepare for it. You don't have to guess, and you don't have to fear the red zone. You just have to acknowledge that it's different from the climb, and that it requires new tools, new strategies, and in many cases, a new mindset.

SECTION 2: SEQUENCE OF RETURNS, THE SILENT KILLER

When people think about investing, they tend to focus on averages. "The market averages 7 percent a year," they'll say. "If I've saved enough, I should be fine." But averages are like the mirage at the top of the hill—they hide the brutal reality of the terrain beneath your feet. In retirement, what matters most isn't the average return you earn. It's the *sequence* in which those returns show up. That difference can mean the gap between a thirty-year retirement filled with travel, family, and freedom—or a forced downsizing in your 70s because the money didn't stretch far enough.

Sequence of Returns Risk

Same Average, Very Different Outcomes

Both start with $1 million, withdraw $50,000 per year

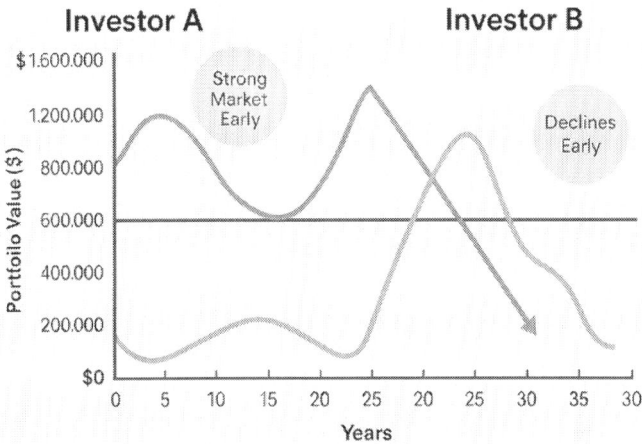

Investor A   Investor B

Strong Market Early

Declines Early

Source: Author's own calculations.

I call this the "silent killer" of retirement plans because most people don't see it coming. They walk into my office with spreadsheets and charts showing that, on paper, their portfolio should last. What those charts don't reveal is how a few bad years at the beginning of retirement can permanently tilt the odds against them, no matter how strong the averages look.

Gloria's story is a perfect example. A 64-year-old teacher from Lansing, Gloria retired in the summer of 2007. She had worked diligently for decades, building a $1.5 million portfolio alongside a modest pension. She felt confident—after all, the markets had been climbing for years. She took her first withdrawal of $60,000, planning to keep spending steady while letting the rest of her portfolio ride the market's gains. Then came 2008.

When the financial crisis hit, the S&P 500 dropped nearly 37 percent. For Gloria, it wasn't just a number on the news ticker. It was her nest egg falling from $1.5 million to under $1 million in less than a year. And because she still needed to live, she kept making withdrawals—selling stocks at the bottom to cover everyday expenses. Every dollar she took out locked in those losses. Even when markets eventually recovered, her account never fully did, because she had fewer shares left to benefit from the rebound.

By 2015, Gloria's portfolio was almost 25 percent smaller than it might have been had the downturn struck later in her retirement. The damage from those early withdrawals was permanent. She ended up going back to work part-time in her 70s—not because she wanted to, but because she *had to.*

Here's the cruel math behind it: two retirees can start with the exact same $2 million portfolio, withdraw the exact same $80,000 a year, and average the exact same 6 percent return over 30 years. If one of them experiences negative returns early in retirement, while the other has strong early years and weaker later years, the **results will be night and day.** The unlucky retiree could run out of money in 18 years. The lucky one could have money left over after 30. Same averages, *completely different outcomes.*

That's sequence of returns risk. And it hits hardest in the red zone, when you're no longer adding to your accounts but taking from them.

I've seen it in more than one profession. A physician who retired right before the pandemic downturn. An attorney who left his firm in 2008, planning to travel, only to watch his accounts fall 40 percent in twelve months. A sales executive who jumped into retirement during the inflation spike of 2022, withdrawing heavily just as the markets sagged. Each had what looked like enough to retire comfortably—$2 million, $3 million, sometimes more—but the sequence of returns risk blindsided them.

So what's the solution? The key is to build insulation around those early years. That might mean keeping two or three years of expenses in cash or bonds, so you aren't forced to sell stocks in a downturn. It might mean using a guaranteed income product to cover the basics, freeing the rest of your portfolio to recover. It might mean starting with smaller withdrawals early and increasing them later once the markets stabilize.

In other words, protecting yourself from the silent killer isn't about chasing the highest return. It's about controlling the order in which you experience returns—and giving yourself a buffer so that bad years don't dictate the rest of your retirement.

Because here's the reality: no one can predict when a downturn will strike. But we do know this—every retiree will face one, probably more than once, during their red zone years. The question is not *if* it happens. *It's how prepared you'll be when it does.*

SECTION 3: SHIFTING MINDSET: FROM ACCUMULATION TO DISTRIBUTION

For decades, the financial advice most people hear is simple: save more, invest steadily, let compounding do the heavy lifting. And for the climb, that advice works. It's how professionals across industries—engineers, doctors, attorneys, CEOs, and business owners—accumulate wealth that reaches into the millions. But once you reach the top of the mountain, the rules change. What got you here isn't necessarily what will get you safely down.

Tom's case made this clear. In his 40s and 50s, his buy-and-hold strategy worked beautifully. He contributed steadily to his 401(k), reinvested dividends, and didn't flinch when markets dipped. Volatility was his friend—stocks on sale meant more growth later. But when he entered his early 60s and started making withdrawals, that same strategy suddenly looked risky. The portfolio that once gave him confidence now made him feel exposed.

This is the mindset shift that every retiree must make: retirement isn't about building wealth anymore. It's about *using wealth* in a way that keeps it sustainable. I've had to explain this to more than one CEO who was used to taking bold risks in business, to attorneys accustomed to thinking in terms of wins and losses, and to doctors who thought of investing like a science experiment. The climb rewarded aggressiveness; the descent rewards caution, balance, and precision.

One of the most persistent myths in retirement planning is the "4 percent rule"—the idea that you can withdraw 4 percent of your portfolio each year, adjusted for inflation, and safely make it through a 30-year retirement. That rule was built in the 1990s, when bond yields were 6 percent and lifespans were shorter. Today, with bond yields closer to 3–4 percent and retirements stretching 30 or 35 years, the math is very different. For many high-net-worth families, the safe withdrawal rate is closer to 3–3.5 percent. That difference may not sound dramatic, but over millions of dollars, it adds up to hundreds of thousands less spending power if you don't adjust.

The descent requires a more nuanced playbook:
- **Cover essentials with certainty.** Housing, healthcare, food, insurance—these aren't optional. They should be backed by guaranteed sources like Social Security, pensions, or fixed income products. I once worked with a retired VP who had $4 million in the markets, but still couldn't sleep at night until we carved out enough guaranteed income to cover his $10,000 monthly baseline expenses. Once that was in place, he finally relaxed and let the rest of his portfolio breathe.
- **Use markets for flexibility.** Discretionary expenses—travel, gifts, hobbies—can be funded with stocks, ETFs, and other growth-oriented assets. This allows the markets to work in your favor without the pressure of covering your daily bills.
- **Build in buffers.** Having two to three years of expenses in cash or short-term bonds acts as a release valve during market downturns. It means you're not forced to sell stocks when they're down, giving your portfolio the space to recover.

Shifting gears isn't always easy. High achievers are often wired to keep climbing, keep chasing growth, keep pushing for the next level. But the descent requires restraint. It's about designing a portfolio that allows you to live well without gambling on perfect market timing.

When clients finally make this shift, something remarkable happens.

The conversations in my office change. Instead of asking, "How much did we make last quarter?" they begin asking, "Can I help my kids buy their first home?" or "Can I take my grandkids to Europe without worrying about the budget?" That's when I know the shift has taken hold—when money stops being a scoreboard and starts being a tool for freedom.

SECTION 4: HEALTHCARE & HIDDEN COSTS

If the red zone is the most precarious stretch of the retirement journey, healthcare is the steepest and most unforgiving part of the trail. You can prepare for market volatility with diversified portfolios. You can plan around sequence of returns with cash buffers. But when it comes to healthcare, the costs are both unpredictable and often staggering.

Most retirees underestimate just how much of their wealth will eventually be consumed by health expenses. It isn't just Medicare premiums or the occasional doctor visit. It's the steady creep of prescriptions, procedures, and the possibility of long-term care that can turn even a multimillion-dollar portfolio into a question mark.

I'll never forget April, a physician who came to see me shortly after retiring from her practice. She had more than $3 million saved, a textbook example of financial discipline. But when we ran the numbers, she was stunned by what Medicare premiums alone would cost her over time. Because her income remained high from required distributions, she triggered IRMAA surcharges—income-related monthly adjustment amounts—that added thousands a year to her Part B and Part D premiums. "I spent my career helping patients manage their health," she said, "and now I feel like the system is taking a scalpel to my retirement."

We restructured her withdrawals, did a series of Roth conversions, and managed her taxable income to bring her below the IRMAA thresholds. That saved her over $5,000 a year in premiums—money she could now redirect toward travel and family instead of handing over to Washington.

Then there's long-term care, the elephant in the room that too few want to talk about. Statistically, **70 percent of people over age 65 will need some form of long-term care.** In Michigan, the average cost for a private room in a nursing facility is over $130,000 a year. Four years of care could easily consume half a million dollars or more. For affluent families, this isn't just about protecting themselves—it's about protecting the legacy they want to leave behind.

Take Rick and Rebecca, a retired business owner and his wife. They had built a fortune—over $5 million between investments and the proceeds of a business sale. "We're set," Rick said confidently. But

Rebecca was diagnosed with early-onset dementia in her 70s, and the cost of her care quickly exceeded $12,000 a month. Within a few short years, Rick realized that without a strategy, he could spend through more than a million dollars of their savings just on care. What shook him most wasn't the cost itself, but the realization that it threatened the secure future he envisioned for his children and grandchildren. We worked together to reposition part of their portfolio into vehicles that included long-term care riders—protection that meant future costs would not jeopardize their financial legacy.

Healthcare is the one category of retirement spending where optimism can be dangerous. Too many people assume Medicare covers "everything." It doesn't. Medicare doesn't cover long-term custodial care. It doesn't shield you from surcharges if your income crosses certain thresholds. And it doesn't protect you from inflation in healthcare costs, which historically outpaces general inflation year after year.

That's why affluent families need to treat healthcare as a core part of their retirement strategy, not an afterthought. Here's what that looks like in practice:

- **Budget realistically.** Assume higher-than-expected healthcare inflation. For many clients, we model annual increases of 5–6 percent in medical costs, not the 2–3 percent used for general expenses.
- **Plan around IRMAA.** Proactive Roth conversions and careful timing of distributions can keep taxable income below the thresholds, saving thousands per year.
- **Use insurance as leverage.** Long-term care riders on annuities or life insurance can stretch dollars farther than paying out-of-pocket.
- **Build flexibility.** Having dedicated healthcare reserves— sometimes a separate account earmarked only for medical needs—creates clarity and prevents healthcare surprises from derailing the rest of the plan.

For many of my clients—executives, doctors, attorneys—their greatest fear isn't running out of money because of vacations or generosity toward their children. It's that a health crisis will consume what they worked so hard to build. I often tell them: markets may go up and down, but healthcare is the one certainty you can't ignore.

If the red zone is the descent, healthcare is the steep slope where footing is most treacherous. But with foresight, strategy, and the right protections in place, you don't have to fear it. You can prepare for it, absorb it, and keep your retirement journey on course.

SECTION 5: THE BEHAVIORAL TRAP: EMOTIONS IN THE RED ZONE

The most sophisticated financial plan can be undone by one very human factor: emotion. Numbers don't lie, but people panic. And when they do, the damage can be worse than any market downturn.

During the accumulation years, emotions are easier to manage. If the market dips in your 40s, you keep contributing, ride it out, and eventually recover. But in the red zone, when you're no longer saving but withdrawing, fear feels magnified. Every market headline sounds personal. Every dip feels permanent. And panic-driven decisions— selling low, shifting entirely to cash, abandoning a strategy halfway through—can do more harm than the downturn itself.

I remember sitting across from Mark, a 66-year-old executive who had built a $2.5 million portfolio. In March 2020, when COVID sent markets tumbling more than 30 percent in a matter of weeks, Mark couldn't sleep. "I can't afford to lose everything," he told me, voice tight with worry. Despite my counsel, he sold most of his equities at the bottom. What had been a temporary paper loss became a locked-in $750,000 setback. The market rebounded within months, but Mark's portfolio never fully recovered. The real loss wasn't caused by the market—it was caused by fear.

Behavioral risk doesn't just show up as panic selling. Sometimes it's overconfidence. I've worked with sales executives who thrived in high-pressure environments, believing they could outsmart the markets with "just a few tactical moves." Others, like attorneys, lean on their analytical training, convinced they can out-research or out-argue volatility. Doctors often think of investing like medicine—diagnose the problem, apply the treatment, and expect predictable results. But markets aren't patients, and they don't follow protocols. Overconfidence can be just as dangerous as panic, leading to oversized bets, concentration in a single sector, or timing strategies that unravel under stress.

The psychology behind this is well documented. Behavioral economists like Daniel Kahneman and Amos Tversky showed that human beings feel the pain of losses twice as intensely as the joy of gains. In retirement, that pain is magnified because you don't have the same margin for error. Losing $500,000 in your 40s might sting, but you have 25 years to recover. Losing $500,000 in your 60s, while drawing $100,000 a year to live on, can fundamentally alter the trajectory of your retirement.

That's why one of the most important parts of my role isn't building spreadsheets—it's building guardrails. For Mark, after his panic-driven losses, we restructured his portfolio so that 30 percent of his income came from guaranteed sources: an annuity and bond ladder that provided $5,000 a month no matter what the market did. The other 70 percent remained in growth assets, but with clear rules about when to rebalance and how much risk he was willing to take. Those guardrails kept him from making the same mistake again, even when volatility resurfaced in 2022.

Guardrails can take many forms. For some, it's a "no panic rule"—a commitment that they won't sell without a 48-hour cooling period and a conversation with their advisor. For others, it's aligning their portfolio to a Risk Number, ensuring the mix of assets matches both their tolerance and capacity for risk. For still others, it's having enough guaranteed income to cover essentials so they never feel forced to sell growth assets in a downturn.

The point isn't to eliminate emotion—that's impossible. The point is to anticipate it and plan for it. Just like a mountain climber ropes in before the descent, retirees need psychological safety nets before the red zone volatility hits.

Time and again, I've seen how this transforms retirement. Once clients know their essentials are covered and their guardrails are in place, the conversations change. They stop obsessing over market swings and start focusing on what really matters—spending time with family, traveling, building legacies, or pursuing passions they put off during their careers.

Because the real behavioral trap isn't just panic or overconfidence. It's letting fear or ego steal the joy from retirement. A well-designed plan does more than protect wealth—it protects peace of mind. And in the red zone, that peace of mind may be the most valuable asset of all.

SECTION 6: YOUR DESCENT PLAYBOOK

If climbing the mountain of wealth requires endurance, grit, and consistency, then descending it safely requires preparation, balance, and the right equipment. No mountaineer would start a descent without a harness, ropes, or a map. Yet too many retirees step into their red zone with nothing more than hope and a spreadsheet. That's not a plan—it's a gamble.

Over the years, I've come to think of retirement planning as equipping clients with a *descent playbook*. It's not about predicting the future—it's about being ready for whatever the mountain throws at you: sudden storms, loose footing, or hidden cliffs. The playbook doesn't just reduce risk; it creates the freedom to enjoy the journey without fear.

Here's how the playbook comes together.

1. Assess the Terrain

Every descent begins with surveying the landscape. For retirement, that means running stress tests. How does your portfolio perform in a bear market? What happens if inflation spikes? How long does your money last under different withdrawal rates?

I use tools like Monte Carlo simulations not to scare clients, but to reveal the range of possible outcomes. When a CEO or attorney sees how sequence of returns risk could wipe out millions, it's like shining a flashlight into a dark cave. Once they see the risk, they're motivated to plan for it.

2. Build Your Harness: Guaranteed Income

The first rule of a safe descent is simple: cover your essentials with guarantees. Housing, food, insurance, healthcare—those are the non-negotiables. If those needs are met by steady income sources—Social Security, pensions, annuities—everything else becomes less stressful.

I worked with a retired vice president who had $5 million in the markets but still woke up at 3 a.m. worrying. When we carved out $12,000 a month in guaranteed income to cover his family's lifestyle, he finally exhaled. The rest of his portfolio could swing up or down, but he knew the roof over his head and the refrigerator in his kitchen weren't at the mercy of Wall Street.

3. Pack an Emergency Kit: Cash & Bonds

Even the most seasoned climbers keep supplies for the unexpected. In retirement, that means holding two to three years of living expenses in cash or short-term bonds. This buffer ensures you don't have to sell stocks in a downturn.

Think back to Gloria, who retired right before 2008. If she'd had a $150,000 reserve set aside, she could have avoided locking in losses during the crash. That buffer would have given her portfolio the breathing room to recover.

4. Choose the Right Pace: Flexible Withdrawals

Climbers know that rushing down the mountain is as dangerous as standing still. The same is true for retirement withdrawals. Instead of sticking rigidly to the old "4 percent rule," modern retirees need flexible strategies that adjust with the markets. Some years you might spend a little less, others a little more—but the key is aligning withdrawals with reality, not with outdated formulas.

I had a client, a successful attorney, who was adamant about withdrawing $200,000 annually no matter what. When we showed him how that would deplete his $3 million portfolio in 18 years if markets turned against him, he softened. By adopting a flexible spending rule and cutting back modestly during downturns, he preserved both his wealth and his lifestyle.

5. Plan for the Storm: Healthcare & LTC

Every mountain has weather patterns. Some you can see coming, others arrive without warning. In retirement, healthcare is that storm. It's not optional, and it can hit harder than expected. Budget generously. Account for Medicare surcharges (IRMAA). Protect against long-term care expenses with insurance solutions or dedicated reserves. Clients who treat healthcare as an afterthought often face the hardest falls. Those who prepare walk through storms with confidence.

6. Set Guardrails: Behavioral Protection

Even the best climbers make mistakes when fear sets in. Guardrails prevent small slips from turning into disasters. In retirement, guardrails might be:

- A "no-panic rule" requiring 48 hours before any major sale.

- Portfolios tied to a Risk Number that keeps exposure within comfort zones.
- Guaranteed income streams that reduce the emotional urge to sell in downturns.

Mark, the executive who sold at the bottom of 2020, now has these guardrails in place. The result? When volatility returned in 2022, he stayed calm—and his portfolio stayed intact.

7. Work with a Guide

Finally, no one descends Everest alone. A fiduciary advisor serves as your climbing guide—someone who's seen every type of weather, every type of terrain, and knows how to adjust the route in real time. My role isn't just managing money; it's walking beside clients, helping them avoid hidden crevices, and ensuring they enjoy the journey instead of fearing it.

The Power of the Playbook

When clients embrace this playbook, something powerful happens. The anxiety fades. Instead of white-knuckling every market downturn, they relax. Instead of wondering whether they can afford to help their children or travel abroad, they know exactly what their wealth can support. Instead of obsessing over CNBC headlines, they focus on sunsets, family dinners, and legacies.

The descent doesn't have to be a white-knuckle ride. With the right plan, it can be steady, confident, even joyful. And that's the point of all the years of climbing in the first place—not just to reach the summit, but to come down safely and enjoy the view.

CLOSING THE CHAPTER: THE SAFE LANDING

Tom's question still echoes in my mind: *"How do I get down without breaking my neck?"* It's the same question that every retiree faces, whether they've saved $1.5 million, $5 million, or more. The truth is, reaching the summit is an achievement—but it's not the finish line. The real measure of success is in the descent.

I've walked this trail with hundreds of families: engineers who built careers in Michigan's auto industry, attorneys who fought through decades of courtroom battles, doctors who saved lives, executives who built companies, and business owners who poured everything into their work. Different careers, different stories, but when they enter the red zone, their concerns sound strikingly similar:

Will my money last?

What happens if the market crashes?

How do I protect my family if healthcare costs explode?

The good news is, you don't have to walk this path blindly. You can prepare. You can build a playbook that protects against sequence of returns risk, that covers healthcare with foresight, that keeps emotions in check with guardrails, and that turns your hard-earned wealth into paychecks you can rely on.

When clients embrace this shift, the transformation is remarkable. Fear gives way to confidence. Anxiety turns into peace of mind. Instead of checking market tickers every morning, they check flight schedules for long-postponed vacations. Instead of worrying about being a burden, they start thinking about what kind of legacy they want to leave. Instead of clinging to the top of the mountain, they descend with assurance, knowing their footing is secure.

That's what Tom discovered when we restructured his plan. Today, he's sailing Lake Huron with his wife, enjoying the very retirement he once doubted was possible. His portfolio is no longer a source of stress—it's the engine powering his freedom.

And that's the goal for you, too. Retirement isn't about holding your breath and hoping you don't run out of money. It's about creating a path that lets you exhale, relax, and enjoy the view.

As we move into the next chapter, we'll go deeper into aligning your investments with your personal "speed"—your risk tolerance and capacity—so that your descent feels not only safe, but tailored to the pace that lets you live fully. Because the truth is, a safe landing doesn't happen by accident. It happens by design.

CHAPTER FOUR

Driving at Your Speed:
Matching Investments to Your Risk Tolerance

Ever meet someone who drives like they own the road? Take Marjorie, an 89-year-old spitfire from Farmington Hills, who rolled into my office with a portfolio that could rival a NASCAR driver's fuel tank. A widow and retired nurse, she loves the thrill of hitting the casinos and trading tech stocks like they're slot machines. "Jordan," she laughed, gripping her cane like it was the wheel of her old Corvette, "I'm driving my money at 90 miles an hour—give me growth or give me nothing!"

Her $1.4 million nest egg was parked almost entirely in volatile growth ETFs, and when the market dipped 10 percent in early 2025, she shrugged it off like it was nothing more than a pothole on Telegraph Road.

Now compare her to Connor, a 32-year-old software developer from Wixom, who inherited his grandfather's $600,000 farm trust. "I'm at 25 miles an hour, steady and slow, no risks," he told me, his voice cautious, almost fearful. Connor refused to let even a single dollar drift toward stocks, clinging instead to bonds and CDs.

Then there's Dr. Patricia, a 55-year-old physician from Bloomfield Hills with more than $3 million saved. Her income and capacity for risk are enormous, but her tolerance is low. After living through both the dot-com bust and the 2008 crash, she carries emotional scars that keep her more conservative than her portfolio can afford.

Each of these people came in with a different "speed limit" for their money. None of them were wrong. None of them were right. The truth is, the key to building and preserving wealth isn't about racing ahead or crawling along—it's about finding **the speed that matches both your emotions and your financial reality**. That's what this chapter is all about: matching your portfolio to your personal speedometer so you can cruise into retirement without running off the road.

Risk tolerance isn't just a Wall Street buzzword—it's how much market turbulence you can handle before your emotions take the wheel. Too aggressive, and a sudden dip can wreck decades of savings. Too conservative, and inflation quietly eats your money like rust under a Michigan car. In my decades of guiding professionals across Oakland, Macomb, and Livingston counties—engineers in Sterling Heights, teachers in Howell, executives in Troy—I've seen it all. The portfolios that last aren't always the flashiest or the most cautious; they're the ones that match the driver to the car, the speed to the road.

EDUCATIONAL DEEP DIVE: RISK TOLERANCE VS. RISK CAPACITY

One of the most misunderstood parts of retirement planning isn't how much you've saved, what products you own, or even when you plan to retire. It's something more fundamental: **your relationship with risk**. Not risk in the vague sense of "I'm aggressive" or "I'm conservative," but risk in measurable, practical terms.

There are really two kinds of risk: **tolerance** (how much risk you're willing to take) and **capacity** (how much risk you can actually afford to take). They're like the two dials on a dashboard — turn one too far without adjusting the other, and your financial vehicle is heading for trouble.

1. Risk Tolerance: The Psychology of Risk

Risk tolerance is emotional. It's about how much market turbulence you can live with without panicking or second-guessing yourself. It's shaped by your personality, your past experiences, your generation's story, even the way you saw money handled growing up.

Take Jamal, a 47-year-old automotive engineer from Berkley. He earns a strong six-figure salary and has accumulated about $2.2 million between his 401(k), brokerage accounts, and Roth IRAs. On paper, he should be able to take on market risk comfortably. But Jamal grew up watching his father lose his pension when the company he worked for restructured in the 1980s. That early experience scarred him. So when the market dropped 20 percent in 2022, Jamal's fear took over — he slashed his equity exposure at the exact wrong time, turning paper losses into permanent ones.

That's tolerance in action: it's not about what you can afford; it's about what your heart and stomach can handle.

Tolerance can be measured a few different ways:

- **Risk questionnaires**, which present "what if" scenarios. For example, if your $1.5 million portfolio lost $150,000 in a month, how would you react?
- **The Risk Number® (Nitrogen)**, which assigns a score from 1 to 100 based on your comfort with volatility.
- **Behavioral finance profiling**, which looks at biases like *loss aversion* (we feel the pain of loss about twice as strongly as the joy of gains), *anchoring* (getting stuck on past market highs), or *overconfidence* (believing we're immune to downturns).

But here's the catch: ***what people say*** and ***what they actually do*** in stressful markets don't always match. A client might claim they're fine with a 20 percent dip — until it happens, and suddenly they're ready to sell everything.

2. Risk Capacity: The Math Behind the Emotions

While tolerance is psychological, **capacity is mathematical**. It's your financial ability to take risk. In other words: if the market drops, how much damage can you absorb without derailing your retirement?

Think of it like shock absorbers on your car. A smooth ride depends on having enough cushion to handle the bumps in the road.

Capacity is influenced by:

- **Cash flow** — Do you have income that comfortably covers expenses? If so, you can take more risk than someone living month-to-month in retirement.
- **Time horizon** — The longer until you need the money, the more time you have to recover from downturns.
- **Liquidity** — Ample emergency reserves increase capacity.
- **Debt** — Lower liabilities mean greater flexibility.
- **Guaranteed income sources** — Pensions, Social Security, or annuity accounts reduce the pressure on your investments.

Take Margaret, a 65-year-old retired teacher from Sterling Heights. She's got $850,000 saved, plus a pension covering most of her essential expenses. Her risk tolerance is low — she's a worrier by nature — but her capacity is higher than she realizes. Because her pension covers the basics, she could safely take more investment risk.

Yet her fear has her over-weighted in bonds and CDs, which risks her money being eaten away by inflation over the next 25 years.

On the other side is Dr. Patricia from Bloomfield Hills. With more than $3 million saved and a high income, her *capacity* is enormous. But emotionally, she remains conservative. If her allocations are too cautious, she risks undershooting her long-term goals — things like healthcare costs, travel, and leaving a legacy for her children.

Capacity is measured with tools like:

- **Monte Carlo simulations**, which run thousands of possible "market life stories" to see the probability of a plan succeeding.
- **Net worth and liability mapping**, showing assets and debts in context.
- **Income replacement ratios**, ensuring retirement income covers essential expenses, even in bad markets.

3. When the Two Gears Don't Match

This is where danger sets in.

- **High tolerance + low capacity** = catastrophic losses you can't recover from.
- **Low tolerance + high capacity** = underperformance, falling short of your retirement goals.

Picture two gears that need to turn smoothly together. If one spins too fast while the other lags, the system grinds down.

For example: Remember Connor in Wixom with his $600,000 inheritance? At 32, his *capacity* is high — he has decades to recover from downturns. But his *tolerance* is extremely low, so he hides in bonds. The result? His portfolio barely keeps up with inflation. Thirty years down the road, his money risks losing purchasing power.

Now flip it. Eleanor, a 70-year-old widow from Howell, has a $1.1 million IRA. She claims she can "handle risk" because she's seen it all. Her tolerance is high, but her capacity is shrinking — she's now drawing from her account every month with no paycheck to replenish it. If markets drop early in her retirement, her withdrawals will accelerate losses — the classic sequence of returns risk.

Both mismatches can derail even the best-intentioned retirement plan.

HISTORICAL PERFORMANCE BY RISK CATEGORY

Charts and tables can tell one story, but they don't capture the real-life emotions of clients living through downturns. To make these categories real, let's walk through how investors in Oakland, Macomb, and Livingston counties might have experienced them over the past two decades.

CONSERVATIVE:
(20 percent stocks / 60 percent bonds / 20 percent cash)
- **Average return:** ~5.5 percent
- **Worst year loss:** –5 percent

Conservative portfolios are built like a sturdy sedan — slow and steady, not flashy, but unlikely to break down in a storm.

Take Jason, a 72-year-old retiree from Clinton Township. In 2008, his $1.3 million conservative portfolio fell about 5 percent. He didn't enjoy seeing his balance slip, but compared to his neighbor — who was down 30 percent — Jason slept fine. His pension and Social Security checks covered most of his expenses, so the portfolio acted like backup fuel.

The trade-off? Over 20 years, Jason's portfolio returned less than half of what a growth allocation would have delivered. He avoided deep pain but also missed out on long-term growth that could have supported bigger gifts to his grandchildren or a legacy for his church.

BALANCED:
(50 percent stocks / 40 percent bonds / 10 percent cash)
- **Average return:** ~7.5 percent
- **Worst year loss:** –15 percent

Balanced portfolios are like a reliable crossover SUV — good mileage, decent speed, but still steady on rough roads.

In 2020, Alice, a 64-year-old teacher from Brighton, watched her $1.6 million balanced portfolio lose around 12 percent in the first quarter when the pandemic hit. For a moment, she panicked. But by the end of the year, markets recovered, and her account closed higher than it started. The lesson? Balanced portfolios have enough growth to recover from shocks — as long as the investor stays buckled in and doesn't jump out mid-ride.

GROWTH:
(70 percent stocks / 25 percent bonds / 5 percent cash)
- **Average return:** ~9.0 percent
- **Worst year loss:** –25 percent

Growth portfolios are like sports cars — fun to drive, but you'd better know what you're doing when the road turns icy.

In 2008, Jan of Auburn Hills had $1.5 million in a growth allocation. When Lehman Brothers collapsed, his account lost over 20 percent in months. Jan admitted he nearly sold everything — but he held on. By 2010, his portfolio had fully recovered, and over the next decade it grew to over $3 million. The catch? If he had panicked and sold in late 2008, he would have permanently locked in losses and likely delayed his retirement by years.

AGGRESSIVE GROWTH
(90 percent stocks / 10 percent bonds)
- **Average return:** ~10.5 percent
- **Worst year loss:** –43 percent

Aggressive portfolios are like race cars — thrilling when conditions are right, but dangerous if you hit a pothole at high speed.

Take Donnie from Livonia, age 34, who poured his $800,000 inheritance into an aggressive ETF mix in late 2021. By the end of 2022, tech stocks crashed, and he was down nearly 30 percent. On paper, Donnie still had time to recover. But emotionally, he wasn't ready — he pulled back to 40 percent stocks at exactly the wrong time. By mid-2023, when markets rebounded, he'd already missed much of the recovery.

This is the classic pitfall of aggressive portfolios: they often perform best in the long run, but only if you stay invested. The greatest danger isn't the market itself — it's the investor's reaction to it.

THE TAKEAWAY:

Every portfolio "speed" comes with its own highs and lows. The conservative investor avoids stomach-churning crashes but risks outliving their money. The aggressive investor may accumulate the most wealth but often struggles to stay disciplined when volatility strikes.

The lesson for clients across Oakland, Macomb, and Livingston counties — from retirees in Sterling Heights to executives in Bloomfield Hills — is that **there's no universally right allocation. The right one is the one you can stick with.** If you can't sleep at night, the returns don't matter. And if you never grow enough, you'll run out of fuel before your journey ends.

RISK IN ACTION: THE RIPPLE EFFECT ACROSS THE RIPT FRAMEWORK

Understanding risk in isolation is like knowing the horsepower of your car but ignoring the road conditions. Horsepower matters, but not if the pavement is icy or the brakes are worn. Risk tolerance and capacity only become meaningful when we see how they ripple through the rest of the RIPT framework: **Income, Portfolio, and Taxes**.

Think of RIPT as an ecosystem. Adjust one element, and the others respond.

Risk and Income: Aligning Stability or Variability

Income is where risk tolerance often collides with reality. If your essential retirement income depends on assets that fluctuate wildly, your lifestyle may swing with the markets.

Consider Mark, age 62, from Troy. A retired automotive executive, Mark receives a generous military pension that covers 80 percent of his household expenses. Because his "income floor" is already stable, his risk capacity is high. With that cushion, he's able to tie more of his discretionary income to equities, dividends, and growth-oriented withdrawals. Market downturns don't threaten his lifestyle because his essentials are locked in.

Contrast that with Alice from Brighton, who relies entirely on Social Security and her $1.4 million IRA. Her tolerance for risk is moderate, but her capacity is lower, because every dollar she withdraws must come from volatile assets. A bear market early in her retirement could devastate her plan if she were too aggressive. For Alice, income stability is paramount. That's why we structured a "floor and upside" model: fixed income sources (annuities, bonds, Social Security) cover the essentials, while a smaller growth bucket fuels travel and extras.

THE TAKEAWAY:

Income stability must match emotional comfort. Too much variability with low capacity invites disaster. Too little variability with high-capacity risks underspending or undershooting legacy goals.

Risk and Portfolio: Tax-Efficient Positioning

Risk doesn't just decide how much you invest in stocks, bonds, or annuities — it also decides **where you hold them**. This is the art of **asset location**.

Take Patricia, the physician from Bloomfield Hills with $3 million in savings. Her tolerance is low, but her capacity is high. We positioned her riskier growth assets inside her Roth IRA, where the tax-free growth compounds without future tax drag. Meanwhile, we placed income-producing assets like bonds inside her traditional IRA, deferring the taxes until she draws them later. The result: less volatility in her taxable accounts and a stronger after-tax growth engine in her Roth.

Now look at Sven in Sterling Heights. He has a moderate tolerance and a long horizon. By strategically placing high-volatility holdings in his taxable account — where long-term capital gains rates are favorable — we preserved his flexibility while still aligning with his comfort zone.

Morningstar research shows that smart asset location can add the equivalent of 0.5 to 0.75 percent annually in net returns. Over decades, that's hundreds of thousands of dollars — simply from matching risk decisions to tax positioning.

Risk and Taxes: Roth vs. Traditional Strategy

Risk tolerance and capacity also play an underrated role in one of the most common questions: *"Should I lean toward Roth or Traditional retirement accounts?"*

- A high-tolerance, long-horizon investor is often more willing to fund Roth accounts aggressively. They accept the upfront tax hit,

knowing their money can compound tax-free for years.
- A risk-averse retiree may prefer the upfront tax deduction of Traditional contributions, locking in certainty today rather than betting on high returns tomorrow.

But here's where capacity matters most:

Take Eleanor from Howell. At 70, she has $1.1 million in an IRA and a high tolerance. She likes the idea of Roth conversions, but her capacity is low. Every tax dollar she spends on conversions reduces her retirement cushion. For her, full-scale conversions would be reckless. Instead, we structured smaller, opportunistic conversions in market downturns — balancing her comfort with her true financial ability.

Compare that with Darren from Novi. At 32, he has decades to recover from volatility. His tolerance is low, but his capacity is enormous. With guidance, we nudged him into heavier Roth contributions while explaining the long-term benefit: locking in tax-free growth now, while he's in a lower tax bracket.

THE TAKEAWAY:

Roth vs. Traditional isn't just a tax decision — it's a risk decision. The right balance depends on both emotional comfort and mathematical ability. Check out our tax calculator on Roth conversions: www. maintaxbill.com – free for anybody to use.

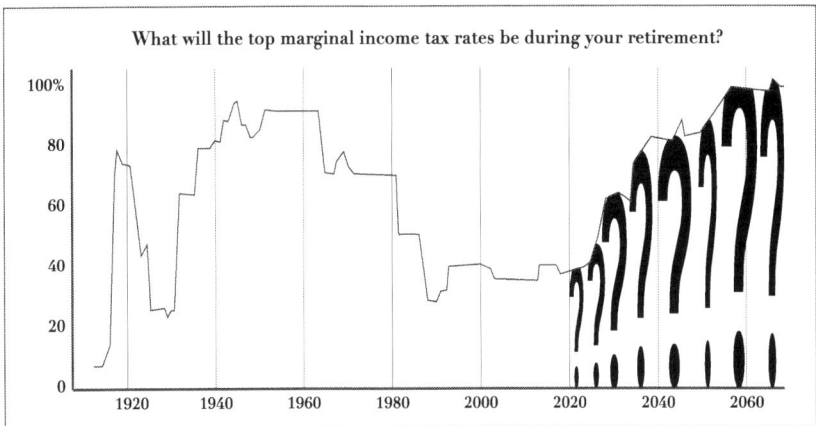

Source: Magellan Financial using data from the Urban-Brookings Tax Policy Center, "Historical Individual Income Tax Parameters: 1913 to 2018"

The First Domino

When clients across Oakland, Macomb, and Livingston counties understand their true speed — their blend of tolerance and capacity — every other decision becomes clearer. Income plans align with reality. Portfolios are positioned for growth *and* tax efficiency. Tax strategies become proactive rather than reactive.

Risk is the first domino in the RIPT framework. Get it right, and the rest fall into place in order. Get it wrong, and the whole plan wobbles.

YOUR SPEED PLAYBOOK: HOW TO MATCH YOUR MONEY TO YOUR MILE-PER-HOUR

If your risk score is your financial speedometer, then your Playbook is the driver's manual. Without it, you're like a race car on I-96 without a map—capable of high speeds but unsure when to accelerate, when to brake, and when to pull into the pit stop for maintenance.

This Playbook is about turning an abstract "risk number" into a concrete plan of action.

Step 1: Confirm Your True Speed

Most people think they know their speed, but behavior tells the real story.

Take Kevin, a 58-year-old auto supplier from Troy. He swore he was "a 70 MPH investor"—comfortable with swings. But when his $2 million portfolio dropped $300,000 during the 2020 pandemic, he sold almost everything. His behavior revealed he was closer to 40 MPH.

Action: Review how you reacted in past downturns. If you've never lived through a major drop with significant assets, run stress tests with your advisor. Don't just trust what you think—trust your track record.

Step 2: Align Income Stability with Speed

Your income plan should match your emotional comfort.

- **High tolerance (70+ MPH):** You may accept variable income streams—dividends, growth-based withdrawals—because you have other safety nets.
- **Moderate tolerance (50–69 MPH):** You'll likely benefit from a hybrid model—stable income for essentials (annuities, pensions, Social Security) with a growth bucket for extras.

- **Low tolerance (<50 MPH):** You'll sleep best knowing your essentials are covered by predictable income, even if that means less upside.

Case Study: Laura, 66, from Bloomfield Hills, had $1.8 million saved and a moderate tolerance. We placed half in a fixed-indexed annuity to guarantee income and the rest in a balanced portfolio. She now knows her bills are paid regardless of markets—and she can enjoy her grandkids without obsessing over CNBC.

Step 3: Position Your Portfolio by Speed Zone

Your mix of assets should reflect your combined tolerance and capacity:

- **Fast lane (high tolerance + high capacity):** More equities, alternatives, tax-efficient placement (growth assets in Roths).
- **Middle lane (moderate tolerance or capacity):** Balanced mix—often 50/50 or 60/40.
- **Slow lane (low tolerance + low capacity):** Conservative positioning with guarantees and short-term bonds.

Case Study: Simon, 32, from Saline, had a low tolerance but high capacity. We placed growth assets inside Roth accounts—where he wouldn't see the day-to-day swings—and gave him a modest bond ladder in his taxable accounts. He stayed invested because his "visible" money felt safer, even though his long-term growth engine was still running.

Step 4: Link Your Tax Plan to Your Speed

Taxes and risk go hand-in-hand.

- **High tolerance:** You might be comfortable converting large sums to Roth during downturns—accepting short-term pain for long-term gain.
- **Moderate tolerance:** Partial, phased conversions make sense—small enough to avoid big tax surprises.
- **Low tolerance:** Conservative approach—keep more in Traditional, convert slowly or opportunistically.

Case Study: Mark, 62, from Troy, was a 75 MPH investor with pensions covering his essentials. When markets dipped in 2022, we converted $400,000 to Roth, paying the taxes from non-retirement cash. Mark viewed it as a "tax buying opportunity"—locking in future tax-free growth while valuations were down.

Step 5: Test and Adjust Your Speed

Your speed isn't fixed. Life changes it. Retirement, health issues, inheritances, job losses—they all reset your dashboard.

Rule of Thumb: Reassess at least once a year. Don't overreact to headlines. Adjust gradually, not with knee-jerk reactions.

Case Study: Eleanor, 70, from Howell, once had a high tolerance. But when she started drawing from her IRA, her capacity fell. We recalibrated her plan—adding stable income sources and reducing equity exposure—to match her new "road conditions."

QUICK SELF-CHECK QUIZ: IS YOUR SPEED ALIGNED?

Answer "Yes" or "No" for each:
1. My essential income is stable enough that market dips don't scare me.
2. My portfolio allocation feels right—I'm not losing sleep at night.
3. I understand how much I could lose in a downturn—and I'm comfortable with it.
4. My tax strategy matches my risk style (e.g., Roth vs. Traditional balance).
5. I've reviewed my risk number within the last 12 months.
6. I have 6–12 months of emergency savings.
7. I know my withdrawal rate in retirement—and it's sustainable.
8. I could explain my portfolio to my spouse or kids in plain English.
9. I've lived through a downturn with significant assets and stayed disciplined.
10. My plan connects risk, income, portfolio, and taxes in writing.

SCORING:
- **9–10 Yes answers:** You're in sync—keep cruising.
- **6–8 Yes answers:** Minor tune-ups needed—adjust where mismatches exist.
- **0–5 Yes answers:** Pull into the pit stop—it's time for a serious review.

CLOSING THE CHAPTER: THE TAKEAWAY

The Playbook proves that risk isn't a single decision—it's a series of coordinated moves across income, portfolio, and taxes. Like driving, you don't just pick a speed once; you adjust to the conditions around you.

The winning strategy isn't "fast" or "slow." It's consistency. Match your true speed, stick with it, and your wealth will carry you farther than you ever imagined.

CHAPTER FIVE

Outsmarting Uncle Sam:
Tax Planning for a Wealthier Retirement

It was one of those gray Michigan mornings where the clouds hang low enough to brush the rooftops in Farmington Hills. Across my desk sat Ray, a 62-year-old executive who had just wrapped up a long career running operations for a mid-sized auto supplier. He'd built what many would consider a textbook retirement plan: $2.4 million tucked into his 401(k), a healthy pension on the way, and Social Security waiting down the road.

On paper, Ray looked bulletproof. But as he slid a thick folder of statements across the table, his voice carried the weight of unease.

"Jordan," he said, "I did what they told me—maxed my 401(k), took the company match, deferred as much as possible. But now that I'm running the numbers, it feels like Uncle Sam owns half my retirement."

Ray wasn't exaggerating. Like thousands of others in Metro Detroit, he had followed the old playbook: delay taxes as long as possible. That playbook worked well in the accumulation years, but retirement tells a different story. Between required minimum distributions (RMDs), Social Security taxation, and Medicare premium surcharges, Ray's "bulletproof" retirement plan looked more like a tax minefield.

And now, with Congress passing the One Big Beautiful Bill Act (OBBBA) in 2025, the rules of the game had shifted yet again. Brackets were locked in, deductions had been reshaped, and seniors gained some new advantages—but the traps didn't disappear. They just changed shape.

In fact, this is where many smart, disciplined savers get blindsided. They spend decades focusing on investment returns and account balances, only to discover in retirement that their biggest expense isn't the market—it's taxes.

That morning, I walked Ray through the same reality check I've given to countless others. You can't avoid taxes, but you can outsmart them.

With the right strategy, you don't just keep more of your hard-earned money—you gain freedom. Freedom to travel, to give, to retire on your terms without watching Washington siphon off more than its share.

This chapter is about turning confusing IRS rules and fresh legislation into a roadmap you can actually use. We'll uncover the four biggest tax traps in retirement—RMDs, Social Security taxation, Medicare surcharges, and the legacy tax bomb—and show how proactive planning, especially Roth conversions in the new OBBBA landscape, can transform your future.

Because at the end of the day, the real measure of wealth isn't just what you've saved—it's what you get to keep.

TRAP #1 – THE RMD AVALANCHE

RMDs—Required Minimum Distributions—are the IRS's polite but firm way of saying, *"We've been patient long enough; now it's our turn to get paid."* For decades, you've been feeding your Traditional IRA or 401(k), enjoying the tax deduction on the way in, watching it grow tax-deferred, and telling yourself you'd "figure out the taxes later."

Later is here.

Starting at age 73, the IRS looks at the balance of your tax-deferred accounts and demands a slice every single year—whether you need the money or not. Withdrawals count as ordinary income. That means they don't just create a tax bill; they can also push you into higher brackets, make your Social Security more taxable, and trigger higher Medicare premiums two years later.

The OBBBA didn't touch RMDs. If anything, it quietly raised the stakes. By increasing the standard deduction and creating the senior deduction, it gave retirees more room to convert or withdraw money early at lower rates. But if you wait too long, those benefits vanish—and the avalanche hits.

Bob the Engineer – Clarkston, Michigan

Bob retired at 74 after a career designing bridges and highways. His IRAs totaled $1.8 million. When his first RMD hit, it came to more than $68,000. That withdrawal—money he didn't need—bumped him from the 22 percent to the 24 percent bracket, made 85 percent of his Social Security taxable, and raised his Medicare premiums by nearly $2,000.

Bob could have used the OBBBA's larger deduction in his late 60s to do modest Roth conversions each year. With a $43,500 standard + senior deduction (for a married couple), he could have moved $40,000–$60,000 annually to Roth status without breaking into a higher bracket. Instead, he postponed, and the avalanche buried him in taxes later (www.maintaxbill.com – check it out!).

Candice the Nurse – Sterling Heights

Candice was a nurse for nearly 40 years, careful with money, and proud of her $900,000 IRA at retirement. She disliked the idea of "paying taxes early" and avoided Roth conversions. By 73, her account had grown to $1.3 million. Her first RMD: $49,000. Combined with her pension and Social Security, her taxable income was higher in retirement than it had been in her final working years.

The irony? OBBBA's new senior deduction would have allowed her to move tens of thousands each year into Roth status at little or no tax cost. But without planning, she ended up paying *more* at age 74 than she ever did at age 64.

Daniel the Small Business Owner – Howell

Daniel sold his auto repair shops at 66. He and his wife planned to live modestly off savings and wait until 70 to take Social Security. Their plan looked solid—until the RMD avalanche. At 73, Daniel faced a required withdrawal of nearly $55,000, which combined with his wife's income from a part-time job, triggered Medicare IRMAA surcharges two years later.

Had Daniel structured partial Roth conversions in the years right after selling his business, the OBBBA's larger deductions and higher SALT cap would have shielded much of the income. Instead, the avalanche rolled over him, increasing his taxes *and* his premiums.

THE TAKEAWAY:

RMDs aren't evil. They're simply the government collecting on a decades-old IOU. But the danger isn't just the withdrawal—it's the ripple effect it creates. The OBBBA gave retirees new tools—larger deductions and temporary senior benefits—to manage their taxable income earlier. Those who use them can turn the avalanche into a light snowfall. Those who don't risk being buried.

TRAP #2 – THE SOCIAL SECURITY TAX SURPRISE

Few things frustrate retirees more than discovering their Social Security—something they already paid into—is taxable. "How can they tax it twice?" is a question I hear weekly. The answer is simple: Congress changed the rules in 1983, allowing taxation if your income is "too high."

Here's the kicker: the thresholds set in 1983 have never been adjusted for inflation. They're frozen in time. Meanwhile, everything else—from wages to pensions to RMDs—has climbed. The result is that more retirees fall into the trap every year.

The OBBBA expanded deductions and raised SALT caps, but it didn't touch Social Security thresholds. So, while retirees may feel a bit of relief when filing their 1040, they still stumble into this invisible tax.

Aaron the GM Retiree – Troy

Aaron spent decades at General Motors and retired comfortably with a pension and a seven-figure IRA. He called me one April, frustrated. "Jordan, my tax bill is four grand higher than I expected. I didn't change anything!"

The culprit? A modest cost-of-living adjustment on his pension, plus a slightly larger RMD. That little bit of extra income pushed more of his Social Security across the threshold. The tax on that new chunk of taxable Social Security was enough to create his "surprise" bill.

Jasmine the Realtor – Rochester

Jasmine, a widowed realtor, drew $2,000 a month from Social Security and about $50,000 annually from her IRA. She was shocked to discover that 85 percent of her Social Security was being taxed. Worse, her provisional income put her within a whisker of an IRMAA threshold.

We restructured her withdrawals—using Roth conversions in her 60s while the OBBBA senior deduction was in place, then blending Roth and taxable withdrawals later. The result: her taxable Social Security dropped to around 50 percent of her benefits, saving her about $2,000 a year and keeping her Medicare premiums flat.

Steven & Michelle – Bloomfield Hills Attorneys

This couple came to me after both retiring from successful law practices. Their household income was still strong—over $180,000 between pensions, investments, and RMDs. They were stunned to find that nearly all of their Social Security was taxable.

With their high income, OBBBA's larger deduction barely moved the needle. What did help was sequencing: they delayed Social Security until after several years of Roth conversions. By using the temporary senior deduction (2025–2028) to shift hundreds of thousands of dollars to Roth IRAs, they lowered their future RMDs and dramatically reduced their exposure to Social Security taxation.

The Tax Torpedo

Social Security taxation creates what I call the "tax torpedo." As income rises past the frozen thresholds, each extra dollar can cause more of your Social Security to become taxable. That means the marginal tax rate on those dollars can be far higher than your official bracket—sometimes 27 percent, 40 percent, even 50 percent.

OBBBA didn't fix this. In fact, it made it easier for some retirees to earn more without paying higher income tax—yet those same extra dollars still pulled more Social Security into taxation.

THE TAKEAWAY:

Social Security was meant to be a foundation, not a revenue stream for Washington. But without planning, it becomes exactly that. Retirees who use the OBBBA's deductions wisely—converting to Roth before benefits start, diversifying withdrawals—can sidestep the torpedo. Those who ignore it risk watching their promised safety net unravel into just another tax bill.

TRAP #3 – MEDICARE IRMAA SURCHARGES

If there's one retirement cost that consistently catches people off guard, it's Medicare's Income-Related Monthly Adjustment Amount—better known as IRMAA.

IRMAA is essentially a stealth tax. It doesn't show up on your tax return, but it appears in your Medicare bill. Cross certain income thresholds, and your Part B and Part D premiums jump—sometimes by thousands per year.

The OBBBA didn't change the way IRMAA is calculated. In fact, it arguably made the trap sneakier: by increasing the standard deduction and giving seniors an extra $6,000 deduction (per person), retirees can often withdraw or convert more money while staying in the same tax bracket. That feels like a win—until they realize IRMAA is based on MAGI (Modified Adjusted Gross Income), which ignores deductions.

In other words: you can still be in the 22 percent bracket, but if your MAGI creeps above the threshold, you'll pay higher Medicare premiums two years later.

Ron & Sue – Business Owners from Brighton

Ron and Sue sold their family landscaping business at 66, walking away with nearly $2 million in retirement accounts. They decided to do a $150,000 Roth conversion in one year, assuming their new deductions under OBBBA would shield them. Tax-wise, they were right: they stayed in the 24 percent bracket.

But two years later, their Medicare premiums jumped by $4,500 for the year. Why? Their MAGI—before deductions—crossed an IRMAA threshold. Had they split that conversion into two or three years, they could have used OBBBA's expanded deductions each year and avoided the premium hike.

Cathy the Teacher – Macomb County

Cathy, a retired teacher, thought she was safe with her "tax-free" municipal bond interest. After all, it wasn't taxable for federal income. But when she added $90,000 of muni bond interest to $140,000 of other retirement income, her MAGI exceeded the IRMAA line. Suddenly, her Medicare premiums jumped by $1,600.

Her reaction summed it up: *"So tax-free wasn't really tax-free?"* That's the lesson. For IRMAA, municipal bond interest still counts toward MAGI—even under OBBBA.

Harold the CEO – Birmingham

Harold, a retired CEO with a substantial portfolio, knew he was always going to be above the base Medicare premium. But he didn't realize how "sticky" IRMAA tiers are. After a one-time $250,000 Roth conversion at age 68, his MAGI spiked. Two years later, he paid nearly

$9,000 more in Medicare premiums. Even though his income dropped again, the surcharge stuck for the full calendar year.

THE TAKEAWAY:

IRMAA is a reminder that retirement planning isn't just about federal tax brackets. It's about understanding every lever—taxable income, provisional income, and MAGI. The OBBBA gave retirees new room to maneuver, but if you don't coordinate that maneuvering with Medicare thresholds, you can end up giving it all back in hidden surcharges.

TRAP #4 – THE LEGACY TAX BOMB

Many clients dream of leaving a financial legacy. But if most of that legacy is in tax-deferred accounts, what you're really leaving your kids or grandkids is a tax problem.

The Tax Traps Lurking in Your Nest Egg

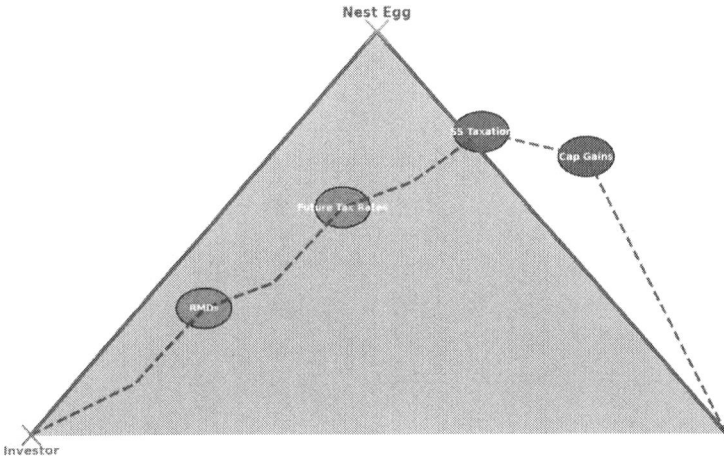

Source: Main Financial Group.

The SECURE Act eliminated the "stretch IRA" for most non-spouse beneficiaries. Now, adult children must empty inherited IRAs and 401(k)s within 10 years—and every withdrawal is taxed as ordinary income. The OBBBA didn't touch this. That means the Legacy Tax Bomb is alive and well.

Rachel the Attorney – Royal Oak

Rachel inherited a $1 million IRA from her father. Already earning $250,000 as a practicing attorney, she had to take $100,000 per year for ten years. Those withdrawals pushed her into the 35 percent bracket, costing her roughly $350,000 in federal taxes over the decade. What looked like a million-dollar gift shrank to $650,000 after taxes.

Molly & Marcus – The Sibling Split

Molly, a high school teacher in Macomb County, inherited half of her mother's $800,000 IRA. Her brother Marcus, a surgeon in Troy, inherited the other half. Molly's withdrawals stayed in the 22 percent bracket. Marcus's withdrawals were taxed at 37 percent. Same inheritance, wildly different outcomes—all because of timing and tax brackets.

Eleanor – Brighton Widow Who Planned Ahead

Eleanor, a 70-year-old widow, had a $1 million IRA and two children in high tax brackets. Using OBBBA's senior deduction, she began converting $200,000 per year for five years into Roth IRAs. She paid about $250,000 in taxes during her lifetime but saved her children over $400,000 in taxes they would have owed. By the time she passed, the entire IRA had been converted. Her heirs still had to empty the Roth within ten years, but every dollar came out tax-free.

Becky – Legacy IRA, Another Option

Becky sat across from me in the Brighton office, her hands folded neatly on top of a leather folder that contained years of careful saving. At 68, she had worked hard, lived within her means, and accumulated more than enough to cover her own retirement needs. "Jordan," she said with a thoughtful smile, "I don't need all of this money for me. What I want is to make sure my kids and grandkids have something meaningful to remember me by."

Like many retirees, Becky's biggest concern wasn't running out of money—it was leaving a legacy that wouldn't get swallowed up by taxes.

That's when I introduced her to what we call the **IRA Legacy** strategy. Instead of leaving her $350,000 IRA in a position where her heirs would be forced to pay income taxes on every dollar they received, Becky repositioned it into a fixed income annuity. That annuity provided guaranteed payments, which were then used to purchase a permanent life insurance policy.

The outcome was remarkable: her $350,000 IRA was transformed into a $1,240,000 tax-free benefit for her family. When Becky saw the numbers, she leaned back, let out a breath of relief, and said, "This is exactly what I wanted—a way to multiply what I've worked for, without Uncle Sam taking such a big bite."

For Becky, it wasn't about the dollars alone—it was about the meaning behind them. She pictured her grandchildren using part of that tax-free inheritance to pay for college, buy a first home, or start a business. Her simple act of financial foresight turned into a powerful gift, one that carried her love and hard work far beyond her own lifetime.

THE TAKEAWAY:

Without planning, the Legacy Tax Bomb turns a generous gift into a burden. With planning, you can shift the tax cost to yourself—when deductions and brackets are favorable—and spare your heirs.

The OBBBA didn't change the rules for inherited IRAs. However, it gave today's retirees a window to use larger deductions and smoother conversions to defuse the bomb before passing wealth down, or the option to do an IRA Legacy that can produce significant tax-free funds.

ROTH CONVERSIONS IN THE OBBBA ERA

If there's one tool that has become even more valuable after the One Big Beautiful Bill Act, it's the Roth conversion. In plain English, you're moving money from the "IRS's Future Claim" bucket into the "Tax-Free Forever" bucket.

Roth Conversions: Your Tax Shield Strategy

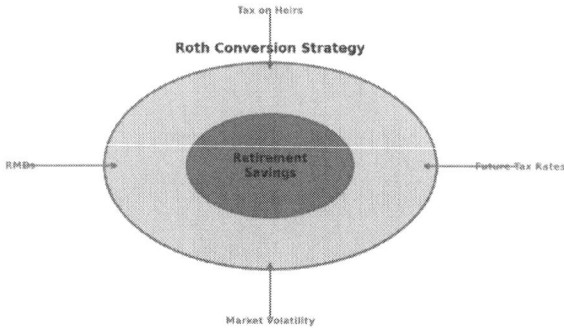

Source: Main Financial Group.

Under OBBBA, seven tax brackets are locked in. The standard deduction is larger. Seniors get an extra $6,000 deduction per person through 2028. And the SALT cap is higher. The net effect? Retirees can often convert *more* money each year without spilling into the next bracket.

Peter & Lydia – Sterling Heights

Peter and Lydia, both 67, have $80,000 in pension and investment income. Their new standard + senior deduction totals $43,500. That means they can convert roughly $43,000 of IRA money each year before owing a single dollar in federal tax. Over a decade, they'll move nearly their entire IRA to Roth status—on their terms, not the IRS's.

Dr. Patrice – Bloomfield Hills Physician

Dr. Patrice retired at 60 after a successful medical career. With $3 million in retirement accounts, she worried about the RMD avalanche and the Legacy Tax Bomb. Using OBBBA's expanded deductions, she began a five-year Roth conversion ladder of $200,000 annually. Each year, she stayed within the 24 percent bracket, avoided IRMAA spikes, and shifted a million dollars to tax-free status.

Tim – Waterford Engineer

Tim, 57, started converting $150,000 annually from his IRA into Roths. By timing conversions in "gap years" before Social Security and RMDs, he avoided the tax torpedo and saved an estimated $250,000 in lifetime taxes.

THE TAKEAWAY:

Roth conversions remain one of the few strategies where you decide when and how much tax to pay. OBBBA didn't make them less powerful—it made them less rushed. Instead of racing against a 2026 "sunset," retirees can now spread conversions over years, filling up their chosen brackets strategically.

THE RIPT FRAMEWORK IN ACTION

At Main Financial Group, we use the RIPT framework—Risk, Income, Portfolio, Taxes—to make tax planning practical.

- **Risk** – Tax risk is as real as market risk. A portfolio that looks safe on paper can create massive RMDs that push you into higher brackets.
- **Income** – The source of withdrawals matters as much as the amount. Drawing the wrong income at the wrong time can trigger Social Security taxation or IRMAA surcharges.
- **Portfolio** – Asset location matters. High-growth assets belong in Roth accounts, while tax-inefficient ones belong in tax-deferred.
- **Taxes** – Taxes aren't a one-time event; they're a lifetime strategy.

By treating taxes as a gear in the machine—not an afterthought—you gain control. OBBBA's new rules only make the gears spin differently. The principle stays the same: integrate taxes into every retirement conversation.

YOUR TAX PLAYBOOK:
TURNING STRATEGY INTO ACTION

A good tax plan isn't static—it adapts to laws, markets, and life. Here's how retirees in Oakland, Macomb, and Livingston counties are applying these lessons.

10+ Years Before Retirement

- Build multiple "tax buckets": taxable, tax-deferred, and tax-free Roth.
- Max out Roth 401(k) options if your employer offers them.
- Use lower-income years to seed Roth IRAs early.

5–10 Years Before Retirement

- Run a multi-year tax projection.
- Plan a Roth conversion ladder—fill brackets each year with conversions.
- Rebalance portfolios with asset location in mind.

Early Retirement (Before Social Security and RMDs)

- Delay Social Security to keep provisional income low.
- Use OBBBA's senior deduction to convert aggressively between 65–68.
- Stay mindful of IRMAA thresholds when converting.

RMD Age and Beyond

- Use Qualified Charitable Distributions (QCDs) to reduce taxable income.
- Blend Roth and taxable withdrawals to keep income steady.
- Continue partial conversions if it benefits heirs.

CLOSING THE CHAPTER:
OUTSMARTING UNCLE SAM

Remember Ray, the executive from Farmington Hills who feared Uncle Sam owned half his retirement? Together, we built a multi-year Roth conversion ladder, using OBBBA's senior deduction to move nearly a million dollars into Roth status. We restructured his withdrawals so his Social Security stayed mostly tax-free. We kept his MAGI just under IRMAA thresholds. And we defused the legacy tax bomb so his children would inherit tax-free accounts instead of a compressed tax bill.

A year later, Ray called me from Kensington Metropark. He was out fishing, his grandkids splashing along the shore. His voice carried none of the unease I'd heard in my office. "Jordan," he said, "it feels good to know Uncle Sam isn't my biggest partner anymore. For the first time, I feel like I'm in control."

That's the payoff of proactive tax planning. It isn't just about saving money—it's about peace of mind. And in retirement, peace of mind may be the most valuable asset of all (check out www.maintaxbill.com to see how much you could save).

CHAPTER SIX
Beating the Inflation Monster: Keeping Your Money's Value

Picture this: It's a warm July afternoon in Michigan. The kind where the sky is that perfect postcard blue, the lemonade glass sweats faster than you can drink it, and you're swatting away mosquitoes the size of hummingbirds. Retirement should feel like that kind of day—comfortable, slow, and enjoyable.

But lurking in the shade, there's a pest far worse than any mosquito. You can't hear it buzzing, you can't smack it away, but it can drain your retirement one bite at a time. That pest is inflation—the invisible villain that slowly erodes the buying power of your money. It's not dramatic like a stock market crash or a sudden health emergency. It works in whispers, not shouts, quietly making everything you buy cost just a little bit more each year… until one day, you realize your cozy nest egg has become a shrinking puddle.

I've seen it happen too many times.

THE DAY BETTY MET THE MONSTER

Back in 2022, when inflation in the U.S. hit **9.1 percent—the highest since 1981**—I had a client named Betty walk into my Brighton office. She was 72, a retired schoolteacher from Livonia, and she looked like she had just read her grocery receipt and found it twice as long as last month's. She clutched her purse like it was holding the last dollar she'd ever see.

"Jordan," she said, "I thought my savings were safe in bonds. But the prices at Meijer are rising faster than weeds in my garden. My fixed income feels like it's on a diet."

Betty had done everything right—or so she thought. Forty years of diligent saving had built her a $500,000 IRA, almost all in bonds yielding a safe-but-measly 2 percent. That "safe" portfolio was losing the inflation fight by 7 percent that year alone. In other words, the real value of her money—what it could actually buy—was shrinking at a pace she'd never experienced.

We reworked her portfolio. Forty percent went into a mix of dividend-paying equities and Treasury Inflation-Protected Securities (TIPS), investments designed to adjust with inflation. The result? By 2025, she was earning 2–3 percent above the Consumer Price Index, enough to not just hold the line but actually grow her purchasing power.

Now, Betty spends more time enjoying her grandkids and less time worrying if she can afford the good ice cream instead of the generic stuff. And that's the point of this chapter—to make sure your retirement, like Betty's, can stand toe-to-toe with the Inflation Monster and win.

WHY INFLATION IS RETIREMENT'S SILENT THREAT

Inflation isn't just an economic term for talking heads on cable news. It's a **thief in the night**—stealing a little more of your purchasing power each year. Gas, groceries, housing, healthcare—nothing is immune.

Here's the simplest way to think about it: If inflation averages 3 percent a year, your $100 bill will only buy $74 worth of goods in 10 years. At 5 percent, it drops to $61. The numbers sound small until you remember that retirement often lasts **20 to 30 years**. That's a long time for the monster to keep nibbling away.

In 2025, the Bureau of Labor Statistics reported that food prices rose by 2.2 percent and housing by 3.5 percent. Those numbers might not sound scary—but compound them over decades, and they're devastating. A 2025 Transamerica survey found that **69 percent of retirees fear outliving their money**, with inflation topping the list of threats—even more than market volatility.

I learned early from my dad—also a schoolteacher—that inflation is like a slow leak in a tire. You don't notice it at first, but keep driving on it, and one day you'll find yourself stranded on the shoulder, wondering what went wrong.

THE LONG VIEW:
WHAT INFLATION CAN REALLY DO

Over my 20-plus years advising retirees—doctors, engineers, factory workers, small business owners—I've seen inflation erode dreams in ways that still surprise me. The saddest cases aren't the ones where someone lost money in the market. They're the ones where people thought they were safe… only to watch their standard of living shrink year after year.

Imagine you're 65, freshly retired, and you have a $60,000 annual budget. If inflation averages 3.5 percent, you'll need over $100,000 a year just 20 years later to live the exact same lifestyle. That's without adding any new luxuries or unexpected medical costs. If your investments don't keep pace—or better yet, beat inflation—you're essentially **walking down a slowly descending escalator**, wondering why you're getting lower despite feeling like you're standing still.

Chapter Roadmap: What We'll Cover

In this chapter, we're going to:

1. **Expose** the sneaky ways inflation erodes your wealth.
2. **Look back** at the wild inflation of the 1970s and 1980s—and the lessons it still teaches us today.
3. **Unpack strategies** that not only protect against inflation but can actually grow your buying power over decades.
4. **Show real retiree stories**—both cautionary tales and success stories—that bring the numbers to life.
5. **Give you an actionable "Inflation Playbook"** so you know exactly what steps to take next.

By the end, you won't just understand inflation—you'll be ready to face it head-on, shield up, sword in hand, and maybe even a little swagger in your step.

THE INFLATION MONSTER'S SNEAKY WAYS: HOW IT ERODES YOUR WEALTH

Inflation doesn't show up in your mailbox with a big red warning stamp. It doesn't announce itself on your front porch like a thunderstorm rolling in over Lake Michigan. No—this monster prefers the slow approach. It hides in your weekly grocery run, in the renewal notice from your insurance company, in the sneaky service fees that seem to grow each year.

I once heard someone say inflation is like an uninvited houseguest who quietly raids your fridge. At first, you barely notice—a yogurt cup here, a slice of cheese there. But come back a month later and half your pantry is gone.

In retirement, this is especially brutal because you're not replenishing your pantry with a paycheck anymore. You're drawing from a fixed supply—your savings—and every "yogurt cup" inflation takes is one you can't get back.

A Tale of Two Retirements

Let me introduce you to two individuals: Tom and Hilary. They were both 68 when they retired in 2005 and had identical $1 million portfolios. Tom kept his money in long-term CDs and bonds, earning about 3 percent annually. Hilary built a more diversified portfolio with a mix of dividend stocks, TIPS, and some real estate exposure.

At first, Tom felt like the smarter one—his income was predictable, his principal untouched. But as the years passed, the cost of everything climbed. Gas prices doubled. Grocery bills crept up. Medicare premiums inched higher. By 2025, Tom's safe, fixed income wasn't enough to cover his lifestyle without dipping heavily into his principal. His $1 million nest egg had the purchasing power of about $600,000 compared to when he retired.

Hilary, on the other hand, saw her diversified investments grow faster than inflation most years. She still had market ups and downs, but by 2025 her portfolio had not only kept up with costs—it had grown in real terms. She wasn't just surviving; she was still traveling, still helping her grandkids with college, and still buying the good wine without guilt.

Same starting point. Two completely different endings. *The difference?* How they handled inflation.

HOW INFLATION WORKS AGAINST YOU

The **Consumer Price Index (CPI)**—the most common measure of inflation—tracks a "basket" of goods and services: food, housing, clothing, transportation, healthcare, and more. Think of it as the nation's collective shopping list. In June 2025, CPI was up 2.7 percent from the year before, a small number compared to the 9.1 percent of 2022, but still enough to matter. At 2.7 percent, your dollar loses nearly a third of its buying power over 15 years.

The problem is that CPI is an average. Your personal inflation rate could be much higher depending on what you spend money on. If you travel a lot, rising airfare will hit you harder. If you have ongoing health issues, the 4–6 percent annual rise in medical costs will sting more than the national average. And if you're helping adult children financially, you're exposed to inflation in their cost of living, too.

The Fixed-Income Trap

A common mistake I see—especially among conservative investors—is assuming that "safe" means "secure." A retiree with a $50,000 pension might feel solid on day one. But at 3.5 percent inflation, that pension loses half its purchasing power in just 20 years.

Let's make it more concrete:

Year	Annual Pension (No Adjustment)	Purchasing Power (in Today's Dollars)
1	$50,000	$50,000
10	$50,000	$35,600
20	$50,000	$25,400

That's like going from buying steak dinners to eating dollar-menu burgers, even though the checks are the same size.

Real-World Price Creep

Let's rewind to 1980. A movie ticket averaged $2.89. In 2025, that's closer to $10. A gallon of gas? Around $1.19 in 1980—$3.65 in 2025. A dozen eggs? 91 cents in 1980—$3.29 today. These might sound like small differences, but remember: you're not buying just one movie ticket, one gallon of gas, or one carton of eggs. You're buying hundreds, maybe thousands, over decades.

And here's the kicker—those examples only reflect average CPI inflation. Many essentials for retirees, like healthcare and long-term care, have historically risen at **twice the CPI rate**.

Healthcare: Inflation's Silent Partner

If inflation is the monster in the living room, healthcare is the one hiding in the closet. According to Kiplinger's 2025 report, healthcare costs for retirees have been climbing at 4.5 percent annually—well above the CPI. And Medicare, while helpful, doesn't cover everything.

I worked with a couple from Grand Rapids, Harvey and Diane, who were in great health when they retired at 65. By 75, Harvey had a chronic heart condition that required multiple medications and regular specialist visits. Even with insurance, their out-of-pocket medical costs rose 60 percent in just eight years. Their biggest financial worry wasn't market volatility—it was the slow, relentless rise of co-pays, deductibles, and uncovered treatments.

Why Inflation Hits Retirees Harder

When you're working, your wages often rise with inflation—or at least have the potential to. But in retirement, most income sources are fixed. Social Security has cost-of-living adjustments (COLAs), but those often lag behind real-world cost increases. Investments can outpace inflation, but only if they're structured with that goal in mind.

In short: **when inflation rises, your expenses grow, but your income doesn't**—*unless you make it happen.*

Lessons from the 1970s–1980s: When Inflation Roared

Ask anyone who lived through the 1970s about prices, and you'll see a certain look come over their face—a blend of disbelief and exhaustion. It was a decade when the price tags in stores seemed to change faster than the weather. And for retirees on fixed incomes, it was a gut punch they never saw coming.

To set the stage, imagine walking into a grocery store in 1970. A gallon of milk cost 62 cents. A loaf of bread was 25 cents. A gallon of gas? Just 36 cents. People felt relatively secure—if you had a modest pension or a few savings bonds, you could get by comfortably.

Fast forward just 10 years to 1980:

- Milk: $1.54
- Bread: 50 cents
- Gas: $1.19 (and often rationed)

Those jumps didn't happen gradually—they came in waves, often sudden and steep, like a rogue tide hitting the shore.

The Numbers Behind the Pain

The Consumer Price Index (CPI) rose from **5.5 percent in 1970 to a staggering 14.4 percent in 1980** (Federal Reserve History 2025). To put that in perspective, if you had $100,000 in savings in 1970 and just stuck it in a bank account earning 5 percent interest, by 1980 your money could buy *only half of what it once did.*

The causes were a perfect storm:

1. **OPEC Oil Shocks** – In 1973, an embargo by the Organization of Petroleum Exporting Countries tripled oil prices almost overnight. This rippled into every corner of the economy—transportation, manufacturing, agriculture.
2. **Wage-Price Spirals** – As prices rose, unions demanded higher wages, which led companies to raise prices even more to cover labor costs, creating a self-feeding loop.
3. **Loose Monetary Policy** – The Federal Reserve, trying to keep unemployment low, kept interest rates too low for too long, flooding the economy with money.
4. **Psychology** – Once people expected higher prices, they started making purchasing decisions to "beat" inflation, like hoarding goods, which ironically made shortages and price hikes worse.

Retirees in the Crossfire

For retirees, this was a nightmare. If your pension was fixed, you had no way to keep up. Social Security's cost-of-living adjustments didn't exist until 1975, and even then, they often lagged behind actual inflation.

I once spoke with Dean, a 78-year-old client from Grand Rapids, who remembered the period vividly.

"Jordan, back then gas prices doubled so fast it made your head spin. My savings shriveled like a prune. I had CDs paying 5 percent, but inflation was at 13.5 percent. It was like bailing water out of a boat with a hole in the bottom—you just couldn't keep up."

He wasn't exaggerating. By 1980, the interest on "safe" fixed investments was far below the inflation rate, meaning retirees were losing ground every single year—even as they thought they were being prudent.

The Volcker Shock

The turning point came when Paul Volcker, appointed Federal Reserve Chair in 1979, decided to take a baseball bat to the inflation monster. He raised the federal funds rate to **a jaw-dropping 20 percent** in 1981. That made borrowing nearly impossible—mortgage rates hit 18 percent—but it squeezed inflation down to 3.2 percent by 1983.

The medicine worked, but it was bitter. The early 1980s saw a sharp recession. Unemployment climbed above 10 percent. Businesses shuttered. Retirees who relied on selling assets for income often had to sell in a depressed market.

The Quiet Legacy

Today, inflation rates are nowhere near the extremes of the late 70s, but the danger is still real. The 1970s taught us a few lessons that remain critical for anyone planning retirement:

1. **Inflation Can Move Fast** – You can go from "manageable" to "panic" in just a couple of years. Waiting until it's obvious is too late.
2. **Fixed Income Alone is Dangerous** – Relying solely on bonds, CDs, or fixed pensions leaves you exposed to purchasing power erosion.
3. **Diversification Is Survival** – Stocks, inflation-protected securities, real estate, and other growth assets are essential for long retirements.
4. **Policy Matters** – Central bank decisions can change the game overnight. Keeping an eye on interest rate trends isn't just for economists—it affects your portfolio directly.

Sarah's Story: A Second Chance

Sarah, a 68-year-old from Midland, Michigan, had lived through the 1980s and still remembered the sting.

"My pension back then bought a steak dinner every Friday. Now, if I stuck with it as my only income, it would barely cover a burger and fries."

When we reviewed her portfolio in 2024, we added a ladder of TIPS and shifted a portion of her assets into a balanced stock-and-dividend portfolio. By 2025, she wasn't just keeping up—her real (inflation-adjusted) income was growing. Sarah told me, "It's not about reliving the past. It's about making sure the past doesn't happen to me again."

This historical backdrop sets the stage for the next part of the chapter—**how to actually beat the inflation monster** with modern, diversified strategies that balance growth and safety. That's where we'll open the toolbox and get specific.

STRATEGIES TO BEAT THE MONSTER: INVESTMENTS THAT OUTPACE INFLATION

The good news about inflation? It's not unbeatable. The bad news? You can't beat it by doing nothing. Beating the Inflation Monster requires choosing assets and strategies that grow *faster* than the rise in prices over the long haul.

There's no single magic bullet, but there are proven weapons you can carry into the fight. And the strongest battle plan blends multiple ones, so if one stumbles, another can pick up the slack.

1. EQUITIES: THE LONG-TERM GROWTH ENGINE

When you look back over decades of market history, one fact stands tall: stocks have historically outpaced inflation by a comfortable margin. Vanguard's research shows the **real return on equities** (after inflation) has averaged about 7 percent annually over the last century.

Why They Work:

Companies can raise prices on their goods and services when inflation rises—passing costs to customers while still growing earnings. This pricing power helps stocks keep pace with, and often exceed, inflation.

How to Use Them in Retirement:
For retirees, the sweet spot isn't 100 percent in stocks—it's finding the right allocation that provides growth without making you lose sleep. Fidelity suggests that for many retirees, 40–60 percent equities strike the balance between opportunity and volatility control.

Real-Life Example: Betty's Equity Boost
You met Betty earlier—the retired schoolteacher who was stuck in low-yield bonds. By moving 40 percent of her portfolio into dividend-paying large-cap equities, she went from losing ground against inflation to earning 2–3 percent more than CPI each year. And because she held dividend stocks, she got both potential price appreciation and steady income.

Pro Tip: Use equity funds or ETFs with a history of consistent dividend growth. Even in volatile markets, dividends can provide a "paycheck" that rises over time.

2. TIPS: INFLATION-PROTECTED SAFETY NETS
Treasury Inflation-Protected Securities (TIPS) are government bonds designed specifically to fight inflation. Their principal value adjusts with changes in the CPI, so your interest payments and maturity value rise when prices rise.

Why They Work:
Unlike traditional bonds, which can lose real value when inflation rises, TIPS maintain their purchasing power. The interest rate is fixed, but the amount it's applied to increases with inflation.

How to Use Them in Retirement:
Many retirees ladder TIPS—buying bonds that mature at different times—to create a steady stream of income while keeping pace with inflation.

Real-Life Example: Sarah's TIPS Ladder
When Sarah from Midland added TIPS to her portfolio, we staggered maturities over 5, 10, and 15 years. This ensured she had inflation-

adjusted income arriving regularly while keeping part of her portfolio in growth-oriented equities.

3. FIXED-INDEXED ANNUITIES: GROWTH + PROTECTION

Annuities have a bad reputation in some circles, but that's often because people lump them all together. Fixed-Indexed Annuities (FIAs) can offer a unique combination: downside protection and growth potential linked to market indexes like the S&P 500.

Why They Work:

FIAs let you capture part of the market's upside without risking your principal to market downturns. Some include income riders that increase payouts over time, helping you fight inflation during retirement.

How to Use Them in Retirement:

- Allocate 20–40 percent of your portfolio to FIAs as part of the Income section of your RIPT plan.
- Choose products with inflation-adjusted income options or generous income growth riders.

Real-Life Example: Harold's FIA Shift

Harold, who lived through the 1970s, wanted protection but feared another inflation wave. We used an FIA with an income rider that increased payouts by 6 percent annually until activated. When inflation spiked in 2022, Harold's income base was already high enough to keep him ahead.

HOW THE FIXED-INDEXED ANNUITY PROTECTS FROM MARKET STORMS

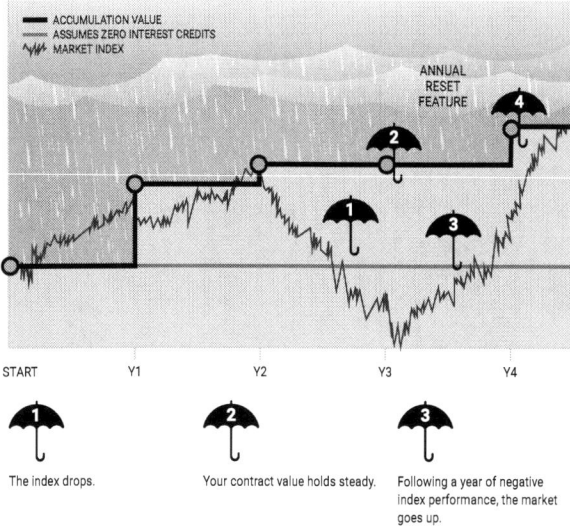

ACCUMULATION VALUE
ASSUMES ZERO INTEREST CREDITS
MARKET INDEX

ANNUAL RESET FEATURE

START   Y1   Y2   Y3   Y4

This hypothetical example is provided for illustrative purposes only and does not reflect any surrender charges or market value Adjustments (MVAs) that may be assessed. With the purchase of any additional-cost riders, the contract's value will be reduced by the cost of the rider. This may result in a loss of principal and interest in any year in which the contract does not earn interest or earns interest in an amount less than the rider charge. If there is no indexed interest, the value would be the money you put into the annuity.

1 The index drops.

2 Your contract value holds steady.

3 Following a year of negative index performance, the market goes up.

4 Your accumulation value can increase any year during which a positive index change occurs thanks to annual reset.

Source: Magellan Financial.

4. REAL ESTATE & REITS: TANGIBLE INFLATION HEDGES

Real estate tends to rise in value over time, often faster than inflation. Even better, rental income can be adjusted upward to keep pace with rising costs.

Why They Work:

Real assets like property are limited in supply, so as the cost of living rises, so does the demand—and price—for usable space.

How to Use Them in Retirement:

· Direct ownership if you want hands-on control (and don't mind being a landlord).
· Real Estate Investment Trusts (REITs) for a hands-off, diversified approach.

Real-Life Example: The Johnsons' Income Boost

The Johnsons, a retired couple in Traverse City, owned two small rental units. By modestly raising rents each year to keep up with inflation, they maintained steady purchasing power. For liquidity, they also held REITs that yielded 5–7 percent, providing inflation-sensitive income without the landlord headaches.

5. SHORT-TERM BONDS & CDS: PARKING WITHOUT PENALTY

While long-term bonds can get crushed by rising interest rates, short-term bonds and CDs can be rolled over more frequently, letting you adjust to higher yields as they appear.

Why They Work:

You're not locked in for decades at a low rate, so when inflation pushes interest rates higher, your returns can adjust quickly.

Pro Tip: Pair short-term bonds with higher-growth assets. They're not designed to beat inflation on their own, but they can be part of a balanced strategy that stays flexible.

6. TAX-SMART MOVES THAT AMPLIFY YOUR INFLATION DEFENSE

Inflation steals from you in one way, but taxes can double the theft if you're not careful. That's why the Taxes portion of your RIPT framework is so critical here.

Roth Conversions

By shifting assets from tax-deferred accounts (like traditional IRAs) into Roth IRAs, you're locking in today's tax rates and creating tax-free income for the future—a powerful hedge when inflation pushes you into higher nominal brackets.

Asset Location

Place growth assets in tax-advantaged accounts and income assets in taxable ones to reduce the annual tax drag on returns.

Bracket Management

Monitor how inflation-driven income increases (like higher Social Security COLAs or annuity payouts) could push you into higher tax brackets, and plan withdrawals accordingly.

RIPT FRAMEWORK: INFLATION IN ACTION

Inflation-proofing your retirement isn't just about one or two moves—it's about integrating your entire plan:

- **Risk:** Balance enough equities to grow without taking on "keep-you-up-at-night" volatility.
- **Income:** Use annuities and dividend growth stocks to create rising paychecks.
- **Portfolio:** Diversify with TIPS, REITs, commodities, and short-term bonds.
- **Taxes:** Minimize Uncle Sam's bite so inflation isn't stealing from taxed dollars.

When Sarah's plan incorporated all four, she had a portfolio that not only met her spending needs but kept increasing her real purchasing power—even if inflation averaged 3–4 percent for decades.

Your Inflation Playbook

1. **Learn History** – Study past inflation spikes so you recognize the early warning signs.
2. **Diversify by Design** – 40 percent equities, 30 percent TIPS, 20 percent annuities, 10 percent real assets is a starting point, not a rule.
3. **Use Inflation-Linked Income** – FIAs, dividend stocks, and rental income that can rise over time.
4. **Adjust Annually** – Review your portfolio every year to ensure your growth rate exceeds inflation.
5. **Stay Flexible** – The Inflation Monster changes tactics; so should you.

Slaying the Monster

Betty didn't set out to become a warrior. She just wanted her retirement to feel secure, her ice cream budget intact, and her grandkids' visits worry-free. But when inflation came knocking, she adjusted, diversified, and took control—and now she's winning. Harold, scarred from the 1970s, refused to relive the same mistake. Sarah, still haunted by her pension's shrinking value, learned to weave together annuities, TIPS, and equities so her purchasing power could grow, not wither.

These aren't just financial adjustments—they're mindset shifts.

Beating the Inflation Monster is about recognizing that your retirement isn't static. It's a living, breathing stage of life that needs ongoing attention and adaptation. The same strategy that works today might need tuning tomorrow.

Inflation is relentless, but it's not invincible. Like any monster, it can be studied, anticipated, and outmaneuvered. When you arm yourself with a diversified portfolio, inflation-protected income streams, and a tax plan that minimizes erosion, you don't just fend it off—you make it work for you. Rising prices mean companies raise revenues, which can lift your investments. Proper planning turns what could be a retirement-killer into a challenge you're equipped to meet head-on.

THE TAKEAWAY:

Here's the truth: If your money isn't growing faster than inflation, you're falling behind—whether you notice it now or not. But you have the tools, strategies, and historical lessons to avoid that fate.

Your goal isn't just to survive inflation. It's to **outpace** it, to live the retirement you've envisioned without watching your lifestyle shrink year after year.

And remember:

- **Growth matters.** Without it, even the largest nest egg will eventually lose buying power.
- **Balance matters.** Too much risk invites disaster; too little risk guarantees erosion.
- **Review matters.** Inflation's pace changes—your plan must adapt alongside it.

CLOSING THE CHAPTER: THE TRANSITION TO WHAT'S NEXT

With your inflation defenses in place, you're ready for the next great pillar of a successful retirement: **maximizing Social Security**.

Because here's the thing—Social Security isn't designed to cover all your expenses, and it's not immune to inflation's bite. In the next chapter, we'll explore how to optimize your benefits, coordinate them with your other income streams, and make sure you're squeezing every possible dollar from a program you've spent a lifetime paying into.

If inflation is the monster in the shadows, Social Security is the loyal but sometimes underappreciated ally you'll want by your side—provided you know how to get the most from it.

CHAPTER SEVEN

Social Security Smarts:
It's Not Your Whole Plan

It was one of those crisp, golden Michigan fall mornings where the air smells faintly of woodsmoke, the kind of day that makes you want to grab a flannel shirt and a steaming cup of coffee. From my Brighton office window, I could see maple leaves fluttering down like confetti, each one painted in the reds, oranges, and golds that only October can deliver.

I was reviewing a client's retirement plan when Hannah and John walked in, a pleasant suburban couple from Canton in their late sixties. Hannah was a retired nurse who had spent four decades caring for patients with equal parts skill and compassion. John, a former auto worker, still had the sturdy build of a man who had spent years on the factory floor. But the way they shuffled into my office, hands in pockets, told me something was off.

They sat down, and Hannah let out a sigh so heavy you could almost see it.

"Jordan," she said, "we've paid into Social Security for 40 years. This has to be our golden ticket, right? Enough for golf trips, spoiling the grandkids, maybe even a cruise or two?"

It was a hopeful question, but one I've heard before — and I already knew where the conversation was headed. "Well," I replied gently, "let's look at the numbers together."

THE REALITY CHECK

Their combined monthly benefit was $3,500. Respectable, sure — until you compare it to their $5,800 monthly expenses. That's a 40 percent shortfall every single month. And to make matters worse, their IRA withdrawals pushed their provisional income high enough that **85 percent of their Social Security benefits were taxable**, costing them roughly $500 a month in federal taxes alone.

When I explained this, John's jaw tightened. "So, you're saying we basically worked all these years just to give some of it back to Uncle Sam?" "Not exactly," I said, "but Social Security was never designed to be your whole plan. It's a tool — a good one — but it's not the entire toolbox."

We worked through an optimization strategy: delaying Hannah's benefit until age 70 for an 8 percent annual increase, using spousal benefits so John could claim half her amount without reducing hers, and strategically managing their IRA withdrawals to minimize taxation. Within months, Hannah's benefit rose by $300 a month, John was receiving spousal benefits, and they'd reduced their annual tax bill.

The next time they came in, they had a different energy — relaxed, laughing, talking about their golf league. They weren't living large, but they were living smart. And that's the point of this chapter: **Social Security is important, but it's only one piece of the retirement puzzle**. If you treat it as your only income source, you risk being blindsided. If you integrate it wisely into a bigger plan, you can make it work for you rather than the other way around.

A Reliable Truck, Not a Luxury Yacht

Think of Social Security as that old, reliable pickup truck. It'll get you

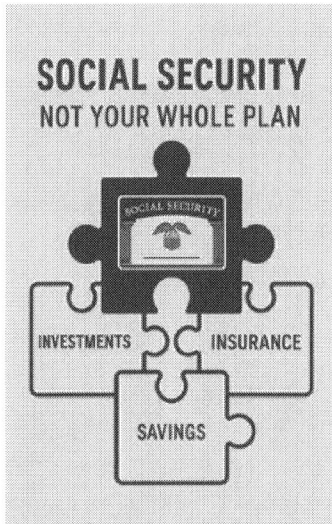

SOCIAL SECURITY
NOT YOUR WHOLE PLAN

SOCIAL SECURITY

INVESTMENTS   INSURANCE

SAVINGS

Source: Main Financial Group

from point A to point B, no problem. But if you're expecting it to haul a mansion, tow a yacht, and pay for all the fuel along the way — you're in for a surprise.

In 2025, the **average monthly Social Security benefit for retirees is $1,976** — a modest 2.5 percent increase from 2024, thanks to the annual Cost-of-Living Adjustment (COLA). For a married couple, that's about $3,952 a month. Not bad, but when the **average annual retirement expense is around $60,000** (per the 2025 Synchrony Bank Retirement Survey), Social Security alone will cover just 30–40 percent of what you'll likely spend.

And you're not alone if you depend on it: according to the **2025 EBRI/Greenwald Research Retirement Confidence Survey**, 94 percent of retirees receive Social Security, but for only 66 percent is it the major source of income. That means roughly one-third are already leaning heavily on pensions, savings, or annuities.

In my more than twenty years advising people from every walk of life, I've seen the same pattern: those who treat Social Security as a foundation do well; those who treat it as the whole building eventually face cracks in the walls.

My business partner's father (the Shermanator), says: "Social Security is a safety net, not a hammock." You can rest on it, but you can't build your whole retirement on it.

HOW WE GOT HERE: A BRIEF, EYE-OPENING HISTORY OF SOCIAL SECURITY

To really understand why Social Security can't be your whole plan, it helps to step back in time — all the way to 1935, in the depths of the Great Depression. Imagine breadlines stretching around city blocks, farms failing across the Midwest, and unemployment rates north of 20 percent. For millions of older Americans, there was no retirement "plan" at all. If you couldn't work, you relied on your children, your church, or — more often — charity.

President Franklin D. Roosevelt and Congress set out to change that. The **Social Security Act of 1935** created a safety net for older Americans, funded by payroll taxes from current workers to pay benefits to current retirees. It was never designed to fully replace a paycheck. In fact, the architects of the program assumed that retirees would supplement Social Security with savings, pensions, or part-time work.

At the time, the math worked beautifully. In 1940, when the first monthly checks were issued, the **average life expectancy was only 61 for men and 65 for women** — meaning many people never collected a penny. For those who did, the average retiree lived only about 12 years after claiming benefits. And here's the kicker: there were **about 42 workers paying into the system for every retiree.**

That worker-to-beneficiary ratio is the heart of the system's stability. The more workers contributing compared to retirees drawing benefits, the easier it is to keep the system flush. But times have changed. In 1960, the ratio had dropped to 5.1 to 1. By 2025? **Just 2.8 to 1.**

From Modest Help to Core Income

In the early years, Social Security was modest. The average monthly benefit in 1940 was $22.54 — roughly $500 in today's dollars. That's barely enough to cover a week's rent on a modest apartment today. But back then, costs were lower, and most retirees had family nearby or modest pensions from employers.

Fast forward to the 1970s, and Social Security began indexing benefits to inflation through the Cost-of-Living Adjustment (COLA). That was a major win for retirees, because it meant your check could keep pace with rising prices.

But here's where the role of Social Security began to shift. As private-sector pensions started disappearing in the 1980s and 1990s, and more people entered retirement without substantial savings, Social Security went from "supplement" to "primary source" for many. Today, the **Social Security Administration estimates** that roughly 1 in 5 married couples and almost half of single retirees depend on Social Security for *90 percent or more* of their income.

The Unspoken Problem

Here's what hasn't changed: Social Security was built to replace **about 40 percent of your pre-retirement income** if you're an average earner. It's still doing that job, more or less. What has changed is the cost of everything else. Healthcare costs have skyrocketed. Housing is more expensive. People are living longer — in some cases 20 to 30 years after retiring.

And yet, **Congress hasn't adjusted the tax thresholds on Social Security benefits since 1983**, which means more retirees get taxed on their benefits every year. Combine that with a shrinking worker-to-beneficiary ratio, and you see why the **2025 Social Security Trustees Report** projects the trust fund could be depleted by 2034, at which point benefits would be cut to about **81 percent of what's scheduled** unless changes are made.

THE TAKEAWAY:

Social Security is one of the most successful government programs in American history. It's kept millions of older Americans out of poverty and remains a guaranteed, inflation-adjusted source of income. But it's a supplement — not a full pension. It's your reliable old pickup truck, not the luxury yacht.

Understanding its original purpose helps explain why relying solely on it is risky. The system was designed for a very different America — one where people didn't live decades in retirement, healthcare didn't consume a third of your budget, and a large workforce supported a smaller group of retirees.

In other words, it's a fantastic base layer. But if you want comfort, flexibility, and freedom in retirement, you'll need more than just this one pillar.

THE SOCIAL SECURITY BASICS: WHAT IT IS (AND WHAT IT ISN'T)

If Social Security were a product sitting on a store shelf, the label might read: *"Funded by payroll taxes. Designed to replace about 40 percent of your pre-retirement income if you're an average earner. Adjusted for inflation annually. Comes with certain claiming rules and tax considerations. Not designed to be your sole source of retirement income."*

The marketing team would probably never approve that as a TV commercial — but it's the truth.

Here's the basic idea: throughout your working life, you and your employer each pay 6.2 percent of your earnings into the Social Security system (up to a maximum taxable wage base — $168,600 in 2025). If you're self-employed, you're both employer and employee, so you pay the full 12.4 percent. That money goes into the trust fund, where it's used to pay current retirees.

Your benefits aren't based on how much you personally paid in, but rather on your **Average Indexed Monthly Earnings (AIME)** over your **35 highest-earning years**, adjusted for inflation. The government then applies a formula to your AIME to determine your **Primary Insurance Amount (PIA)** — the monthly benefit you'd receive at your **Full Retirement Age (FRA)**, which for those born in 1960 or later is 67.

The 35-Year Rule

This is where a lot of people — especially high earners — get surprised. Social Security doesn't just look at your *recent* earnings; it looks at your *highest* 35 years. That means if you have fewer than 35 years of work history, those missing years are filled in as zeros, which can drag down your average significantly.

Even if you've worked more than 35 years, earlier low-income years can still affect your average if your higher-earning years weren't consistent.

The Calculation Formula

Here's how it works in 2025:

1. Find Your AIME

The Social Security Administration indexes each year of your earnings to account for inflation, then takes your highest 35 years, adds them up, and divides by 420 (the number of months in 35 years). This gives you your AIME.

2. Apply the Bend Points

Your PIA is calculated by applying percentages to portions of your AIME:
- 90 percent of the first **$1,253** of your AIME
- 32 percent of the amount between **$1,253 and $7,564**
- 15 percent of the amount above **$7,564**

3. Adjust for Claiming Age

Claim before your FRA? You take a permanent cut — up to 30 percent if you claim at 62. Delay past your FRA, up to age 70, and you earn **delayed retirement credit**s of 8 percent per year.

A Fictional Example: Meet Mark

Let's put some numbers to it. Mark is 67 in 2025 and has just reached his Full Retirement Age. His highest 35 years of inflation-adjusted earnings averaged $90,000 annually.

Step 1: Convert to monthly: $90,000 ÷ 12 = $7,500. That's his AIME.
Step 2: Apply the 2025 formula:
- First $1,253 × 90 percent = $1,127.70
- Next $6,311 ($7,564 − $1,253) × 32 percent = $2,019.52

- Remaining ($7,500 – $7,564) = **negative**, so no third tier.
Total PIA = $1,127.70 + $2,019.52 = **$3,147.22/month** at FRA.
Step 3: Adjust for claiming age:
  - If Mark had claimed at 62, his benefit would be cut by about 30 percent: $2,202/month.
  - If he waited until 70, his benefit would grow by 24 percent: $3,902/month.

That's a $1,700/month swing between claiming early and claiming late — *for life*. That difference could mean the ability to travel, keep up with rising healthcare costs, or simply sleep better at night.

Why This Matters

Understanding how your benefit is calculated helps you make better decisions. You can see how even one or two extra years of work, especially if they're high-earning years, can replace lower-earning years in your 35-year average and raise your benefit.

I've had clients who thought they were "done" working at 63 but decided to keep a part-time consulting job for two more years after seeing how much it would increase their Social Security for life.

Social Security Myth-Busting: Clearing the Fog Before It Costs You

Social Security might be the most widely discussed — and misunderstood — part of retirement planning. Everyone's got a story: the guy at your coffee group who "knows a loophole," the cousin who says it's all going bankrupt, the neighbor who's convinced you're a fool if you wait to claim.

The problem? Much of this "common knowledge" is half-truths at best, outright wrong at worst. Let's bust the biggest myths I hear in my office.

Myth #1: "It's enough to live on by itself."

You already know this one from Hannah and John's story. Social Security was *never* designed to replace 100 percent of your income. It was built to replace about **40 percent for the average worker** — and for higher earners, it replaces even less because of the benefit formula's bend points.

Real-life example: I had a client, Jill, a retired librarian from Northville, who thought her $2,100/month benefit would be plenty. But her Medicare premiums, supplemental insurance, utilities, and groceries ate up nearly all of it — before she even factored in property taxes. She ended up taking a part-time job at the local bookstore. She enjoyed it, but it wasn't part of her original plan.

Myth #2: "Social Security is completely tax-free."

This is one of the most common surprises. Depending on your "provisional income" (half your Social Security + AGI + nontaxable interest), up to **85 percent** of your benefit can be taxable.

Real-life example: Jim and Carol from Plymouth were shocked when their accountant told them their IRA withdrawals pushed 85 percent of their Social Security into the taxable column. "We thought the government was giving us a break for all those years we paid in," Jim told me. I explained that while some retirees pay no tax on their benefits, the income thresholds haven't been adjusted since 1983 — so more retirees get caught every year.

Myth #3: "It's guaranteed forever, no matter what."

The truth: Social Security is backed by law, but the **trust fund reserves are projected to run out in 2034** unless Congress acts. At that point, ongoing payroll taxes would still cover about **81 percent of promised benefits** — but you'd take a 19 percent cut. That's not a doomsday scenario, but it's not nothing either.

Real-life example: When I explained this to Nathan, a 59-year-old engineer from West Bloomfield, he said, "So you're telling me the check won't disappear, but it could be smaller?" Exactly. That's why building additional income sources is so critical.

Myth #4: "I should grab it as soon as I'm eligible — you never know when you'll die."

This one is part logic, part fear. Yes, if you claim at 62 and pass away at 65, you "win" — you collected something. But most people underestimate their life expectancy. For a healthy couple at 65, there's a

50 percent chance one of them will live past 90.
The longer you live, the more waiting pays off.

Real-life example: Jonathan, a retired auto plant supervisor from Flint, claimed at 62. He's now 78, in great health, and regrets the choice every month when his check is hundreds less than it could have been. "I was scared of missing out," he told me. "Turns out I'm missing out for the rest of my life."

Projected Benefits Based on a $2,000 Income at Full Retirement Age

AGE	BENEFIT %	BENEFIT $
Actuarial Reduction		
62	75.0%	$1,500
63	80.0%	$1,600
64	86.7%	$1,733
65	93.3%	$1,866
Full Retirement Age		
66	100%	$2,000
Delayed Retirement Credits		
67	108%	$2,160
68	116%	$2,320
69	124%	$2,480
70	132%	$2,640

Source: RetirementYou source materials.

Myth #5: "If I keep working while collecting, I'm just throwing money away."

Not exactly. If you claim before your Full Retirement Age and earn above the annual earnings limit ($22,320 in 2025), yes — some benefits are withheld. But they aren't gone forever; they're added back into your benefit calculation at FRA, often resulting in a permanent boost.

Real-life example: Nancy, a school administrator from Grand Rapids, kept working after claiming at 64. She was upset when benefits were withheld, but two years later, her monthly check was adjusted upward. "I wish someone had told me it wasn't just lost forever," she said.

Myth #6: "High earners don't need to care about Social Security."
Even if it's not your main income source, it's still a guaranteed, inflation-adjusted stream of money for life. For high earners, the bigger challenge is often tax planning around Social Security to keep more of it in your pocket.

Real-life example: Dr. Maya, a cardiologist in Troy, saw her $4,000/ month benefit heavily taxed because of large required minimum distributions. We used Roth conversions to reduce her future RMDs, saving her thousands in lifetime taxes.

Myth #7: "If I'm divorced, I can't collect on my ex's record."
If your marriage lasted 10 years or more, you can be eligible for spousal benefits based on your ex's work history — even if they've remarried (as long as you haven't).

Real-life example: Janet from Traverse City didn't know she could claim a benefit equal to half of her ex-husband's at FRA, which was more than her own record. It boosted her retirement income by $700 a month, and it didn't reduce his benefit one cent.

Why Busting Myths Matters
The cost of acting on bad information isn't small — it can be thousands of dollars a year for the rest of your life. If you take one thing away from this section, it's this: **learn the rules before you claim, not after.**

THE TAXATION TRAPS: WHEN SOCIAL SECURITY BITES BACK
Mary from Lansing thought she had her retirement finances under control. She'd worked as a nurse for 35 years, had a modest IRA, and was finally enjoying her mornings with coffee and crossword puzzles. Then, one chilly March afternoon, she opened a letter from the IRS.

It wasn't a thank-you note. It was a bill for $4,672 in additional taxes.

The culprit? Her Social Security benefits — the very checks she thought were "tax-free."

She called me in a panic: "Jordan, why am I paying tax on money I already paid taxes on when I earned it?"

The answer lies in something the IRS calls **provisional income**, and it's a trap far too many retirees walk into.

The IRS's Secret Math Formula

Provisional income is the IRS's way of deciding whether — and how much — of your Social Security gets taxed. The formula looks like this:

$$+ \quad \begin{array}{l} \text{Your adjusted gross income} \\ \text{Non-taxable interest income} \\ \text{Half of your Social Security income} \end{array}$$

$$= \quad \text{Your provisional income}$$

Once you know that number, the IRS compares it to these income thresholds:
- **Single Filers:**
  - $25,000–$34,000 → up to 50 percent of benefits taxable
  - Over $34,000 → up to 85 percent taxable
- **Married Filing Jointly:**
  - $32,000–$44,000 → up to 50 percent taxable
  - Over $44,000 → up to 85 percent taxable

And here's the kicker: **those thresholds haven't been adjusted since 1983**. Back then, $25,000 was a comfortable middle-class income. Today? It's barely above the poverty line for a couple. That means more retirees get pulled into paying taxes on their benefits every single year — simply because wages, investment returns, and pensions have grown with inflation, but the tax brackets for Social Security haven't budged.

Two Quick Examples
Let's say Christopher and Dina, a married couple, receive $42,000 a year in combined Social Security benefits.

Scenario 1: Low Other Income
- Half of Social Security: $21,000
- Other taxable income: $5,000
- Provisional income = $26,000 → *below the 50 percent threshold* → No tax on benefits.

Scenario 2: IRA Withdrawals
- Half of Social Security: $21,000
- IRA withdrawals: $50,000
- Provisional income = $71,000 → *well above the 85 percent threshold* → 85 percent of Social Security taxed.

Same benefit amount, completely different tax result.

Hannah & John's $6,000 Lesson
You remember Hannah and John from earlier in the chapter — the couple from Canton who thought Social Security would be their "golden ticket." Their real trap wasn't just the income gap; it was the tax hit.

Their $100,000 in annual IRA withdrawals pushed their provisional income well above $44,000, meaning **85 percent of their Social Security was taxable**. That translated to about $500 a month in extra taxes — **$6,000 a year gone**.

Our fix? We started converting $50,000 a year from their IRA to a Roth IRA during years when their income was lower, and we replaced part of their cash flow with a fixed-indexed annuity that didn't increase their AGI. The result: less taxable income, lower provisional income, and thousands saved in taxes each year.

The IRMAA Surprise
Provisional income isn't the only landmine. Medicare has its own surcharge system called **IRMAA** — the Income-Related Monthly Adjustment Amount.

If your modified AGI exceeds certain thresholds ($103,000 for singles, $206,000 for married couples in 2025), your Medicare Part B and Part D premiums jump. These surcharges can range from **$1,000 to over $5,000 a year** per person.

Example: Tim, a 65-year-old engineer from Clawson, retired in December and claimed Social Security in January. Between his benefits and a large one-time IRA withdrawal to pay off his mortgage, he pushed himself over the IRMAA threshold. Result: an extra $3,000 in Medicare premiums for the year. We could have avoided it entirely with better timing — splitting that withdrawal over two tax years or doing smaller Roth conversions in advance.

State Tax Gotchas
While the majority of states don't tax Social Security benefits, a handful still do in certain situations — and the rules can be quirky. For example:
- **Colorado** taxes some benefits if your income exceeds certain limits.
- **Nebraska** is phasing out its tax, but not fully until 2025.
- **West Virginia** taxes benefits for higher-income retirees.

If you're considering moving in retirement, check the state's tax treatment of Social Security before you pack the moving van.

STRATEGIES TO KEEP MORE OF YOUR SOCIAL SECURITY
Here's what works for many of my clients:

1. **Roth Conversions** – Move money from pre-tax IRAs into Roth IRAs during lower-income years. Roth withdrawals don't count toward provisional income, so they don't trigger more taxation of Social Security.
2. **Qualified Charitable Distributions (QCDs)** – If you're over 70½, donate directly from your IRA to a qualified charity. It counts toward your Required Minimum Distribution but doesn't increase your taxable income.
3. **Timing Your Claim** – Sometimes it makes sense to delay claiming Social Security until after large, one-time withdrawals (selling a business, doing a major home renovation from savings, etc.).

4. **Income Smoothing** – Spread taxable events over multiple years to avoid spiking into higher tax brackets or IRMAA tiers.
5. **Diversified Income Sources** – Balance taxable, tax-deferred, and tax-free accounts so you can pull income strategically.

Your "Tax Defense" Mindset

The single biggest mistake I see is retirees making decisions in isolation — claiming benefits, taking withdrawals, or selling investments without looking at the tax ripple effects. Social Security taxation isn't just about what you *get*; it's about what you *keep*.

I tell clients: "It's not what Uncle Sam gives you that matters — it's what he lets you keep."

When you understand provisional income, IRMAA, and the other traps, you can design a plan that keeps more of your Social Security in your pocket and less in Washington's coffers.

Optimization Strategies: Getting the Most from Your Benefits

If Social Security were a chess game, claiming early without a plan is like moving your queen in the first move — sure, you *can*, but it's probably not the smartest long-term play.

I've seen too many retirees think of Social Security as a "set it and forget it" decision. The truth is, when you claim, how you coordinate with a spouse, and how you handle your other income can add or subtract **tens of thousands — sometimes hundreds of thousands — of dollars over your lifetime.**

HERE IS HOW THE SMART PLAYERS WIN.

1. Delaying Your Claim for Bigger Checks

The rule: For every year you delay claiming benefits past your Full Retirement Age (FRA) — up to age 70 — your monthly check grows by about 8 percent. That's a guaranteed return backed by the U.S. government, and it's hard to beat that kind of certainty anywhere else.

The story: Hannah from earlier in this chapter delayed her claim to age 70 while John took spousal benefits in the meantime. Her monthly check grew by $300, which may not sound huge — until you multiply it out: that's $3,600 more a year, every year, for as long as she lives. Over a 25-year retirement, that's $90,000 in extra income — and that's *before* cost-of-living adjustments.

The mistake to avoid: Thinking you'll "break even" only if you live to some magic age (often quoted around 78–80). The reality is, if you have a long life-expectancy, delaying can make an enormous difference in lifetime benefits and in spousal survivor benefits.

2. Leveraging Spousal Benefits

The rule: If you're married, you can claim a benefit based on your own work record or up to 50 percent of your spouse's FRA benefit — whichever is higher. The key is timing: you only get the full 50 percent if you wait until your FRA to claim.

The story: John, married to Hannah, didn't have as high an earnings history. Rather than taking his own reduced benefit at 62, he claimed a spousal benefit worth $1,750/month at his FRA while Hannah delayed her own claim to 70. This gave them income now without cutting into her growing benefit.

The mistake to avoid: Thinking spousal benefits add on top of your own — they don't. You get the higher of the two, not both.

3. Maximizing Survivor Benefits

The rule: When one spouse passes away, the survivor gets the higher of the two benefits. That means the decision of the higher earner to delay benefits can significantly boost the survivor's lifetime income.

The story: Samantha, a widow from Midland, didn't realize she could switch from her own reduced benefit to her late husband's higher one. When we made the change, her monthly income jumped by $800. Over the next 15 years, that will add roughly $144,000 to her retirement income.

The mistake to avoid: Claiming early without considering the survivor benefit impact — especially if you're the higher earner.

4. Working the 35-Year Rule

The rule: Benefits are based on your highest 35 years of indexed earnings. Any missing years count as zeros, and low-earning years can pull down your average.

The story: Dave, a doctor from East Lansing, had several low-income residency years in his record. We ran the numbers and found that just two more years of part-time consulting at $100,000 would replace two of those low-earning years, boosting his Social Security by over $500/ month for life.

The mistake to avoid: Retiring a year or two early without checking how many low-earning years are in your 35-year record.

5. Divorced? Know Your Rights

The rule: If your marriage lasted 10+ years and you haven't remarried, you may be able to claim spousal benefits on your ex-spouse's record — even if they've remarried.

The story: Janet from Traverse City, divorced after 15 years of marriage, was set to take her own $1,100/month benefit. She was stunned to learn she could claim $1,800/month based on her ex's record. Over 20 years, that's an extra $168,000 in her pocket.

The mistake to avoid: Assuming divorce disqualifies you entirely from spousal benefits — the rules are more generous than many think.

6. Coordinating with Your Other Income

The rule: Your Social Security interacts with your other income sources — IRAs, pensions, annuities, even part-time work. Poor coordination can trigger higher taxes, Medicare surcharges, or benefit reductions.

The story: Tim, the engineer, would have triggered a $3,000 IRMAA surcharge if he'd claimed Social Security in the same year as a large IRA withdrawal. We delayed his claim by one year, kept him under the threshold, and he avoided the surcharge entirely.

The mistake to avoid: Treating Social Security in isolation. It's not just about the size of your check — it's about what you keep after taxes and surcharges.

7. Using Software to Fine-Tune the Plan

The rule: Tools like *Maximize My Social Security* or *Social Security Solutions* can model thousands of claiming scenarios in seconds.

The story: A couple from Northville had three possible claiming strategies. Running them through software revealed a coordinated delay/spousal approach that would increase their lifetime income by over $120,000 compared to the "default" plan they were considering.

The mistake to avoid: Assuming the SSA office will recommend the best strategy. They'll explain your options, but they won't give personalized advice.

Why This All Matters

Optimizing Social Security isn't about "beating the system." It's about making sure you don't leave money on the table. Every extra dollar of guaranteed, inflation-adjusted income is one less dollar you have to pull from savings — and one more dollar working for you in retirement.

WHY SOCIAL SECURITY ISN'T THE WHOLE PLAN: THE GAPS EXPOSED

Imagine building a house with just the foundation. No walls, no roof, no plumbing. Sure, it's a start — but you're going to have a hard time staying dry when the rain comes.

That's what relying solely on Social Security is like. It's the base of your retirement "house," but it can't shelter you from everything life throws your way.

The Numbers Don't Lie

The **2025 Synchrony Bank Retirement Survey** pegs average annual retirement expenses around **$60,000**. The average married couple's combined Social Security benefit in 2025 is roughly **$3,952 a month** ($47,424 a year). That leaves a **$12,500 annual gap** — before we even factor in taxes, healthcare, or big one-time expenses like a new roof or helping a grandchild with college.

And for higher earners, the gap is often much larger because Social Security replaces a smaller percentage of pre-retirement income.

Case Study 1: Over-Reliant Olivia & Sam

Olivia and Sam are both 67, retired, and drawing Social Security. They have no pensions and very modest savings — about $50,000 in a joint savings account. Their combined Social Security is $3,800/month, which covers basic living expenses but leaves little room for the unexpected.

- When Olivia's car broke down, they had to take out a high-interest loan to cover repairs.
- When Sam needed dental implants (not covered by Medicare), they drained $12,000 from savings.
- Inflation has slowly eroded their buying power, forcing them to cut back on travel and dining out.

They aren't destitute — but every financial hiccup feels like a crisis.

Case Study 2: Diversified Dan & Maria

Dan and Maria also draw $3,800/month in Social Security, but that's just one piece of their plan. They also have:

- $1,500/month from a fixed-indexed annuity.
- $800/month from a small pension.
- The flexibility to take $1,000–$1,500/month from their investment portfolio in good markets.

When Dan needed knee surgery, they paid the $5,000 out-of-pocket cost without touching their annuity or pension income. Their Social Security covers the basics, while the other income streams give them freedom and security.

THE FOUR INCOME PILLARS

When I talk to clients about building retirement income, I frame it as **four sturdy pillars**:

1. **Social Security** – The reliable, inflation-adjusted base.
2. **Pensions / Annuities** – Guaranteed monthly income, regardless of market conditions.
3. **Investments** – Flexible, growth-oriented assets to fight inflation and fund discretionary spending.
4. **Part-Time or Passive Income** – Consulting, rental properties, royalties, or other side income.

The more pillars you have, the less you rely on any single one — and the steadier your "retirement house" stands.

THE HEALTHCARE & LONGEVITY GAP

Even with all four pillars, one of the biggest retirement expenses is healthcare. Fidelity's 2025 estimate says a 65-year-old couple will spend **$315,000 on healthcare over their lifetime** (not including long-term care).

And long-term care is its own beast: the **Genworth 2025 Cost of Care Survey** pegs a semi-private nursing home room in Detroit at **$134,454/year**. Medicare covers very little of this. If you think Social Security can handle it, think again.

THE INFLATION FACTOR

Social Security has built-in cost-of-living adjustments (COLAs), but they're tied to the **CPI-W index**, which doesn't always reflect seniors' actual expenses. Healthcare, for example, often rises much faster than the COLA. Over a 25-year retirement, even modest inflation can cut your buying power in half.

SIDE-BY-SIDE: 20-YEAR PROJECTION

Here's what 20 years might look like for two hypothetical couples starting with the same Social Security benefit:

Year	SS-Only Couple	Diversified Couple
1	$3,952/mo	$7,252/mo (SS + annuity + pension + portfolio)
10	$4,803/mo (COLA applied)	$8,803/mo (COLA + annuity + portfolio growth)
20	$5,842/mo	$10,432/mo

By year 20, the diversified couple has far more flexibility — and less stress when unexpected expenses hit.

Client Story: The $2,000 Gap

Allen and Jules from Novi had Social Security covering 70 percent of their expenses, but they were still short $2,000/month. They didn't want to take on market risk in their later years, so we built a plan with:

- Annuities for guaranteed income.
- Roth conversions to reduce taxable income later.
- A conservative investment portfolio for growth.

Now, instead of wondering each month where the shortfall will come from, they know their income covers 100 percent of their needs — with Social Security as just one piece of the puzzle.

Why This Matters Now

The Social Security Trustees Report warns that without reform, the system will only be able to pay about **81 percent of scheduled benefits starting in 2034.** If that happens, and you're relying solely on Social Security, you could see an immediate drop in income with no backup plan.

If you treat Social Security as the *foundation* of your plan, you can build walls, a roof, and maybe even a nice porch to enjoy your retirement years. But if you treat it as the *entire* plan? You're standing out in the rain hoping it doesn't storm.

RIPT FRAMEWORK:
SOCIAL SECURITY IN THE MIX

When we build retirement plans at Main Financial Group, we use the RIPT framework: Risk, Income, Portfolio, and Taxes. Think of it as a four-lane highway — Social Security drives in all four lanes, but it doesn't dominate the road.

R – Risk: Stability, But Not Immunity

Social Security is one of the most stable income sources you'll ever have. It's backed by the U.S. government, indexed to inflation, and continues for life. That makes it an essential "low-risk" asset in your retirement mix.

But stability doesn't mean immunity from risk:

- **Inflation risk** – Your COLA may not keep pace with rising healthcare or housing costs.
- **Legislative risk** – Without reforms, benefits could be cut to 81 percent in 2034.
- **Longevity risk** – Living longer means you need more than Social Security to maintain your lifestyle.

Example: Hannah and John's Social Security gives them a baseline income floor, but their annuity and investments absorb the shocks from inflation and market swings. Without those other tools, their risk of outliving their money would be much higher.

I – Income: The Base Layer of the Retirement Paycheck

We often talk about "creating your retirement paycheck." Social Security is your base layer — the guaranteed deposit that arrives every month like clockwork.

The key is what you stack on top of it:

- **Annuities** for guaranteed lifetime income.
- **Pensions** if you're fortunate to have one.
- **Investment withdrawals** timed for tax efficiency.

Example: Tim, the engineer (from our IRMAA example), uses Social Security for fixed expenses like utilities, property taxes, and Medicare premiums. His annuity covers discretionary expenses, and his portfolio is there for travel and emergencies. The blend lets him enjoy retirement without wondering if he can afford a vacation.

P – Portfolio: Positioning for Growth and Flexibility

Knowing Social Security is there allows you to be more strategic with your investment portfolio. You can take the right amount of risk without worrying about meeting your basic needs.

But here's the mistake some make: they think Social Security replaces the need for growth investments. That's dangerous in a 20–30 year retirement where inflation can cut your buying power in half.

Example: Dave from East Lansing (the doctor) delayed Social Security until 70, giving his portfolio eight extra years to grow without withdrawals. That growth cushion means he can ride out market downturns without cutting back on essentials.

T – Taxes: The Hidden Lever in Maximizing Social Security

Taxes are the most overlooked part of Social Security planning.
- Up to 85 percent of your benefits can be taxable.
- Claiming too early while still working can push you into higher brackets.
- Large Required Minimum Distributions (RMDs) from IRAs later in life can spike your tax rate and Medicare premiums.

Example: Samantha (the Midland widow) didn't just switch to her higher survivor benefit — we also paired that move with Roth conversions in low-income years to keep her future tax rate low. By controlling her AGI, we reduced how much of her Social Security gets taxed, and she keeps more of every check.

THE RIPT PAYOFF

When Social Security is integrated into all four lanes of the RIPT highway:
- **Risk** is reduced because you have a stable income floor.
- **Income** is coordinated so your paycheck covers needs *and* wants.
- **Portfolio** growth can be maximized without jeopardizing essentials.
- **Taxes** are managed so you keep more of what you earn.

When we apply this framework, Social Security becomes a *strategic asset*, not just a check in the mail.

YOUR SOCIAL SECURITY PLAYBOOK: 7 STEPS TO OPTIMIZE YOUR BENEFITS

Think of this as your *field manual* for Social Security. If you follow it step-by-step, you'll avoid the most common mistakes, keep more of your benefits, and make smarter decisions that last the rest of your life.

Step 1: Know Your FRA and Projected Benefits

What it means: FRA (Full Retirement Age) is the age when you can claim your full benefit with no reduction — 67 for those born in 1960 or later.

Why it matters: Claiming before FRA means a permanent cut; delaying past FRA grows your benefit.

Example: Carol from Plymouth thought she'd get $2,400/month at 65. Her SSA statement showed that was her FRA benefit at 67. If she claimed at 65, she'd lose about $160/month for life.

Do:
- Create an account at SSA.gov to view your actual earnings history and benefit estimates.
- Check for errors — incorrect earnings years can reduce your benefit.

Don't:
- Assume "full" means 65; that's outdated.

Self-check question: Do I know exactly what my benefit will be at 62, FRA, and 70 — and what the monthly difference is?

Step 2: Delay If Possible

What it means: Each year you delay past FRA adds roughly 8 percent to your monthly check, up to age 70.

Why it matters: That's a guaranteed lifetime return, adjusted for inflation.

Example: Hannah delayed from 67 to 70, increasing her benefit by $300/month. Over 25 years, that's $90,000 more — before COLAs.

Do:
- Delay if you have other income sources to cover expenses.
- Use part-time work or withdrawals from savings to bridge the gap.

Don't:
- Delay without considering life expectancy, health, and survivor benefits.

Self-check question: Could I cover my needs for 1–3 more years without claiming Social Security?

Step 3: Leverage Spousal and Survivor Benefits

What it means: You may be entitled to benefits based on your spouse's work record — up to 50 percent for spousal and up to 100 percent for survivor.

Why it matters: Coordinating these benefits can significantly boost lifetime income.

Example: John claimed spousal benefits at FRA while Hannah delayed her own to 70. Samantha switched to a survivor benefit after her husband's death, adding $800/month.

Do:
- Time spousal benefits to allow the higher earner's benefit to grow.
- Consider survivor benefit implications before the higher earner claims.

Don't:
- Assume you can take both your benefit and your spouse's — you only get the higher of the two.

Self-check question: Have I coordinated my claims to maximize both lifetime and survivor income?

Step 4: Manage Taxes and IRMAA

What it means: Your benefits can be taxed up to 85 percent and can push you into higher Medicare premiums (IRMAA).

Why it matters: Poor tax planning can erase much of your benefit.

Example: Tim avoided a $3,000 Medicare surcharge by delaying his claim one year and spreading IRA withdrawals over multiple years.

Do:
- Use Roth conversions to lower future taxable income.
- Keep provisional income below IRMAA thresholds when possible.

Don't:
- Take large taxable withdrawals in the same year you start Social Security without running the numbers.

Self-check question: Do I know my provisional income — and how it changes if I claim Social Security?

Step 5: Diversify Your Toolbox

What it means: Social Security is one tool — not the whole kit. Layer in annuities, investments, and pensions.

Why it matters: Diversification protects you from legislative risk, inflation, and market downturns.

Example: Dan and Maria use Social Security for basics, an annuity for travel and fun, and their portfolio for long-term growth.

Do:
- Use guaranteed income sources for essentials.
- Keep growth assets for inflation protection.

Don't:
- Rely solely on Social Security to cover all retirement expenses.

Self-check question: If Social Security was cut by 20 percent, could I still meet my essential expenses?

Step 6: Review Annually

What it means: Your Social Security strategy isn't "set it and forget it." Life changes, and so should your plan.

Why it matters: Health, taxes, and laws can shift the optimal strategy.

Example: Mark was planning to delay until 70, but a new diagnosis prompted him to claim earlier and enjoy the income while he could travel.

Do:
- Review your SSA statement yearly.
- Recalculate if you change jobs, have a health change, or get married/divorced.

Don't:
- Assume last year's plan is still the best this year.

Self-check question: Have I reviewed my Social Security strategy in the last 12 months?

Step 7: Work with a Fiduciary Advisor

What it means: The SSA will explain your options but won't tell you which is best for your situation.

Why it matters: Coordinating Social Security with the rest of your plan requires a full financial picture.

Example: A Northville couple increased their lifetime income by $120,000 after an advisor coordinated their Social Security claims with Roth conversions and annuity purchases.

Do:
- Choose an advisor who understands tax planning, not just investments.
- Use planning software for precise scenario modeling.

Don't:
- Rely solely on SSA reps or "rules of thumb" from friends.

Self-check question: Has my Social Security strategy been integrated with my tax, investment, and income plans?

CLOSING THE CHAPTER: YOUR PLAYBOOK SUMMARY

When done right, optimizing Social Security is like tuning a finely crafted engine. Every adjustment — delaying, coordinating with a spouse, managing taxes — makes it run more efficiently for years to come.

And the best part? Once you get it right, you can stop worrying about it and start enjoying the retirement you worked so hard to earn.

CHAPTER EIGHT

The Great Wealth Transfer:
Leaving a Legacy Without a Tax Bomb

Picture this: It's a crisp, sun-splashed morning in Brighton, Michigan, the kind where the air feels like it was washed overnight and the coffee in your mug somehow tastes a little richer. My office sits just off Main Street, where the small-town storefronts still carry that "we've been here for decades" authenticity—hardware store, diner, barber.

On this particular morning, the bells above my office door jingled, and in walked Dorothy. Seventy years old, with silver hair perfectly set, and an expression that told me she wasn't here for small talk. She had a stack of papers in her hands—thicker than a Detroit phone book back when people actually used them—and the kind of posture that comes from both Midwestern pride and the weight of responsibility.

She eased into the chair across from my desk, placed the stack down with a sigh, and looked me straight in the eye. "Jordan," she said, her voice calm but her eyes carrying the kind of concern you only see from someone who's been thinking about the same problem for far too long, "I've got a mess on my hands."

DOROTHY'S STORY — A WIDOW'S WORRY

Dorothy's husband, Richard, had passed a year earlier after a life spent working for Dow Chemical. He was an engineer's engineer—precise, deliberate, and quietly proud of the $500,000 IRA he had built over decades. To Richard, that account was the family's safety net, their nest egg, and ultimately, the gift they would leave to their two sons, Ben and James.

Ben lived in Grand Rapids and worked as a mechanical engineer. James was in South Lyon, building a career in software. Both had good incomes—good enough, in fact, that they were already paying some of the highest federal tax rates.

"I don't want my boys paying taxes on money their father sweated for," Dorothy continued. "It's like leaving them a pie with half the slices missing."

Now, she wasn't wrong. We ran the math: Under the SECURE Act's rules, her sons would have to drain the IRA within 10 years of her passing. Given their current earnings, each withdrawal would be taxed at rates pushing into the 35–37 percent bracket. On that $500,000 balance, it could mean more than $185,000 evaporating in taxes before either son saw a dime.

That wasn't just a slice missing from the pie—it was the IRS walking away with a family-sized portion.

The Conversation That Changed Her Mind

When I first laid out those numbers, Dorothy frowned. Not at me—at the unfairness of it. "So, what you're telling me," she said, "is that if I do nothing, the government gets a bigger share than my boys?"

"Not exactly bigger," I replied, "but enough to change the story you thought you were writing for them."

That's when we started talking about **Roth conversions**. Over the course of five years, Dorothy could convert the IRA to a Roth while still alive, paying the taxes herself at her current 22 percent rate—far below what her sons would face. The total bill would be about $110,000. Painful, yes, but in return, the account could grow tax-free for the rest of her life. At a reasonable 7 percent annual return, it could be worth around $1.5 million by the time it passed to her sons—and they wouldn't owe a penny in taxes.

"You mean," Dorothy asked, leaning forward, "they could keep the whole pie?" "Every slice," I said. She didn't hesitate. "Then let's bake it."

Why This Chapter Matters

Dorothy's story is one among millions that will play out over the next two decades. **We are living in the early innings of the largest transfer of wealth in history**—$124 trillion moving from baby boomers and the silent generation to their heirs and charities by 2048.

But here's the hard truth: Without thoughtful planning, a significant chunk of that money won't end up with children, grandchildren, or community causes. It will go to the IRS.

That's what this chapter is about—how to make sure your legacy goes where you want it to, without leaving behind a **tax bomb** that explodes in the faces of the people you love.

THE GREAT WEALTH TRANSFER — A BRIEF HISTORY WITH A BIG FUTURE

The concept of passing wealth from one generation to the next is as old as civilization itself. Ancient Rome had its own estate laws, carefully regulating who could inherit land and assets. Medieval England codified inheritance into primogeniture, where the eldest son took the lion's share (and often the whole thing), leaving siblings to seek their fortunes elsewhere. In the United States, the Founding Fathers inherited not just ideas from Europe, but also complex questions about property, taxation, and fairness.

For much of U.S. history, wealth transfers were relatively modest in scale. In the 19th century, the average American farmer might pass on land, tools, and livestock—not portfolios or retirement accounts. Even as late as the 1950s, when corporate pensions were more common than 401(k)s, retirement wealth was often tied to defined benefit plans that ended with the retiree's life.

It wasn't until the late 20th century that **individual retirement accounts**—IRAs, 401(k)s, and other tax-deferred vehicles—became household terms. The Employee Retirement Income Security Act (ERISA) of 1974, followed by the 401(k) boom in the 1980s, created a new phenomenon: millions of Americans building substantial, individually owned retirement accounts. These accounts weren't just supplemental savings—they became the primary nest eggs for an entire generation.

By the turn of the 21st century, two forces converged:
1. **The Baby Boomers**—the largest generation in U.S. history—were entering their peak earning years.
2. **The stock market's long-term rise**—punctuated by volatility but broadly upward—meant that retirement accounts swelled in value.

Fast forward to today, and we find ourselves staring at what economists call the **Great Wealth Transfer**. According to Cerulli Associates' 2025 update, between now and 2048, approximately **$124 trillion** will change hands. About $105 trillion will pass directly to heirs, while another $18 trillion will flow to charitable organizations.

That's not just a big number—it's a number with enormous implications:

- Tax policy will shape outcomes more than market performance for many families.
- The beneficiaries of this wealth aren't just children—they include grandchildren, charitable causes, and in some cases, unintended recipients (the IRS being one of the biggest).
- The decisions you make now will ripple through decades of family history.

Why This Wealth Transfer Is Different

This isn't the first time wealth has moved from one generation to another, but several factors make this era unique:

1. Tax-Deferred Accounts Dominate

In past generations, much of inherited wealth was in real estate, cash, or taxable investment accounts—all of which came with different tax treatment, including the favorable step-up in basis for capital gains. Today, trillions are locked inside IRAs and 401(k)s, where every dollar withdrawn by heirs is taxed as ordinary income.

2. The SECURE Act Changed the Game

Before 2020, non-spouse heirs could "stretch" required minimum distributions (RMDs) from an inherited IRA over their life expectancy, allowing decades of tax-deferred growth. The SECURE Act of 2019 eliminated that option for most beneficiaries, compressing the withdrawal window to just 10 years. This accelerates taxes, often during heirs' highest earning years, making the tax bite much bigger.

3. The Estate Tax Sunset Looms

For years, families braced for the estate tax exemption to be cut nearly in half after 2025, dropping from today's historically high $13.61 million per person down to roughly $7 million. That would have meant more middle-market families with successful businesses, farms, or appreciated real estate suddenly facing a tax once reserved for the ultra-wealthy.

But in a dramatic turn, the recently passed "One Big Beautiful

Bill" scrapped that sunset altogether. Instead, the exemption has been permanently set at $15 million per person, indexed for inflation going forward. While the top estate tax rate of 40 percent remains unchanged, the higher, permanent threshold means fewer estates will be subject to federal estate tax—at least for now. For families approaching that level of wealth, however, thoughtful planning remains critical, because laws can always change again with the stroke of a pen in Washington.

4. Longevity & Multi-Generational Planning
People are living longer. This means more wealth will transfer later in life, often when heirs are in their 50s or 60s and already in high tax brackets—making compressed taxation even more costly.

5. Charitable Giving in the Spotlight
With trillions set to move, nonprofits are positioning themselves as part of the legacy conversation. Planned giving, donor-advised funds, and charitable trusts are becoming central tools for both tax mitigation and impact.

Why You Can't Afford to "Do Nothing"
Let's be blunt: doing nothing is a plan—it's just a terrible one. If you die with a large traditional IRA or 401(k) and no strategy in place, your heirs will inherit a ticking clock and a growing tax bill.

Take an example that's playing out in my office more than you might think:
- Parent leaves a $1 million IRA to a son earning $200,000 a year.
- The son has to drain it within 10 years under the SECURE Act.
- Even if he spreads withdrawals evenly, that's $100,000/year in additional taxable income.
- Result: higher tax bracket, $300,000–$370,000 lost to the IRS.

Now multiply that scenario by millions of households across the country, and you see why this is more than a personal issue—it's a national one.

THE TAX BOMB IN YOUR LEGACY — HOW IRAS EXPLODE FOR HEIRS

Let's start with an uncomfortable truth: That gleaming retirement account balance you've spent decades building—the one that looks so impressive on your statement—may not be the number your family actually gets.

In fact, for heirs of traditional IRAs or 401(k)s, the real number can be 20–40 percent smaller after taxes, depending on their own income level. And the culprit isn't bad investing, a down market, or even poor spending habits. The culprit is the U.S. tax code.

The Illusion of "All Mine"

For most of your working life, a traditional IRA or 401(k) felt like a win. Every contribution lowered your taxable income that year, letting you keep more in your paycheck. The money grew tax-deferred—meaning you didn't pay capital gains or dividend taxes along the way—and you got the psychological lift of watching a bigger number every quarter.

But here's the catch: **"tax-deferred" is not "tax-free."** You haven't escaped taxes. You've postponed them—and by postponing, you've also created a problem for whoever inherits your account. It's like filling a safe with gold bars for your kids, but leaving a note that says, "By the way, 30–40 percent of these belong to the IRS."

The SECURE Act — From Stretch to Squeeze

Before 2020, non-spouse heirs could stretch distributions from an inherited IRA over their own life expectancy. A 40-year-old might have had 40+ years to draw down the account, taking small annual withdrawals and letting the rest grow. Taxes were spread out, and the impact was softened.

That's gone. The **SECURE Act of 2019** (and its 2023 follow-up, SECURE 2.0) condensed the withdrawal window for most non-spouse beneficiaries to **10 years**. Now, the IRS is essentially saying, "You've got a decade—empty it out."

The result? Large chunks of taxable income crammed into a short period, often when heirs are in their highest earning years.

The Math Behind the Explosion

Let's break this down with three scenarios so you can see the difference:

Scenario 1 — The Do-Nothing Plan
- IRA value at death: $1,000,000
- Beneficiary: 45-year-old son earning $200,000/year
- 10-year drawdown: $100,000/year added to income
- New taxable income: $300,000/year

At 2025's tax brackets, that pushes him into the 35–37 percent range for much of that decade. The result? Roughly $320,000 in taxes over the 10-year period.

Scenario 2 — The Roth Conversion Plan
- Parent converts IRA to Roth gradually over 8 years before passing, paying taxes at an average 22 percent bracket.
- Taxes paid upfront: ~$176,000
- Account grows tax-free in the Roth to $1.2 million by time of inheritance.
- Heir withdraws at will—no taxes owed.

Difference in net inheritance: **$324,000** more for the family. But wait, there's more!

Scenario 3 — The IRA Legacy Plan
- Parent determines they do not need their full IRA for retirement income and designates $1,000,000 for legacy purposes.
- IRA is repositioned into a fixed income annuity, which generates guaranteed annual payments.
- Those annuity payments are used to fund a permanent life insurance policy.
- Result: a tax-free life insurance benefit of approximately $3,200,000 to the heirs (based on a healthy 65–70-year-old parent).

Instead of forcing the next generation into higher tax brackets or paying a significant upfront tax bill, this strategy transforms the IRA into a legacy multiplier. By using the annuity as a funding engine, the family creates a tax-free inheritance three times larger than the original IRA—without the burden of income taxes that normally accompany traditional retirement accounts.

REAL PEOPLE, REAL PAIN

Mitchell's Story

Mitchell, a 75-year-old from Livonia, had an $800,000 IRA when he passed away. His daughter, a successful physician earning $250,000, inherited it. Under the SECURE Act, she had to pull roughly $80,000/year for 10 years. Each withdrawal pushed her into a higher tax bracket. By the time the account was emptied, she had paid over $280,000 in taxes—money that could have been saved with a pre-death Roth conversion.

Mitchell wasn't careless—he simply didn't know the rules had changed. When the SECURE Act killed the stretch IRA, his old plan became a tax trap.

Veronica's Story

Veronica, 68, inherited her mother's $300,000 IRA in 2024. She thought of it as a cushion for retirement, but the forced withdrawals meant $30,000/year of taxable income added to her Social Security and pension. This not only pushed her into a higher bracket—it triggered IRMAA surcharges on her Medicare premiums, costing her hundreds more per month. The tax bomb doesn't just shrink inheritances—it can create a cascade of other expenses.

THE RIPPLE EFFECTS OF A TAX BOMB

The cost of an inherited IRA tax bomb can spread far beyond the IRS check:

- **Medicare Premium Hikes:** Higher income from withdrawals can trigger Income-Related Monthly Adjustment Amount (IRMAA) surcharges.
- **College Aid Impact:** If heirs have kids in college, higher reported income can crush eligibility for financial aid.
- **Estate Tax Complications:** Large IRAs add to estate value, possibly pushing it over the exemption threshold after 2025's sunset.
- **Lost Compounding:** Money paid in taxes upfront is gone forever—money that could have continued growing for heirs.

Why Awareness Is the First Step

Most people aren't aware of this problem because it doesn't show up in their own retirement projections. You might know your RMDs, you might have a handle on your living expenses, but unless you model what happens after you're gone, you're missing the full picture.

And here's the thing: **The IRS is counting on your inaction.**

They know trillions in tax-deferred accounts are about to change hands, and they've already tightened the rules to make sure they get their share faster.

ROTH CONVERSIONS — THE TAX-FREE LEGACY SUPERPOWER

If the SECURE Act is the storm cloud looming over your family's inheritance, the Roth IRA is the umbrella that keeps everyone dry. It doesn't just reduce taxes for your heirs—it can eliminate them altogether on inherited retirement accounts.

Here's why Roth conversions are such a powerful legacy tool:

- **Pay Taxes Now, Not Later:** You settle the tax bill during your lifetime—at rates you can control—instead of leaving your heirs to pay at potentially higher rates.
- **Tax-Free Growth:** Once inside a Roth, your investments grow tax-free for the rest of your life and for your heirs.
- **No Required Minimum Distributions (RMDs) for You:** Unlike traditional IRAs, Roth IRAs have no RMDs during your lifetime, giving your money more time to grow.
- **10-Year Rule Still Applies, but with a Twist:** Yes, heirs still have to withdraw Roth funds within 10 years—but withdrawals are tax-free, so timing doesn't matter for tax purposes.

The Roth Conversion Ladder

A full, all-at-once Roth conversion sounds tempting—just rip off the Band-Aid, pay the tax, and be done. But for most people, it's smarter to ladder conversions over several years, staying within lower tax brackets and avoiding unnecessary Medicare premium hikes.

Think of it as moving money through a doorway—wide enough to fit a good chunk each year, but not so much that you jam up the hallway and trigger penalties.

Step-by-Step Laddering Strategy:
1. **Calculate Your Tax Bracket Ceiling**
   Determine the highest bracket you're comfortable filling each year. For many, that's the 22 percent or 24 percent bracket (current 2025 rates).
2. **Estimate Future Tax Rates**
   Consider where rates are headed. With the Tax Cuts and Jobs Act set to sunset in 2026, today's brackets may be the lowest you'll see for a while.
3. **Run the 10-Year Heir Tax Simulation**
   Model what your heirs would pay under the SECURE Act if you do nothing. That's your benchmark for potential savings.
4. **Convert in Annual Chunks**
   Move enough each year to stay within your bracket ceiling, paying the tax with non-IRA money if possible (so you don't shrink the converted amount).
5. **Repeat Until Goal Is Reached**
   Whether it takes 3 years or 10, keep going until you've converted the portion of your IRA you want to protect from future taxes.

Case 1 — The Strategic 22 percent Bracket Fill
Eddie, 72, from Grand Rapids, had a $1.6 million traditional IRA. He was already taking RMDs but wanted his three kids to inherit tax-free. We ran the numbers and found that converting $200,000/year for eight years would keep him in the 22 percent bracket. He paid about $352,000 in taxes over that period. Without the conversion, his heirs—two doctors and an attorney—would have faced $600,000+ in taxes under the 10-year rule.

Net savings: nearly $250,000.

Case 2 — Widow's Compressed Timeline
Marilyn, 68, lost her husband unexpectedly and inherited his $900,000 IRA. She had no pension and modest Social Security, putting her in a lower bracket now than she'd be in later once RMDs started.

We converted $150,000/year for six years, filling her 12 percent and 22 percent brackets while staying below the IRMAA threshold for Medicare.

Her two children, both in high-income tech jobs, will now inherit a Roth instead of a tax bomb.

Case 3 — The Estate Tax and Roth One-Two Punch

A business owner with a $6 million estate in 2025 faced both the looming estate tax sunset and the SECURE Act problem. By converting $300,000/year to Roth and pairing it with a life insurance trust funded from business sale proceeds, we cut both income and estate taxes for the heirs—saving them more than $1 million combined.

The Emotional Side of Roth Conversions

Here's the part people often overlook: when you convert to Roth, you're making a conscious choice to shoulder the tax burden yourself so your family doesn't have to. I've had clients tell me it feels like "writing a love letter in numbers" to their kids—an act of generosity and responsibility that can't be overstated.

And unlike complicated trust structures or hard-to-explain estate maneuvers, a Roth is something your heirs can understand in seconds: **"It's yours, and it's tax-free."**

BEYOND THE NUMBERS — WHEN A ROTH CONVERSION ISN'T RIGHT

It's worth noting that Roth conversions aren't a one-size-fits-all solution.

They work best when:
- You have cash outside your IRA to pay the taxes.
- Your current tax rate is lower than your heirs' likely future rate.
- You expect tax rates overall to rise.

They may be less attractive if you:
- Need every dollar from your IRA for living expenses.
- Are in a very high tax bracket now and expect your heirs to be in lower brackets later.
- Have charitable intentions for the IRA funds (since charities pay no tax on inherited IRAs).

OTHER STRATEGIES — TRUSTS, LIFE INSURANCE, AND CHARITABLE PLANNING

Roth conversions may be the headliner in the "avoid the tax bomb" playbook, but they're not the only tool worth considering. In fact, for many families—especially those with complex estates, multiple heirs, or charitable goals—the most effective approach combines multiple strategies. Think of it like building a house: the Roth is a strong foundation, but you still need walls, a roof, and maybe a few special features to make it exactly the legacy you want to leave.

Trusts — Putting Structure Around Your Legacy

A trust isn't just for the ultra-wealthy. In the context of wealth transfer, a trust is essentially a set of legal instructions for how your money and assets should be managed and distributed after you're gone.

Two Core Types:

1. Revocable Living Trust (RLT)
- You control it during your lifetime, can make changes at any time.
- Primarily used to avoid probate and maintain privacy.
- Doesn't shield assets from estate taxes, but can coordinate asset distribution efficiently.

2. Irrevocable Trust
- Can't be changed after creation (with few exceptions).
- Removes assets from your taxable estate.
- Common for advanced strategies like **Irrevocable Life Insurance Trusts (ILITs)** and **Charitable Remainder Trusts (CRTs).**

The ILIT — Turning Life Insurance into a Tax-Free Legacy

An **Irrevocable Life Insurance Trust** owns a life insurance policy on your life. When you pass, the death benefit is paid to the trust, bypassing your estate and avoiding income tax for heirs.

Example: Marla, a 74-year-old from Birmingham, had $3 million in investments and real estate, putting her above the post-2025 estate tax threshold. By moving a $1 million life insurance policy into an ILIT, she ensured her children received that amount tax-free and outside her estate, saving roughly $400,000 in estate taxes.

The CRT — Giving with a Purpose

A **Charitable Remainder Trust** lets you transfer assets into the trust, receive income from them for life (or a set term), and then leave the remainder to a charity. It's part legacy gift, part tax tool—often used to reduce capital gains taxes when selling highly appreciated assets.

Dynasty Trusts

For families with significant multi-generational wealth, dynasty trusts can keep assets growing tax-efficiently for decades while shielding them from estate taxes each time they pass to a new generation.

Life Insurance — The Tax-Free Equalizer

Life insurance is more than just income replacement—it can be the great equalizer in estate planning.

It can:

- Provide a lump sum to offset taxes heirs will owe on other assets.
- Create liquidity to pay estate taxes without forcing the sale of illiquid assets like a business or family property.
- Equalize inheritances when one heir receives a business or property and another receives cash.

Case in Point: A client of mine left a vacation property to one child and a $2 million life insurance policy to the other. Without the insurance, they would have had to sell the property to "make things fair."

Qualified Charitable Distributions (QCDs) — Giving While Living

If you're over 70½, you can make **Qualified Charitable Distributions** directly from your IRA to a charity—up to $100,000/year per person. These count toward your Required Minimum Distributions but are excluded from taxable income.

The beauty? You reduce your IRA balance (and therefore the future tax bomb) while supporting causes you care about—without triggering taxes on the distribution.

Annual Gifting — The Slow, Steady Transfer

The IRS allows you to give up to **$18,000 per person per year** (2025 limit) without using your lifetime gift/estate tax exemption. For a married couple with two children and four grandchildren, that's $216,000 per year you could transfer completely tax-free, simply by writing checks.

Over a decade, that's more than $2 million moved out of your taxable estate—without filing a single gift tax return (as long as you stay under the annual limit).

Step-Up in Basis — The Unsung Hero of Tax Planning

When your heirs inherit appreciated assets like real estate or stocks, the cost basis is "stepped up" to the value at your death. That means they could sell immediately with little or no capital gains tax.

But here's the trap: this step-up doesn't apply to retirement accounts. That's why a rental property might be a more tax-friendly inheritance than a traditional IRA.

Combining Tools — The Legacy Synergy

The best legacy plans often weave these strategies together:

- Use Roth conversions to eliminate income tax on retirement accounts.
- Pair life insurance (in an ILIT) to cover estate taxes.
- Employ a revocable trust for smooth asset transfers.
- Make annual gifts to gradually reduce taxable estate value.
- Use QCDs to shrink IRA balances while alive.

This isn't about throwing every tool at the wall—it's about aligning the tools with your values and goals.

RIPT FRAMEWORK: LEGACY EDITION

(Risk · Income · Portfolio · Taxes)

When we designed the RIPT framework at Main Financial Group, it was about simplifying retirement planning—breaking it into four critical pillars so clients could see the whole picture. But here's the thing: the RIPT framework doesn't stop when you stop working. It carries right into your legacy planning. In fact, in the context of the Great Wealth Transfer, RIPT becomes even more powerful.

R = Risk — Protecting the Plan and the People

Risk in legacy planning is about more than investment volatility. It's about:
- The risk that taxes will erode your legacy.
- The risk that estate taxes will force a sale of cherished assets.
- The risk of family disputes when the plan isn't clear.

Legacy Risk Tools:
- **Life Insurance** — Provides tax-free liquidity to pay estate taxes or equalize inheritances.
- **Trusts** — Protect assets from creditors, lawsuits, or even heirs' own poor money habits.
- **Clear Documentation** — A will or trust that spells out your intentions, reducing the chance of conflict.

Example: Dorothy's Roth conversion removed the tax risk entirely for her sons. But she also created a revocable trust to ensure the assets passed quickly and privately—avoiding the probate process entirely.

I = Income — Ensuring You're Covered First

One of the biggest mistakes I see is people focusing so much on what they'll leave that they jeopardize their own retirement income. Legacy planning works best when you're certain your own needs are met first.

Legacy Income Strategies:
- **Roth Laddering** — Convert enough to protect heirs without starving your retirement budget.
- **Annuities for Predictable Income** — Freeing other assets for strategic gifting.
- **Charitable Remainder Trusts** — Provide you income for life while earmarking assets for charity later.

Key Point: You don't have to choose between living well now and leaving well later. With the right income plan, you can do both.

P = Portfolio — Structuring Assets for Smooth Transfer

Your portfolio is more than a growth engine—it's a blueprint for how assets will flow to the next generation.

Legacy Portfolio Tactics:
- **Segregate Assets by Purpose** — Retirement income, legacy gifts,

charitable bequests.

- **Use Tax-Friendly Accounts First** — Spend down taxable and traditional IRA funds before Roths to maximize what's left tax-free.
- **Align Investment Strategy with Heirs' Time Horizon** — Younger heirs may benefit from more growth-oriented allocations in inherited Roth accounts.

Example: One client had a $2 million estate split between a Roth IRA, a taxable brokerage account, and real estate. We earmarked the Roth for the grandchildren (long time horizon, tax-free growth), the taxable account for immediate heirs (taking advantage of step-up in basis), and the real estate for a charitable foundation.

T = Taxes — The Final, Decisive Factor

When it comes to legacy, taxes are often the single biggest threat to your goals. If you ignore them, you might unintentionally leave more to the IRS than to your favorite grandchild.

Legacy Tax Strategies:

- **Roth Conversions** — Shift tax burden to your lifetime at favorable rates.
- **Annual Gifting** — Remove assets from your estate without triggering gift tax.
- **QCDs** — Reduce IRA balances while satisfying charitable desires.
- **Estate Tax Planning** — ILITs, GRATs, and other advanced tools for high-net-worth families.

The RIPT Legacy Checklist

Here's how to run a quick RIPT Legacy Review:

1. **Risk:** Have I removed risks to my legacy through insurance, trusts, and clear documentation?
2. **Income:** Am I confident my own retirement needs are covered before committing to legacy transfers?
3. **Portfolio:** Are my assets allocated to minimize taxes and match my heirs' needs?
4. **Taxes:** Have I taken steps to reduce or eliminate the tax burden my heirs will face?

If you can't answer "yes" to all four, your plan isn't complete yet.

YOUR LEGACY PLAYBOOK — PASS WEALTH, NOT BURDENS

When it comes to the Great Wealth Transfer, the difference between a clean, tax-smart legacy and a messy, expensive one comes down to intentional action. You don't need to be an expert in tax law or estate planning—that's what advisors, attorneys, and CPAs are for—but you *do* need to be proactive.

Think of this as your **Legacy Playbook**—a series of coordinated moves designed to make sure your wealth passes where you want it, in the way you want, without leaving your heirs holding a ticking tax bomb.

Step 1 — Take Inventory of Your Wealth Transfer Risks

Before you can fix anything, you need to see the whole picture.

- List all retirement accounts (traditional and Roth), taxable accounts, real estate, life insurance policies, and business interests.
- Identify which assets are tax-deferred (traditional IRAs, 401(k)s) and which are tax-free (Roths, certain insurance).
- Run a projection of what each account might be worth at your expected life expectancy.
- Ask your advisor to simulate what happens to each asset under current tax law if your heirs inherit it *today*.

Why it matters: This is where many people are shocked—seeing the actual dollar amount their heirs could lose to taxes under the SECURE Act's 10-year rule.

Step 2 — Model the 10-Year Rule Impact

Using the SECURE Act rules, calculate what heirs would pay in taxes if they had to drain each tax-deferred account in 10 years. This is where you compare:

- *Do nothing scenario:* Heirs inherit a traditional IRA and pay taxes annually during their peak earning years.
- *Action scenario:* Roth conversion or other planning strategies in place to reduce or eliminate that tax bill.

When you see, in black and white, that your heirs could lose 30–40 percent of the account to taxes, the need for action becomes very real.

Step 3 — Choose Your Primary Tax Strategy

For most families, this will be one of three approaches:

1. **Roth Conversion Ladder** — Gradually shift money from traditional accounts to Roth IRAs while managing tax brackets.
2. **Strategic Charitable Giving** — Use QCDs, donor-advised funds, or charitable trusts to shrink taxable accounts while alive.
3. **Life Insurance + Trust Combination** — Use insurance to create tax-free liquidity, paired with a trust to direct it.

Step 4 — Protect the Plan with the Right Legal Structures

Meet with an estate planning attorney to ensure you have:

- A **revocable living trust** or will that clearly directs your assets.
- **Beneficiary designations** on all accounts updated and aligned with your plan.
- Consider **ILITs** for large life insurance policies and **CRTs** for charitable impact.

These aren't just legal formalities—they're the blueprint for how your plan executes after you're gone.

Step 5 — Align Your Portfolio with Your Legacy Goals

Make sure your investments are positioned for both your retirement and your heirs' future:

- Keep Roth assets in growth-oriented investments (tax-free gains are a gift).
- Spend down taxable and traditional assets strategically to maximize what's left in Roths.
- If leaving assets to charity, fund those gifts with tax-deferred accounts—they pay no tax, so it's the most efficient use of those dollars.

Step 6 — Use Lifetime Gifting to Your Advantage

Start moving assets now using the $18,000 annual gift exclusion ($36,000 per couple, per recipient). This can be especially powerful if:

- You have a large estate and want to reduce its taxable value.
- You want to see your heirs enjoy some of their inheritance while you're alive.

Step 7 — Revisit the Plan Every 1–2 Years

Tax laws change. Life changes. Your health, income, and family situation can all shift—and your plan needs to adapt.

- Schedule a **biennial legacy review** with your advisor, CPA, and estate attorney.
- Keep your heirs informed (at least at a high level) so there are no surprises later.

Dorothy's Full Circle

Let's go back to Dorothy for a moment. When we first sat down, she saw a $500,000 IRA and thought it was her sons' inheritance in full. After walking through the 10-year rule math, she realized the IRS would take a far larger bite than she'd imagined.

Her Roth conversion plan wasn't just about numbers—it was about clarity. She knew exactly what her sons would inherit, how much it would grow, and the fact that it would be tax-free. When the conversion was complete, she told me, "I feel lighter knowing I've already taken care of the hard part."

That's the peace of mind a well-executed legacy plan brings—not just to your heirs, but to you.

CLOSING THE CHAPTER: YOUR CALL TO ACTION

The Great Wealth Transfer is happening whether you plan for it or not. The only question is: will your wealth pass as a gift or as a bill?

Here's the truth—doing nothing is the easiest choice, and the most expensive. The families who thrive in the decades ahead will be the ones who take deliberate, informed steps now to protect their legacies.

So open the conversation with your advisor. Ask the hard questions. Run the simulations. And remember: a legacy isn't just what you leave—it's how you leave it.

CHAPTER NINE

The Second Opinion That Saves:
Why a Fresh Look Matters

It was one of those Michigan summer days where the air felt thick enough to chew. The kind where sweat beads before you even make it from the car to the office door. That's when Dave came barreling into my Brighton office like a man who'd just had enough.

Dave was fifty-five, built like the farm equipment he spent his life running, and he carried the weary look of someone who worked dawn to dusk for decades without ever complaining. But this time, he wasn't carrying a bushel of corn or a wrench—he was carrying a stack of statements thicker than a seed catalog, and he dropped them on my desk with the weight of a man who felt betrayed.

"My bank's advisor pushed me into this thing at a steak dinner seminar," he growled. "Said it would guarantee my retirement. But I'm paying four percent in fees and it's locked up tighter than a silo in January. Is this a scam or what?"

You could hear the frustration in his voice. And truthfully, you couldn't blame him. He had built his life on hard work and trust—trust in the weather, trust in the soil, and trust that when someone in a suit told him something, it was honest. Instead, what he got was a product that worked more like a slow leak in his financial bucket. Those fees—thousands every year—were quietly eating away at his future. The so-called guarantees were flimsy at best, and worse, the product didn't even fit his needs. Dave wanted predictability, income he could count on for the farm and his family. What he got was volatility wrapped in fine print.

We took a step back and gave him something better: a plan that matched his real goals. By moving into a product with no fees, linked to market growth without market losses, his income improved and his peace of mind returned. He walked out lighter, not just because of the dollars saved, but because someone finally sat on his side of the table.

And that, in essence, is what a second opinion is all about.

Why Second Opinions Save

Let's pause here, because this isn't just Dave's story. It's a story I've seen repeated hundreds of times. The characters change—sometimes it's a doctor, sometimes an engineer, sometimes a teacher—but the script is eerily similar. People sit across from me with that same look Dave had: "I thought I was doing the right thing, but now I'm not so sure."

The truth is, most of us don't get second opinions when it comes to money. We'll get one when a doctor delivers a diagnosis, or when a mechanic quotes a price that feels steep. But when it comes to our financial future—the nest egg we spent decades building—too many people take the first answer and hope for the best. That's not just a mistake. It can be the costliest mistake of your life.

Here's why: one wrong decision, one overlooked fee, or one mismatched strategy doesn't just cost you today—**it compounds for years**. Think of it like planting in the wrong soil. If you plant corn in sand, you won't just lose this year's harvest—you've lost all the seasons that seed should have produced.

Second opinions save because they catch those mistakes before they become permanent. They reveal fees nobody explained, risks nobody highlighted, and opportunities nobody mentioned. They give you the chance to align your money with your goals instead of blindly trusting that everything is "fine."

Hidden Dangers of "Trust Me" Advice

A lot of bad financial outcomes don't come from bad people. They come from mismatched incentives. Many advisors operate under rules that allow them to sell you something "suitable." That's not the same as "best." It's the financial equivalent of your doctor prescribing the drug that happens to be on sale from the pharmaceutical rep who brought lunch for the office. It's not illegal. But it's not always in your best interest.

I remember Karen, a sixty-year-old business owner from Rochester. She walked into my office smiling, but underneath the smile was exhaustion. She owned a boutique shop, poured herself into it for decades, and wanted a future where she could slow down without worrying about whether the lights stayed on. Her advisor—someone she'd known for years—had sold her a product that looked safe on paper. But when we peeled back the layers, the reality hit her like a punch in the gut. She was paying over ten thousand dollars a year in fees for a product that locked her money up for nearly a decade.

"It sounded secure," she said softly, staring at the statement like it had betrayed her. "But I feel trapped."

That's what trust-me advice does. It convinces people that something is safe when it's really just expensive. It tells you not to worry, when worry is exactly what you should be doing.

With a second opinion, Karen was able to pivot. We moved her into a plan with no fees, downside protection, and a growth strategy tied to her goals. That decision saved her tens of thousands of dollars over time. But just as importantly, it restored her confidence.

Real Stories, Real People

Let me tell you about Bill. He was a 62-year-old physician from White Lake, sharp as a tack, always the smartest guy in the room. But like many professionals, he was so busy saving lives that he never had the time—or maybe the energy—to double-check his own finances. His advisor ignored the looming tax traps in his retirement accounts. Every year, Bill was losing thousands unnecessarily to taxes he could have avoided with proper planning.

When he finally came to us for a second opinion, we mapped out a tax-smart strategy. By shifting some assets into tax-free vehicles, Bill avoided hundreds of thousands in lifetime taxes. Imagine that—money he had worked for, money meant for his family and legacy, preserved simply because he was willing to ask, "Could there be a better way?"

Then there was Rita, a nurse from Flint. She assumed her advisor was a fiduciary—someone legally bound to put her interests first. He called himself her "trusted advisor," wore the right suit, had the right brochures. But in reality, he was a broker, and his advice was designed more to pad his commissions than to protect her. For years she paid inflated fees on mutual funds that could have been replaced with low-cost alternatives. When she finally realized the difference, it was like pulling the curtain back on Oz. A second opinion didn't just save her money—it gave her clarity.

Fiduciary vs. Non-Fiduciary: The Duty Difference

This is where the rubber meets the road. The difference between fiduciary and non-fiduciary advisors is like the difference between a doctor sworn to "do no harm" and a salesman trying to hit a quota. One is legally bound to put your interests first. The other just has to make sure the product isn't outright harmful.

Most people don't even know which one they're working with. They assume all advisors are fiduciaries. They assume the nice man or woman across the desk is legally required to put them first. But too often, that's not the case.

The problem isn't just the money lost. It's the trust broken. When you hand your future to someone under the belief that they are protecting you, but instead they are protecting their commission, it erodes confidence in the entire system.

A second opinion shines a spotlight on that difference. It forces clarity. It gives you the chance to ask: Who are you really working for—me, or yourself?

THE RIPT FRAMEWORK IN ACTION

At Main Financial Group, we lean on the RIPT framework—Risk, Income, Portfolio, Taxes. It's the lens through which we evaluate every plan. And it's also the lens through which second opinions become most powerful.

- **Risk:** Are your investments aligned with your true tolerance? Not just the number you checked on a form, but the way you actually feel when the market swings.
- **Income:** Do you have reliable income streams, or are you relying too heavily on hope?
- **Portfolio:** Are fees quietly draining your nest egg? Are your

accounts diversified, or are you unknowingly overexposed?

- **Taxes:** Are you ignoring the silent killer of retirement wealth—taxes—or are you using strategies that minimize them?

Every second opinion we give runs through this framework. And almost every time, we uncover opportunities for improvement—sometimes small, sometimes life-changing.

Your Second Opinion Playbook

So, how do you actually get a second opinion? Here's the playbook I give clients:

1. **Gather Everything.** Every statement, every policy, every account. Don't just look at the headline numbers—look at the details.
2. **Find a Fiduciary.** Ask outright: "Are you legally required to act in my best interest at all times?" If the answer isn't a clear yes, keep looking.
3. **Ask the Hard Questions.** What are the fees? What conflicts exist? What alternatives have you considered?
4. **Stress-Test the Plan.** What happens if the market drops 20 percent? What happens if tax rates rise? What happens if you live five years longer than expected?
5. **Compare Options.** Don't just look at return potential. Look at risk, income, and taxes.
6. **Act.** Don't let fear of change keep you from making a better choice. That's the path to clarity. That's the way to take back control.

Behavioral Blind Spots

One of the biggest reasons people don't seek a second opinion is pride. Nobody likes to admit they might have been misled. Others stay loyal to their advisor, even when the advice is costing them thousands, because they don't want to rock the boat. Still others are simply afraid of change.

But here's the truth: seeking a second opinion doesn't mean you've failed. It means you're wise enough to protect what matters most. Doctors get second opinions. Businesses get second opinions. Why should your life savings be any different?

The Save That Counts

Dave saved $150,000. Karen saved $70,000. Bill avoided $180,000 in taxes. Rita reclaimed $6,000 a year in fees. These aren't abstract numbers. They are family vacations, college tuition, medical bills, and retirement dreams.

Every dollar saved is more than just money. It's peace of mind. It's freedom. It's knowing you did everything possible to protect yourself and those you love.

CLOSING THE CHAPTER: WHY IT'S WORTH IT

At the end of the day, a second opinion is about more than numbers. It's about respect—respect for the work you put into building your wealth, respect for the future you want to create, and respect for the people who depend on you.

If you've ever wondered, "Am I really on the best path?"—that's your cue. Get a second opinion. Not because you don't trust yourself. But because you care enough to double-check the map before you take the trip of a lifetime.

Your future is too important to leave to chance. One fresh look can change everything.

CHAPTER TEN

The LIST of Dangers:
Stress-Testing Your Retirement Plan

It was one of those raw Michigan winter afternoons when the sky hangs heavy and gray, and the cold settles into your bones like regret. From the window of my Brighton office, I could see snow drifting sideways across the parking lot, but inside, my desk was scattered with papers that would soon tell a story far more chilling than the weather outside.

George had come in that day.

At 68, George carried himself with the confidence of a man who had commanded an operating room for decades. He was a respected surgeon, the kind of person who had made life-and-death decisions daily, who had trained interns, mentored colleagues, and stood steady under pressure that would buckle most. He moved with brisk certainty, still trim and upright, his tailored winter coat hung neatly on the rack. He shook my hand with the firm grip of someone who had been in control of his world for a very long time.

But when he sat down and spread out his financial statements like surgical instruments across my desk, I noticed something else. Behind his crisp demeanor, behind the rehearsed smile, his eyes betrayed him. They were tired—lined with worry. This was not the look of a man staring down his next complex surgery. This was the look of someone who, for the first time in his life, didn't feel in control.

"Jordan," he began, his voice steady but tinged with unease, "I've got this figured out. Two million in the portfolio. Four percent a year in withdrawals. A balanced mix of stocks that should beat the market. If I just keep steady, I can make this last. Done deal, right?"

He paused, and then his tone shifted. "But…what if it's not?"

That's when the floodgate opened.

He admitted he'd been lying awake at night thinking about his father, who had lived to 95. What if he inherited those same genes? He worried about another market crash like 2008—or even the sudden drop in 2022 when portfolios across America shed 20 percent almost overnight. And then there were the whispers in the back of his mind: inflation, which had just been roaring at levels not seen since the early '80s, and healthcare costs that seemed to spiral upward year after year.

"I'm starting to feel," he said quietly, "like I've been operating without a safety net."

Now, if you've ever sat across from a surgeon, you know they're not the kind to admit vulnerability easily. Their training is about certainty, precision, and calm under fire. But here was George—someone who had navigated the human body's most delicate risks—confessing that when it came to his retirement, he wasn't sure he'd stitched together the right plan.

Running the Stress Test

I slid his statements closer, and together we began peeling back the layers of his assumptions. On paper, it looked fine: $2 million, invested heavily in equities, pulling out 4 percent a year. That had been the "safe withdrawal" rule of thumb for decades. But rules of thumb can be dangerous when they're applied to unique lives.

So, we stress-tested his plan. Not a quick back-of-the-envelope calculation, but a full, scenario-driven review.

- **What if the market dropped 20 percent in the first two years of retirement withdrawals?** His nest egg, already bruised, would bleed further as he pulled income from a shrinking base. That's sequence of returns risk—the danger of hitting turbulence at the very start of your flight. In his case, it could wipe ten years off his portfolio's life expectancy.
- **What if he lived to 95, like his dad?** The math showed he'd need an extra half-million dollars beyond what he had planned. That's longevity risk—the marathon, not the sprint.
- **What about inflation?** Even a moderate 3 percent annual increase meant that his $80,000 of withdrawals would need to grow to more than $120,000 over 20 years just to buy the same groceries, pay the same bills, and live the same lifestyle.
- **And healthcare?** A conservative projection put his lifetime out-of-pocket costs north of $300,000.

The numbers told a sobering story. His "done deal" wasn't done at all. It was a plan standing on a shaky scaffold, vulnerable to any strong wind.

George sat back in silence, his hands folded. For a moment, he looked less like the surgeon and more like the patient.

Rebuilding for Confidence

But here's the thing: stress-testing isn't about scaring people. It's about giving them clarity. It's like taking your car to a mechanic before a cross-country drive. You don't want to hear that your brakes are worn down or your oil is leaking—but you'd rather know before you're stranded on the side of the highway.

For George, the stress test became the turning point. Together, we rebuilt his plan. We shifted about 40 percent of his portfolio into fixed annuity accounts that guaranteed him a predictable income stream—his "safety net" for the essentials. We layered in Treasury Inflation-Protected Securities (TIPS) to hedge against rising costs. We mapped out a Roth IRA conversion strategy to reduce the tax bite later, especially since he'd likely be pulling money for another three decades.

The transformation was remarkable. What had started as an exercise in anxiety ended as a blueprint for security. When we finished, he leaned back, and this time the look in his eyes was different—steady, relieved, even a little hopeful.

"I can live with this," he said, almost to himself. "I can sleep at night again."

And he has. In the months since, George has shifted his energy back to mentoring young doctors, volunteering his time, and planning trips with his wife. The stress test didn't just shore up his portfolio; it gave him back his peace of mind.

Why Stress-Testing Matters

George's story isn't unique. In fact, I'd argue that most people walking into my office have a version of the same blind spot. They've built their retirement plan on a simple assumption: the future will look like the past. Markets will behave, inflation will stay tame, taxes will remain steady, and their health will hold up.

But the future has a way of throwing curveballs. A surprise recession. A tax code overhaul. A medical diagnosis. A longer-than-expected life. Each of these can take a plan that looks fine on the surface and expose cracks underneath.

That's where stress-testing comes in. It's not a Wall Street gimmick or some overengineered financial fad. It's common sense. It's the equivalent of pressure-testing the welds on a bridge before the first car crosses, or running emergency drills in a hospital before the first real crisis arrives.

When you test your plan against the real dangers—before life does—you can find the weaknesses and fix them. And that's where the LIST framework comes in.

INTRODUCING THE LIST

Think of the LIST as your retirement mechanic's checklist. Just like a good road trip requires checking your tires, oil, brakes, fuel, and engine, a good retirement plan requires testing against the four big dangers:

- **Longevity** – Will you outlive your money?
- **Inflation** – Will rising costs eat away at your lifestyle?
- **Stock Market Risk** – Will volatility gut your nest egg at the wrong time?
- **Taxes** – Will Uncle Sam's share grow larger than you expected?

Miss even one of these, and you could find yourself stranded on the roadside of retirement, wondering how it all went wrong.

Longevity: Planning for a Marathon, not a Sprint

When you think about retirement planning, the first instinct is often to imagine a neat twenty-year window. Retire at 65, enjoy life until 85, and exit stage left. But the reality is more complex. What happens if you beat the averages? What if "living well into your 90s" isn't an exception in your family—it's the norm?

Longevity can be both a blessing and a financial landmine. It's like signing up for a half-marathon and discovering on mile 12 that the race is actually 26 miles. Unless you planned for the longer distance, you're going to hit the wall hard.

Cash's Story: The Wealthy Consultant Who Planned Too Short

Cash wasn't an engineer, though he had the same analytical streak. At 62, he had spent his career as a high-level business consultant, advising Fortune 500 companies on strategy and leadership. His work had taken him across the country, and with it came an enviable income. By the time he walked into my office in Troy, he'd accumulated a $1.8 million nest egg, split across brokerage accounts, a large 401(k), and Roth IRAs.

On paper, it looked solid. Cash had built his plan assuming a 25-year retirement window—enough, he thought, to get him comfortably to age 87. But there was one problem: longevity ran in his family. His father had made it to 96, his mother to 94. "We're like marathon runners," he joked, "except none of us trained for it financially."

We ran the stress test. If he only lived to 87, his plan worked fine. Push the projection to 95, though, and the math started to buckle. His portfolio would face a significant drawdown, leaving him with income gaps just when he'd be least able to adapt.

For Cash, the solution was to lock in some guarantees. We shifted part of his portfolio into protected vehicle accounts designed to provide lifetime income. That gave him a financial floor he couldn't outlive, no matter how many birthdays he celebrated. The rest we kept invested for growth, but now with less pressure. For the first time, his retirement plan was marathon-ready.

Sonya's Story: The Attorney Haunted by Her Mother's Final Years

Sonya was 69 when she came to see me in Macomb County. She wasn't a nurse or a teacher—she'd spent decades as an attorney, building a career that was both demanding and successful. By retirement, she had accumulated $1.2 million in savings, plus a home she intended to keep.

But money wasn't her only concern. What weighed on her was her mother's story. Her mom had lived to 98, but spent her final decade in decline, needing care that eventually cost the family nearly $200,000. Sonya feared history repeating itself.

"I've planned until 85, maybe 90," she admitted. "But what if I'm like Mom? What if my health stretches on and the bills keep coming?"

The stress test confirmed her fears. With a plan only covering 85, she had a reasonable chance of success. Extend it to 95, and her probability of running out of money dropped dramatically. It was a chilling thought—having the health to live but not the money to live well.

The fix wasn't just about products; it was about reshaping her mindset. We extended her plan to 95, built in long-term care contingencies, and shifted some assets to guaranteed income products. We also carved out part of her portfolio for inflation protection. Instead of fearing longevity, she began to see it as a possibility to embrace. For the first time, she could picture living to 95 without dreading the cost.

The Longevity Lesson

Cash and Sonya's stories underscore a truth I see every day: longevity is no longer an outlier. Half of today's 65-year-olds will live into their 90s. That's not a fringe scenario—it's the baseline. Yet too many people plan as though 85 is the finish line.

The danger of outliving your money isn't just a theoretical risk; **it's the most common blind spot in retirement planning**. But the good news is this: with the right adjustments, it's preventable. By combining growth investments with lifetime income guarantees, and by extending planning horizons well into the 90s, you can turn longevity from a financial curse into a blessing.

Inflation: The Silent Thief That Shrinks Your Dollar

If longevity is the marathon risk, inflation is the invisible headwind you feel with every step. It's subtle at first—you hardly notice it—but over time it steals distance from your stride. It can creep in quietly, 2–3 percent at a time. But over decades, it erodes purchasing power until the money you thought was ample can barely cover your lifestyle.

For retirees, inflation is personal. It doesn't just make gas or groceries more expensive; it turns fixed income into shrinking income.

Jacqueline's Story: The Sales Executive Who Loved Her Lifestyle

Jacqueline was 64 when she retired from a long career as a regional sales executive. Her drive and charisma had helped her climb the corporate ladder, and she was proud of the $1.5 million she'd built between her 401(k) and brokerage accounts. She wanted retirement to feel like a reward: golf trips with friends, fine dining with her husband, and the ability to spoil her grandchildren without second-guessing the price tag.

When Jacqueline sat down with me, she was confident. "I only need about $80,000 a year," she said, "and I've got more than enough saved." She wasn't wrong—at least, not in year one. But when we modeled her plan over 25 years with a modest 3 percent annual inflation rate, her $80,000 lifestyle ballooned to $162,000 by age 89. Suddenly, the math didn't look as neat.

She had never thought about inflation that way. "I've lived through high prices before," she shrugged, "but I didn't realize it could double my cost of living in retirement."

The fix for Jacqueline was balance. We carved out a portion of her assets for equities—because historically, equities are the best long-term hedge against inflation—and supplemented with Treasury Inflation-Protected Securities (TIPS). That gave her the growth potential to keep pace with rising costs, without exposing her whole plan to market swings. She walked away relieved, knowing she could protect the lifestyle she'd worked so hard to build.

David's Story: The Physician Who Feared Another 2022

David, a 67-year-old cardiologist from Oakland County, had lived comfortably on a high income for decades. He'd built a retirement portfolio of $3.2 million and assumed that was more than enough. But when inflation spiked in 2022—driving up the cost of everything from groceries to medical insurance—he became uneasy. "I'm not worried about running out of money tomorrow," he told me, "but I can't stand the thought of living well now and then struggling later just because prices kept climbing."

We stress-tested his plan with an 8–9 percent inflation shock, similar to 2022. Even with millions saved, the impact was sobering. His planned withdrawals, once comfortable, began to put significant pressure on his portfolio if high inflation persisted for even a few years.

The solution for David was to diversify his income sources. We created a "bucket strategy": a short-term bucket of cash and bonds for stability, a mid-term bucket of TIPS and dividend-paying stocks, and a long-term growth bucket designed to outpace inflation. By layering his strategy, he could weather short-term price surges without sacrificing his long-term security.

For the first time since 2022, he felt at ease. "I can handle the market," he said with a smile, "as long as I'm not blindsided by inflation again."

The Inflation Lesson

Jacqueline and David show two sides of the same coin. Inflation isn't just about numbers—it's about quality of life. For some, it threatens the ability to maintain their lifestyle; for others, it challenges even large portfolios with unexpected strain.

The key is to plan for both the gradual creep and the occasional spike. Retirement is a 20–30 year journey, and over that horizon, costs can double or even triple. Without inflation protection built in, what feels generous today could feel meager tomorrow.

That's why inflation belongs second on the LIST. It's not dramatic like a market crash or a tax bill, but it's relentless. And unless you plan for it, you won't notice the thief until your retirement lifestyle has already been robbed.

Stock Market Risk: Volatility That Can Gut Your Nest Egg

Markets don't move in straight lines. They surge, they crash, they rebound—and sometimes they take years to recover. For retirees, that volatility isn't just an inconvenience, it's a potential disaster. Pulling money from your portfolio during a downturn is like bailing water out of a sinking boat while the storm is still raging. You lose twice: once from the market drop, and again from the withdrawals.

This is known as **sequence of returns risk**—hitting a bad market stretch early in retirement can shave a decade off your portfolio's lifespan. And yet, I see it all the time: clients assume that because the market averages 7–8 percent over time, they'll be fine. But no one lives on averages. You live on what happens year by year.

Linda's Story: The Corporate VP Who Thought She Was Safe

Linda retired at 60 after a long career as a vice president at a Fortune 500 company. She was smart, disciplined, and financially savvy, with $2.4 million invested—most of it in a mix of index funds and company stock. She felt confident that her portfolio would carry her and her husband comfortably through retirement.

"I know the market has ups and downs," she told me, "But I'm in it for the long haul. If it's good enough advice for my 401(k), it should work in retirement too."

We stress-tested her plan. In a "normal" sequence of returns, she was fine. But when we modeled her retiring into a downturn like 2000–2002 or 2008, the cracks showed. Even with an eventual recovery, her early withdrawals amplified the damage, leaving her at risk of running short in her later years.

Linda was stunned. "I thought being aggressive was the smart move," she said.

The solution was to buffer her plan against the market's mood swings. We carved out two years of cash reserves, plus a ladder of bonds, so she wouldn't need to touch her equities during a crash. That simple move transformed her retirement plan. Now, instead of panicking during downturns, she had the confidence to ride them out.

Frank's Story: The Small Business Owner Who Couldn't Sit Still

Frank, 66, had run a successful construction business in Livingston County for decades. He sold the company at retirement, netting $1.6 million after taxes, and rolled most of it into investments. But unlike Linda, Frank didn't have a calm relationship with the market. Every dip made him anxious, and every surge made him greedy.

When 2022 hit and markets dropped 20 percent, Frank did what so many do: he sold at the bottom. By the time he returned to the market, prices had already rebounded, and he'd locked in his losses. His portfolio, once solid, was now limping.

When he came to see me, he admitted, "I know I'm my own worst enemy. I don't want to keep making emotional mistakes."

For Frank, the solution wasn't just financial—it was behavioral. We built a portfolio that included guaranteed income streams so that he didn't feel every market swing in his gut. We set up a "growth bucket" he could ignore for years and a "spending bucket" that covered his immediate needs. The combination gave him peace of mind and kept him from pulling the trigger in panic.

The Market Lesson

Linda and Frank's stories prove that stock market risk isn't just about numbers; it's about timing and temperament. The market can be a powerful engine for growth, but it can also derail a retirement if withdrawals and volatility collide at the wrong time—or if emotions take the wheel.

The antidote is preparation. Cash reserves, bond ladders, and income guarantees create buffers that let your long-term investments do their job without being raided during downturns. The market rollercoaster doesn't have to derail your retirement—but only if you build a plan sturdy enough to keep you strapped in when the ride gets bumpy.

Taxes: Uncle Sam's Cut That Compounds

If longevity is the marathon and inflation the headwind, taxes are the weight strapped to your back that gets heavier every mile. Most people think of taxes as something they'll leave behind once they stop working. But retirement doesn't mean escaping Uncle Sam. In fact, for many, retirement is when taxes become most painful.

Withdrawals from 401(k)s and traditional IRAs are taxed as ordinary income. Required Minimum Distributions (RMDs) kick in whether you need the money or not. Add Social Security taxation, Medicare surcharges, and state taxes, and suddenly that "nest egg" looks more like a government co-owned account. The IRS doesn't just want a slice—it wants a share every single year.

Robert's Story: The Executive with a $4 Million Problem

Robert, a 63-year-old former auto industry executive, had spent decades earning a high salary and maxing out his 401(k). By the time he retired, he had $4 million tucked into tax-deferred accounts. On paper, he felt proud: he had saved diligently, invested wisely, and now had more than enough to live comfortably.

But when we ran his tax projections, the picture changed. By the time he reached age 73 and RMDs kicked in, his required withdrawals would push him into one of the highest tax brackets. Even if he didn't need the income, the IRS would force him to recognize hundreds of thousands in taxable withdrawals every year.

"That's crazy," Robert said, shaking his head. "I worked for this money—how is the government now telling me how and when I have to spend it?"

The solution was proactive: Staged Roth conversions during his 60s, before RMDs began. By converting pieces of his 401(k) into Roth IRAs while tax rates were still historically low, Robert could reduce future RMDs, control his taxable income, and leave tax-free assets to his heirs. It wasn't about eliminating taxes—it was about controlling them. For Robert, the difference amounted to hundreds of thousands of dollars over his lifetime.

Elaine's Story: The Widow and the Survivor Tax Penalty

Elaine was 72, living in Oakland County, and had recently lost her husband, Bill. Together, they had built a comfortable retirement, relying on his pension, Social Security, and $1.3 million in savings. While they were both alive, their tax situation was manageable.

But after Bill passed, Elaine was shocked to discover the **"survivor tax penalty."** As a single filer, her tax brackets were compressed, meaning her income was suddenly taxed more aggressively—even though her lifestyle hadn't changed much. Add in her RMDs and the taxation of her Social Security benefits, and Elaine's tax bill ballooned.

"I never realized being a widow would make me pay more," she said quietly. It was a double blow: the grief of losing her husband and the sting of higher taxes.

To help Elaine, we restructured her withdrawals, leaning on her Roth accounts first and smoothing out her taxable income over time. We also explored qualified charitable distributions (QCDs) from her IRA, which allowed her to satisfy RMDs while lowering taxable income. These strategies didn't erase her grief, but they did ease her financial stress, giving her room to focus on family and healing.

WHAT WILL YOUR NEW TAX RATE BE?

TAX RATE	FOR SINGLE FILERS	MARRIED FILING JOINTLY
10%	$0 - $11,925	$0 - $23,850
12%	$11,926 - $48,475	$23,851- $96,950
22%	$48,476 - $103,350	$96,951 - $206,700
24%	$103,351 - $197,300	$206,701 - $394,600
32%	$197,301 - $250,525	$394,601 - $501,050
35%	$250,526 - $626,350	$501,051 - $751,600
37%	$626,351 or more	$751,601 or more

83% INCREASE

Source: Created by Magellan Financial using IRS 2025 tax rates.

The Tax Lesson

Robert and Elaine's stories illustrate two of the biggest tax traps in retirement: RMDs and the survivor penalty. Both are predictable, but too often ignored until it's too late. The truth is, taxes don't retire when you do. Without planning, they can consume a shocking portion of your wealth.

But with proactive strategies—Roth conversions, income smoothing, charitable distributions, and careful timing—you can take back control. Taxes are the one danger on the LIST that come with a guarantee: they will be there. The question is whether you'll let them dictate your plan, or whether you'll design your plan to outsmart them.

Healthcare: The Silent Danger That Lurks Outside the LIST

The four dangers in the LIST—Longevity, Inflation, Stock Market Risk, and Taxes—are like the big flashing warning lights on your dashboard. They're easy to see, easy to name, and you know you have to deal with them. But there's another danger that doesn't quite fit neatly into the acronym, and yet it looms larger than almost anything else.

Healthcare.

It's the silent danger. The one most people don't talk about because it's uncomfortable. No one likes picturing themselves frail, sick, or dependent. But the truth is, even for the healthiest, healthcare costs in retirement can pile up shockingly fast. Medicare doesn't cover everything. Out-of-pocket costs, premiums, deductibles, prescription drugs, dental, vision, hearing, and—most expensive of all—long-term care.

It's not just a budget item. It's a storm that can sweep through your plan and undo decades of savings.

Lila's Story: Independence at a Cost

Lila was 72, a retired small business owner from Grand Rapids. She was proud of her independence, living alone in the home she and her late husband had built, with $550,000 in retirement savings. For years, she'd managed just fine. But arthritis crept in, and eventually she needed in-home care. It wasn't full-time nursing—just a few hours a day for help with chores, cooking, and errands. Still, it cost nearly $50,000 a year.

When she came to see me, she was rattled. "I thought Medicare would cover more," she said. "But I'm writing checks every month, and I don't know how long I can keep this up."

The stress test revealed what she already suspected: without a plan, healthcare costs would eat away her savings in less than a decade. The fix was adding a long-term care rider to her annuity account, which immediately gave her a pool of funds she could draw on if her needs increased. That one step transformed her outlook. She no longer feared losing her independence—or her home.

Victor's Story: The Successful Entrepreneur Caught Off Guard

Victor was different. At 65, he had just sold his logistics company for a healthy sum and had $2.8 million to his name. He considered himself set for life. "I'm covered," he said confidently when we talked about healthcare. "I'll just pay cash if I need to."

But when we ran the numbers, his tune changed. At current projections, he and his wife could face $350,000–$400,000 in healthcare and long-term care expenses over a 25–30 year retirement. If one of them developed dementia or needed extended nursing care, the tab could easily climb into seven figures.

For Victor, the risk wasn't that he'd run out of money entirely—it was that healthcare costs could cannibalize the money he hoped to pass to his children and grandchildren. The solution was diversification of protection. We used part of his liquidity to fund a hybrid life insurance policy with a long-term care benefit, creating a pool of money specifically earmarked for healthcare needs. That way, if he never needed it, the value would still flow to his heirs.

He walked away surprised but grateful, admitting, "I never thought healthcare would be my biggest risk."

The Healthcare Lesson

What makes healthcare the silent danger is that it doesn't announce itself. Taxes arrive with forms. Inflation shows up in prices at the pump. Market risk flashes across your TV screen. But healthcare sneaks in quietly, often triggered by a diagnosis, an accident, or the slow creep of aging. And by the time it arrives, it's too late to put a plan in place.

That's why it deserves its place alongside the LIST, even if it doesn't fit neatly into the acronym. Healthcare costs have the power to derail a plan, rob independence, and consume a legacy. The antidote is not denial but preparation—whether through Medicare supplements, HSAs, long-term care riders, or hybrid policies that give you options.

In retirement, you can't afford to ignore the silent danger. Because when it strikes, it doesn't just affect your finances. It affects your dignity, your independence, and your family's future.

YOUR STRESS-TEST PLAYBOOK

By now, you've met a cast of characters—George the surgeon, Cash the consultant, Sonya the attorney, Jacqueline the sales executive, David the physician, Linda the corporate VP, Frank the small business owner, Robert the executive, Elaine the widow, Lila the small business owner, and Victor the entrepreneur. Their careers, portfolios, and personalities are different, but they share one common truth: retirement is fragile if you don't test it against life's curveballs.

Stress-testing is about facing those curveballs before life throws them. Just like George discovered on that snowy afternoon in my Brighton office, the cracks only show up when you push your plan beyond the easy scenario. And that's exactly what the LIST—and the silent danger of healthcare—helps us do.

So what's the playbook? How do you stress-test your own retirement? Follow the steps below.

Step 1: Longevity – Plan for a Marathon

Don't build a 20-year plan when you might live 30 or 35 years. The odds are too high. Stress-test to age 95 at a minimum, and ask: *If I live that long, does my plan hold?* If the answer is no, add guaranteed income sources or adjust your withdrawal strategy until it does.

Step 2: Inflation – Don't Let the Silent Thief Win

Project not just what you spend today, but what it will cost in 20 years. If groceries, healthcare, and travel double in cost, will your lifestyle survive? Build in growth assets like equities and inflation hedges like TIPS to make sure your income rises as your expenses do.

Step 3: Stock Market Risk – Don't Ride the Rollercoaster Without a Seatbelt

Markets are volatile. They will go up and down, and if you're withdrawing during the downs, the damage can be permanent. Stress-test your portfolio against a repeat of 2008 or 2022. If you can't cover expenses without selling at the bottom, build cash reserves, bonds, or income guarantees to buffer yourself.

Step 4: Taxes – Take Control Before Uncle Sam Does

Your retirement accounts are joint accounts—with you and the IRS as co-owners. Make sure your plan holds up not only under today's tax rates but also under the rising rates ahead. Consider Roth conversions, charitable distributions, and income smoothing strategies to keep more of your wealth in your pocket instead of Washington's.

Step 5: Healthcare – Don't Ignore the Silent Danger

This one doesn't fit neatly into LIST, but it belongs in every serious plan. Stress-test the cost of long-term care, supplemental insurance, and out-of-pocket medical expenses. Assume at least $300,000–$400,000 over a couple's retirement, and prepare with HSAs, hybrid policies, or annuity riders. It's not about scaring yourself; it's about protecting your independence and your family.

The Annual "Fire Drill"

Stress-testing isn't a one-time event. It should be an **annual fire drill** for your finances. Every year, ask yourself:

- If I live five years longer than expected, can my plan handle it?
- If inflation runs 5 percent for the next three years, will my plan bend or break?
- If the market drops 20 percent tomorrow, can I ride it out without panic selling?
- If taxes rise, do I have a strategy in place to adapt?
- If I—or my spouse—need long-term care, where will the money come from?

Running through those questions once a year doesn't just keep your plan alive—it keeps your peace of mind alive.

CLOSING THE CHAPTER: BULLETPROOFING YOUR FUTURE

George walked into my office thinking he had it all figured out. What he left with wasn't just a new plan—it was confidence. Cash, Sonya, Jacqueline, David, Linda, Frank, Robert, Elaine, Lila, and Victor all discovered the same thing in their own ways: retirement isn't just about having enough money; it's about making sure that money survives the dangers ahead.

The LIST—and the silent danger of healthcare—aren't obstacles to fear. They're signals to prepare. And when you prepare, you don't just build a retirement plan. You build freedom—the freedom to live, to give, to enjoy, and to rest easy knowing your plan has been tested against storms.

Stress-test now. Don't wait until life does it for you. Because in retirement, guessing isn't planning. And hoping isn't a strategy.

CHAPTER ELEVEN

Tools in the Toolbox:
Choosing the Right Investments

Ever walk into a hardware store and feel like a kid in a candy shop? Aisles stacked with hammers, drills, saws, sanders — each one promising to fix something. But pick the wrong tool, and instead of a sturdy bookshelf, you've got a wobbly mess that collapses under the weight of your photo albums. Or worse, you've put a hole in the drywall trying to hang a picture.

That's how Karen felt when she stormed into my Brighton office on a blustery Michigan spring afternoon, her scarf whipping in the wind as she clutched a folder of paperwork to her chest. Karen was 58, a small business owner from Rochester, running a catering company that seemed to feed half the weddings in Oakland County. She had the kind of presence that filled a room: flour on her apron, fire in her eyes, and a voice that carried the weight of someone who'd built success with her bare hands.

"Jordan," she said, slamming the folder on my desk like a cutting board in her kitchen, "they told me this annuity was my golden ticket to retirement. Instead, it's draining me faster than a leaky faucet."

I opened the file. It was a variable annuity — the kind of product that often shows up after a free steak dinner seminar, where the sizzle of the ribeye overshadows the fine print in the brochure. Karen had put $750,000 into this contract, thinking it would give her safety and growth. Instead, she was bleeding **$30,000 a year in fees**. Four percent — every single year — skimmed off the top. And here's the kicker: she still carried full market risk. If the market dropped 20 percent, her account would fall right with it.

Imagine walking into a hardware store, buying the most expensive drill, and discovering it comes with a surcharge every time you pull the trigger. That was Karen's annuity. It wasn't just the wrong tool — it was a broken one.

I told her something that Morningstar had published in their 2025 analysis: the average variable annuity carries between **3-5 percent in annual fees**. Over twenty years, that can eat away **20-30 percent of a retiree's potential returns**. For Karen, that was the difference between building a sturdy retirement and watching it crumble like a cake pulled from the oven too soon.

She looked at me, eyes sharp. "So, what do I do? Toss it in the trash?"

Not exactly. The tool wasn't completely useless — it just wasn't the right one for her job. We "refinanced" her retirement plan. We swapped the variable annuity for a **fixed-indexed annuity** with zero annual fees, one tied to the S&P 500. No, it wasn't going to make her rich overnight. But it could generate steady gains averaging 4–6 percent per year (LIMRA's 2025 averages), protect her principal like a storm shelter in a tornado, and most importantly, boost her income by about **$2,200 a month.**

That's real money — the kind that keeps the ovens running, the employees paid, and the retirement dreams alive. Karen left that meeting lighter, as if a burden had been lifted off her shoulders. Her portfolio was no longer a ticking time bomb; it was a set of reliable tools she could build on.

Here's the truth: investing is not about collecting the shiniest gadgets. It's about choosing the right tool for the job at hand.

My dad had a knack for fixing things around the house, and he taught me that lesson early. He wasn't wealthy, but he had duct tape, WD-40, and a toolbox that could solve just about any problem. He'd say, "Son, the fanciest tool doesn't matter if it's not the right one."
And he was right.

In finance, we've got our own toolbox: **stocks, ETFs, bonds, real estate, and fixed income accounts**. Each one has a purpose. Each one has strengths and weaknesses. Use them correctly, and you can build a retirement that lasts. Use them carelessly, and you risk ending up with the financial equivalent of a crooked shelf.

In my twenty-plus years working with Michigan professionals like doctors, engineers, teachers, and small business owners like Karen, I've seen both outcomes. I've seen people rely too heavily on one "tool," convinced that real estate never goes down or that the stock market always bounces back. And I've seen others who, with the right mix, built portfolios that weathered recessions, inflation spikes, and global crises.

That's what this chapter is about: giving you the knowledge to choose the right investment tools, so your retirement plan doesn't just survive storms — it thrives through them.

We'll unpack the essentials:

- **Stocks and ETFs:** the hammer of growth.
- **Bonds:** the screwdriver of stability.
- **Real Estate:** the wrench that hedges against inflation.
- **Fixed & Fixed Income Accounts:** the drill that can lock in income.

And we'll debunk the myths along the way — the noise that keeps too many smart people from making smart choices. Because jargon doesn't build a legacy. Tools — the right tools, used wisely — do.

So, grab your financial toolbox. It's time to lay out the essentials.

THE TOOLBOX ESSENTIALS: KEY INVESTMENT TOOLS EXPLAINED

Here's your lineup, each with purpose, pros, cons, and 2025 insights.

Stocks & ETFs: The Growth Hammer

If the retirement toolbox had a hammer, it would be stocks. Simple, powerful, and capable of building tremendous wealth — but swing it the wrong way, and you can smash your thumb.

Stocks are ownership slices of a company. Buy shares of Apple, and you own a tiny piece of every iPhone, MacBook, and app they sell. Over the long run, stocks have outperformed nearly every other asset class, averaging close to **10 percent annually over the last century**. That's the good news. The bad news? They don't move in straight lines. Markets swing, sometimes violently. One year, you're up 20 percent. The next, down 15 percent.

I remember Sanj, a 62-year-old engineer from Troy who sat across from me, spreadsheet in hand. He had calculated inflation at exactly 3.2 percent per year using Bureau of Labor Statistics data and wanted to ensure his portfolio could outpace it. He was analytical, methodical — the kind of guy who used torque wrenches to tighten his golf clubs.

"Jordan," he said, "I can't build a retirement that loses to inflation. I need growth."

For Sanj, stocks and ETFs were the hammer. Together, we allocated 60 percent of his portfolio to equities, diversified across U.S. large caps, international markets, and a slice of emerging economies. That gave him the growth potential to outpace inflation while balancing the rest of his toolbox with bonds and fixed annuities.

By contrast, let me tell you about Lily. She was just 14 when her dad brought her into our office for a meeting. Wide-eyed, she leaned forward and asked me, 'How do I buy Disney stock? Or Nike? Or Lululemon? I love their stuff.'"

Her question was simple but profound: how do young investors tap into companies they know without risking it all on one pick? The answer was **ETFs** — exchange-traded funds. ETFs bundle dozens, sometimes hundreds, of stocks into one share, like a toolbox organizer that keeps all your screwdrivers in one place. You want Disney and Nike? Buy a consumer discretionary ETF, and you've got them — plus dozens of other household brands.

In 2025, ETFs officially crossed **$10 trillion in global assets** (Investment Company Institute). They've become the retirement hammer of choice, often replacing traditional mutual funds thanks to lower fees and greater flexibility. On average, index equity ETFs carry an expense ratio of 0.14 percent compared to the 0.75–1.25 percent of actively managed mutual funds. That means more of your returns stay in your pocket instead of padding a Wall Street manager's.

But let's be clear: hammers aren't toys. They can build homes, but they can also smash windows. Stocks and ETFs carry volatility. Look back at 2008 when the S&P 500 plunged nearly 40 percent. Or March 2020, when the COVID-19 pandemic erased a third of the market's value in weeks. Clients called in panic. One man told me, "Jordan, I've lost everything." I had to gently remind him: he hadn't lost until he sold. By December of that same year, the S&P had roared back.

The lesson? The hammer works best when you keep swinging steadily. Stop mid-strike in fear, and you may never finish the project.

Back in 2024, the S&P 500 posted double-digit gains, but with plenty of turbulence along the way—sharp swings that reminded investors how fragile confidence can be. Certain sectors, like infrastructure and inflation-linked ETFs, surged, while others, like high-yield bonds, struggled. And the longer-term picture? Morningstar's outlook suggests that over the next decade, returns may moderate, reminding us that not every hammer strike in investing lands perfectly on the nail.

That's where ETFs shine. They smooth out some of the risk. Imagine you're building a deck. You could hammer each nail one by one (picking individual stocks), hoping your aim is true. Or you could use a nail gun (ETFs), hitting dozens of nails at once, faster and with less chance of smashing your thumb.

Pros of Stocks & ETFs:
- **Growth Powerhouse:** Historically, no other tool matches equities for compounding wealth.
- **Liquidity:** Need to sell? You can exit in seconds.
- **Diversification via ETFs:** Exposure to hundreds of companies at once.
- **Low Fees:** Especially with index ETFs.

Cons of Stocks & EFTs:
- **Volatility:** You need the stomach for swings.
- **Behavioral Traps:** Fear and greed cause many to buy high and sell low.
- **Concentration Risk:** Too much in one sector or stock can wreck a portfolio.

One of my clients, John, a retired GM executive, once told me he "couldn't stomach another downturn." He'd been through the 2000 tech crash and 2008 financial crisis. Both times, he panicked, sold at the bottom, and missed the recovery.

"Jordan," he confessed, "I've lost more money selling too early than I ever lost holding on."

Behavioral finance confirms his story. Study after study shows that the average investor underperforms the very funds they invest in because they trade emotionally. It's not the hammer's fault — it's how we swing it.

That's why I emphasize matching stock exposure to **risk tolerance and capacity**. A 35-year-old engineer may afford a 90 percent stock allocation. A 65-year-old retiree living off withdrawals? Not so much. It's about balance — not just how much growth you want, but how much volatility you can withstand without abandoning your plan.

THE TAKEAWAY:

Stocks and ETFs are the hammer in your financial toolbox. They're indispensable for building growth, but they're not a one-size-fits-all solution. Some clients need a heavy-duty framing hammer; others just need a small tack hammer for modest growth. Used wisely, they can build the foundation of a retirement plan. Used recklessly, they can shatter it.

So before you grab the hammer, pause and ask: "What am I building? And do I have the discipline to keep swinging when the market shakes?"

Only then does the hammer become the tool it's meant to be — a builder of wealth that stands the test of time.

Bonds: The Stability Screwdriver

If stocks are the hammer in your financial toolbox, then bonds are the screwdriver. Not flashy, not loud, but indispensable. A hammer might build the frame of your retirement house, but try putting up shelves without a screwdriver. It's the tool that tightens things down, keeps the structure from rattling, and gives you stability when everything else feels loose.

That's what bonds do in a portfolio. They don't deliver the high-octane growth of stocks, but they provide balance, income, and predictability. In retirement, that matters just as much — sometimes more.

What Are Bonds, Really?

At their core, bonds are loans. You lend money to a government, municipality, or company, and in exchange, they pay you interest. Treasury bonds fund highways and defense. Corporate bonds finance new factories. Municipal bonds pave the roads in your town. You're the lender, and in return, you get steady checks in the mail.

Unlike stocks, where your returns depend on company performance, bonds have contractual obligations. If you hold to maturity, you know exactly what you'll get back — principal plus interest. That predictability makes bonds a calming presence in a portfolio.

But even screwdrivers come in different types: flathead, Phillips, torque. Bonds, too, have varieties:

- **Treasuries** (backed by the U.S. government, considered ultra-safe)
- **Investment-grade corporates** (companies with strong credit ratings)
- **High-yield bonds** (a.k.a. "junk bonds," with higher risk and higher returns)
- **Municipals** (issued by states/cities, often tax-advantaged)
- **TIPS** (Treasury Inflation-Protected Securities)

Each has its use, depending on the project.

Marjorie's Lesson in Balance

Not everybody can have the risk tolerance of Marjorie. You might remember her from Chapter 4 — the client who once told me, *"Give me risk or give me nothing."* Now in her late 80s, Marjorie still carries that same fearless approach to investing. While most people her age want nothing more than safety and stability, she thrives on the ups and downs of the market like it's a game she refuses to stop playing.

If it were up to me, I'd change the way she invests at this stage of life. For most retirees, I'd never recommend running with that level of risk. But Marjorie isn't "most retirees." She's rare — a reminder that risk tolerance is deeply personal, and that while some people can stomach volatility even in their 80s, the vast majority of us need a very different balance.

The Current Bond Landscape

For much of the past decade, bonds were the neglected screwdriver. With interest rates near zero, yields were paltry. Retirees saw 1–2 percent returns and asked, "Why bother?"

But today's bond landscape is different. After years of rate hikes and global economic shifts, yields have climbed. A 10-year Treasury in mid-2025 yields around 4.5 percent, levels we hadn't seen since before the financial crisis. Corporate bonds pay even more, though with added credit risk.

JPMorgan's 2025 forecast notes that bonds are finally competitive again, especially in a diversified retirement portfolio. Schwab's outlook highlights tariffs and federal debt debates as potential volatility drivers, but overall, bonds are regaining their place as a core stabilizer.

Pros of Bonds:
- **Predictable Income:** Coupon payments act like steady rent checks.
- **Lower Volatility:** When stocks drop, bonds often hold or rise.
- **Diversification:** Not tied to equity market swings.
- **Flexibility:** Short-term bonds for liquidity, long-term for higher yield.

Cons of Bonds:
- **Interest Rate Risk:** Rising rates push bond prices down (If you sell before maturity, you could lose principal).
- **Inflation Lag:** Bond income often doesn't keep up with rising costs.
- **Credit Risk:** Companies can default, though this is rare for high-grade bonds.

A Historical Perspective

To appreciate bonds, look back at the 1980s. In 1981, Treasury yields topped 15 percent. Retirees could live comfortably off bonds alone. Imagine locking in 12 percent risk-free for 30 years. Those were the golden screwdriver days.

Fast forward to the 2010s, and that same screwdriver looked dull. Yields collapsed, forcing retirees into riskier assets. Many chased stocks or real estate simply because bonds weren't paying the bills.

Now, in the mid-2020s, the screwdriver has sharpened again. It's not the monster tool of the 1980s, but it's once again worth keeping in your belt.

The Psychology of Stability

I often tell clients: "Bonds are not about excitement. They're about sleep."

When the market tumbles, stocks make headlines. Portfolios with no bonds lose 20–30 percent overnight, sending investors into panic. But portfolios with solid bond allocations often hold steady. That stability keeps clients invested — and that, in turn, preserves their long-term growth.

Behavioral finance research confirms this. Investors with balanced portfolios are less likely to panic-sell in downturns. Bonds act as the emotional screwdriver, tightening down nerves when volatility shakes loose confidence.

Practical Uses in Retirement
How do bonds fit into the RIPT framework?
- **Risk:** Bonds reduce portfolio volatility, giving retirees confidence.
- **Income:** Coupon payments provide steady cash flows.
- **Portfolio:** Bonds diversify equity-heavy holdings.
- **Taxes:** Municipal bonds can offer tax-free income.

One client, a retired Ford executive, built his retirement income around municipal bonds. Tax-free interest allowed him to live comfortably without bumping into higher tax brackets. It wasn't glamorous, but it was efficient — and efficiency matters in retirement.

Bond ETFs and Modern Portfolios
For many, buying individual bonds feels daunting. That's where **bond ETFs** come in. These funds pool hundreds of bonds, offering diversification with a single purchase. Fees range from 0.10–0.50 percent, according to Money.com's 2025 review.

Bond ETFs also provide liquidity — you can buy and sell instantly. That's a major advantage over holding individual bonds, which may lock up your money for years unless you sell on the secondary market (often at a discount).

CLOSING THE SECTION:
Bonds may not make you rich, but they can keep you sane. They're the screwdriver in your toolbox — sometimes overlooked, sometimes undervalued, but always necessary when things get wobbly.

As I told Marjorie when she shifted her portfolio: "You don't need the screwdriver every day. But when you do, nothing else will do the job."

That's the essence of bonds in retirement. They tighten your financial structure, steady your income, and give you the confidence to keep building, even when markets shake.

Real Estate: The Hedge Wrench
If bonds are the screwdriver that steadies the plan, then real estate is the wrench — the tool you grab when you need leverage. A wrench gives you torque, the ability to twist and turn stubborn bolts that won't budge.

In retirement, that's what real estate does: it gives you leverage against inflation, helping your money keep its grip when prices start to climb.

Why Real Estate Matters

Real estate has always had a special place in American wealth. It's tangible. You can touch it, walk through it, rent it out, and hand it down to your kids. Unlike a stock certificate that lives in a digital account, a piece of property feels *real*.

For retirees, real estate often plays the role of an inflation hedge. When the price of groceries or gas rises, so does the cost of rent — and if you own the property, you're the one collecting that extra income. The **NCREIF Property Index** shows that over long horizons, commercial real estate has historically returned **5–7 percent annually after inflation**, making it one of the more consistent inflation-beating tools.

But here's the catch: real estate isn't as simple as HGTV makes it look. For every story of a couple retiring early on rental income, there's another of someone dealing with midnight calls about broken furnaces, tenant evictions, or hurricanes wiping out entire properties. That's why, for many retirees, the wrench comes in the form of **REITs (Real Estate Investment Trusts)** — publicly traded companies that own, operate, or finance real estate. With a single share, you get access to diversified properties without the management headaches.

Alex's Farm Trust Story

One client, Alex, inherited farmland up north from his parents. For years, he wasn't sure what to do with it. Selling it felt like betrayal, but managing it himself wasn't realistic. Eventually, we worked out a plan: he transferred the land into a trust and allocated a portion of his portfolio into REITs focused on farmland and infrastructure.

The result? Alex preserved his family's legacy while generating steady income from professional management. "Jordan," he told me, "I don't have to be the farmer anymore. I just get to enjoy the harvest."

The Current Real Estate Landscape

Right Now, real estate looks like a mixed bag:

- **Commercial real estate** is under pressure. Office spaces in big cities are still recovering from the post-pandemic shift to remote

work. Vacancy rates remain elevated, and some office towers in major metros are selling at discounts.
- **Residential real estate**, however, remains resilient. Demand for housing outstrips supply in many regions, keeping rents high and property values climbing.
- **Specialized real estate** — like data centers, logistics hubs, and medical office buildings — has become hot property. As technology advances and populations age, these sectors offer growth opportunities.

For retirees, that means broad exposure through REITs or infrastructure ETFs may be safer than betting the farm (literally) on a single condo or strip mall.

Pros of Real Estate:
- **Inflation Hedge:** Rents and property values tend to rise with inflation.
- **Diversification:** Real estate often moves differently than stocks and bonds.
- **Income Potential:** Rental income or REIT dividends can supplement retirement cash flow.

Cons of Real Estate:
- **Illiquidity:** Unlike stocks, real estate can't be sold with a click.
- **Management Hassles:** Tenants, repairs, taxes.
- **Market Risks:** Hurricanes, floods, or downturns can wipe out value.

The Illusion of Easy Money

I once worked with a couple who wanted to retire early by flipping houses. They had watched the TV shows and thought it looked easy. Within two years, they were exhausted — dealing with contractors who disappeared mid-job, properties that sat unsold for months, and thin margins eaten up by taxes and fees.

Their "wrench" ended up stripping the bolt instead of tightening it. We eventually shifted them toward REITs that gave exposure to real estate without the stress. The lesson was simple: real estate is powerful, but it's not effortless.

REITs in Action

Real Estate Investment Trusts solve many of these problems. They allow everyday investors to own shares of massive property portfolios — shopping centers, warehouses, apartment complexes, even cell towers. In 2025, REIT ETFs charge 0.50–1 percent fees and provide liquidity that direct ownership can't.

For retirees, REITs often deliver dividend yields of 4–6 percent, supplementing income while providing inflation protection. It's like having a wrench with a ratchet function — more efficient, less strain.

How Real Estate Fits in RIPT

- **Risk:** Provides diversification, though sector-specific risks exist.
- **Income:** Rental streams or REIT dividends add cash flow.
- **Portfolio:** Balances equities and bonds with a tangible asset class.
- **Taxes:** Depreciation and 1031 exchanges offer unique advantages for direct ownership. REIT dividends, however, are taxed as ordinary income, so placement in retirement accounts can matter.

CLOSING THE SECTION:

Real estate is the wrench in your financial toolbox — not always needed, but invaluable when inflation loosens the nuts and bolts of your retirement plan. Used wisely, it provides leverage and strength. Used recklessly, it can strip the threads and leave you worse off.

As Alex's farm trust showed, the right kind of real estate exposure can honor the past, strengthen the present, and prepare for the future. Just remember: it's not about swinging the biggest wrench in the store; it's about using the right one for the job.

Fixed & Fixed Income Accounts – aka Annuities: The Income Drill (Fixed Only, No Variables)

If stocks are the hammer, bonds the screwdriver, and real estate the wrench, then annuities are the drill in your retirement toolbox. A drill doesn't just hold things together — it creates the holes you need to anchor into something permanent. In retirement, annuities can do the same: anchor income, lock down guarantees, and give stability where markets can't.

The Reputation Problem

Say the word "annuity" at a cocktail party and watch people roll their eyes. Most folks picture high fees, pushy salespeople, and contracts more confusing than a 1040 tax form. And to be fair, much of that reputation comes from **variable annuities**, with their 3–5 percent annual fees (Morningstar 2025) and market risk that defeats the purpose of safety.

But lumping all annuities together is like saying all drills are junk because you once bought a $19.99 bargain model that burned out after a week. There are bad drills, yes — but there are also professional-grade tools that last decades.

The truth: **fixed annuities and fixed-indexed annuities** (FIAs) can be powerful retirement tools when used correctly. They offer guarantees that stocks and bonds can't. They can create predictable income streams, protect principal, and in some cases, double as long-term care support.

Karen's Drill in Action

We met Karen at the start of this chapter — the small business owner who stormed into my office, fed up with her variable annuity. Her story highlights the difference between a broken drill and the right one for the job.

We replaced her high-fee variable annuity with a **fixed-indexed annuity** tied to the S&P 500. Suddenly, Karen's fees dropped to zero. Her $300,000 was protected against loss, but she still participated in market gains (capped, but with far less risk). Most importantly, it generated **$2,200 a month in guaranteed income** — enough to ease her retirement fears and let her focus on growing her catering business.

When Karen left that meeting, she told me, "Jordan, for the first time in years, I feel like my money is working *for me*, not *against me*." That's the power of the right drill.

How Fixed Annuities Work

There are a few varieties retirees should know:
- **Fixed Annuities (FA):** Think of these like CDs from an insurance company. You put in money, and in exchange, you earn a guaranteed interest rate (say 3–5 percent). Safe, simple, predictable.
- **Fixed-Indexed Annuities (FIA):** These tie growth to a market

index, like the S&P 500, without risking principal. If the market goes up, you share in the gain (up to a cap). If the market goes down, you don't lose a dime. Current averages (LIMRA 2025) show 4–6 percent returns with zero annual fees.

- **Immediate Annuities (SPIAs):** You hand over a lump sum, and the insurer starts paying you monthly income immediately, often for life. Like flipping a switch that turns savings into a pension.
- **Annuities with Income Riders:** Some FIAs offer riders that guarantee income for life or double income if long-term care needs arise. These riders often come with small fees (0.5–1 percent), but for many retirees, they're worth the trade-off.

The Long-Term Care Angle

One feature I particularly like in some modern annuities is the **income doubler for long-term care needs**. Imagine you're collecting $2,000 a month from your annuity. If you can't perform basic activities of daily living (like bathing or dressing), that income could double to $4,000 for several years.

For clients without dedicated long-term care insurance — which is expensive and difficult to qualify for — this rider can be a lifesaver. It's not perfect, but it's often the most practical way to fill the gap.

Pros of Fixed Annuities:
- **Principal Protection:** Market downturn? No losses.
- **Guaranteed Income:** A personal pension, regardless of market performance.
- **Zero or Low Fees:** Unlike variables, most fixed indexed annuities have no annual fees.
- **Tax Deferral:** Growth inside the annuity isn't taxed until you withdraw.

Cons of Fixed Annuities:
- **Illiquidity:** Surrender periods (often 7–10 years) limit access to principal.
- **Caps & Participation Rates:** You don't get all market gains, only a slice.
- **Complexity:** Some contracts are packed with jargon that confuses retirees.

A Case Study: Sanj's Surprise

Remember Sanj, the engineer who loved spreadsheets? He was skeptical of annuities, calling them "expensive insurance gimmicks." But when we modeled his retirement plan, we discovered a gap: his growth portfolio provided plenty of upside, but his income floor — the minimum guaranteed money he could count on every month — was weak.

We allocated part of his savings to a fixed-indexed annuity with an income rider. Suddenly, his guaranteed lifetime income jumped by $40,000 a year. When he saw the numbers, he leaned back and said, "So this isn't replacing my investments — it's securing them."

Exactly. The drill didn't replace the hammer, screwdriver, or wrench. It anchored the plan where other tools couldn't.

The Myth-Busting Moment

Here's where I pause in client meetings and go myth by myth:

- **"All annuities are bad."** Wrong. Variables are fee-heavy, yes, but fixed annuities and FIAs can be efficient, low-cost, and effective.
- **"I'll lose control of my money."** Partly true. Annuities require commitment, but most allow 10 percent free withdrawals annually. You're not locked out — you're just encouraged to stay long-term.
- **"I can get better returns in stocks."** Sometimes, yes. But remember: annuities aren't meant to beat stocks. They're meant to guarantee what stocks can't — income and safety.

How Annuities Fit into RIPT

- **Risk:** They reduce exposure by protecting principal.
- **Income:** They create guaranteed paychecks in retirement.
- **Portfolio:** They complement growth assets with stability.
- **Taxes:** Tax-deferred growth, plus strategic Roth conversions can enhance efficiency.

<u>CLOSING THE SECTION:</u>

At the end of the day, annuities are like a drill. If you've only ever seen the cheap, plastic versions, you'll think they're junk. But if you pick the right one, with the right bit, it can do something no other tool in the box can: create an anchor point.

For retirees like Karen and Sanj, that anchor meant peace of mind. It meant knowing the lights would stay on, the bills would be paid, and the future would be less about fear and more about freedom.

That's what the right tool does.

DEBUNKING MYTHS: TOOLS WITHOUT HYPE

Every profession has its myths. Ask a golfer and you'll hear that buying the latest driver will shave ten strokes off your game. Ask a fisherman and someone will swear there's a "magic lure" that catches every bass in the lake. And in finance? The myths swirl louder than anywhere else.

The problem is, myths don't just waste money — they cost people their financial futures. Let's take a closer look at four of the biggest offenders.

Myth #1: All Annuities Are Bad

This one has been shouted from TV pundits, bloggers, and dinner table debates for years. Somewhere along the line, "annuity" became a dirty word.

But here's the truth: not all annuities are created equal. The bad rap comes largely from **variable annuities**, which — as we've seen — can carry 3–5 percent annual fees, market risk, and confusing riders. No wonder people hate them.

But fixed and fixed indexed annuities? That's a different story. They have zero annual fees, protect principal, and provide lifetime income guarantees. LIMRA's 2025 report even showed fixed indexed annuities outperforming traditional bonds in down markets.

Karen's story drives this home. She thought all annuities were bad — until she discovered the right kind. After her switch, her outlook flipped from frustration to freedom. The myth didn't just fade; it collapsed under the weight of facts.

Myth #2: Stocks Always Win

"Just put it all in the S&P 500 and forget about it." Now that advice has worked well for long-term investors, no doubt. But does it *always* win? Not necessarily.

Morningstar's 2025 forecast projects that stock returns over the next decade may moderate to 4–6 percent annually, compared to their historic 10 percent. And history shows long stretches when bonds or real estate outperformed equities. From 2000 to 2010 — the so-called "lost decade" — the S&P 500 actually lost money after inflation, while bonds quietly delivered steady gains.

That doesn't mean stocks are bad — it means they're not invincible. They're the hammer in the toolbox, not the only tool you should own.

Myth #3: Real Estate Is Easy Money

Buy a rental property, sit back, and collect checks. That's the dream, right?

I worked with a couple who tried just that. They bought three properties with visions of passive income. Within six months, they were dealing with leaky roofs, late rent, and a tenant who turned the living room into a reptile terrarium.

Their "easy money" dream quickly became a second job. Eventually, they sold two properties and shifted into REITs instead, trading headaches for consistent dividends.

Real estate can be a great inflation hedge, but it isn't foolproof. Hurricanes, vacancies, and management costs can strip away profits. The myth of "easy" real estate has bankrupted many would-be moguls.

Myth #4: ETFs Are Risk-Free

ETFs have soared in popularity because of their low fees and diversification. And rightly so — they're an excellent tool. But too many investors now treat them as if they carry no risk at all.

I once met a retiree who had 100 percent of his savings in a single "dividend ETF." He assumed the diversification protected him from losses. What he didn't realize was that the ETF was heavily concentrated in one sector — utilities — and when rates rose, the ETF dropped by 15 percent in six months.

The myth here is not that ETFs are bad. It's that diversification eliminates risk entirely. It doesn't. It spreads it. That's valuable — but it doesn't make you invincible.

The Bigger Danger of Myths

The real danger isn't in the tools themselves. It's in how myths distort behavior. When people believe all annuities are bad, they miss out on income guarantees that could save them. When they believe stocks always win, they may take on more risk than they can stomach. When they chase "easy" real estate, they may end up with sleepless nights. And when they assume ETFs are bulletproof, they may overconcentrate without realizing it.

Each myth is like using the wrong tool for the job — a hammer where you need a wrench, a screwdriver where you need a drill. The result isn't just inefficiency. It's damage.

CLOSING THE SECTION:

At Main Financial Group, I've seen the myths come and go, often recycled with new names. But the truth never changes: no single tool builds a retirement. Myths blind us to nuance. Reality opens our eyes to options.

So the next time someone says, "All annuities are bad" or "Stocks always win," remember: that's like saying every tool in the hardware store is junk except the hammer. A real builder knows better.

RIPT FRAMEWORK: TOOLS ALIGNED

If the retirement toolbox is full of hammers, screwdrivers, wrenches, and drills, then the RIPT framework is the blueprint that tells you which tool to use — and when. Without a blueprint, even the best tools get misused. With it, you know where everything fits, and your plan holds together for the long haul.

RIPT stands for **Risk, Income, Portfolio, and Taxes**. It's the four-part framework we use at Main Financial Group to make sense of the chaos and ensure every decision builds toward stability, not stress.

Risk: Controlling the Speed of the Car

Risk is about how much volatility you can handle — emotionally and financially. Stocks and ETFs, the hammer, offer growth but can swing wildly. Bonds, the screwdriver, tighten things down and reduce risk. Annuities, the drill, can anchor guarantees when you need them most.

Take Karen. Her variable annuity left her exposed to risk she didn't even realize she had. When we shifted her into a fixed-indexed annuity, her risk score dropped significantly. She went from fearing every market dip to feeling secure, knowing her base was protected.

The right tool for risk depends on the driver. A 35-year-old still accelerating toward retirement can afford more "hammer" strikes. A 65-year-old living off their nest egg needs more screwdrivers and drills to keep things steady.

Income: Building Reliable Paychecks

Income is the heartbeat of retirement. Without it, every trip to the grocery store feels like a gamble. That's where the right mix of tools makes all the difference.

- **Annuities** provide guaranteed monthly checks, like pensions.
- **Bonds** deliver coupon payments you can plan around.
- **REITs and dividend-paying ETFs** add supplemental income streams.

Sanj's case illustrates this well. His spreadsheet showed he had growth covered, but when we plugged the numbers into RIPT, we saw his income stream was thin. By adding a fixed-indexed annuity with an income rider, we raised his guaranteed baseline by $40,000 a year. Suddenly, his "what if" scenarios looked a lot less scary.

Income planning is about more than just numbers. It's about peace of mind. It's about knowing the lights will stay on even if the stock market is throwing a tantrum.

Portfolio: Structuring the Mix

The portfolio is the big picture — the sum of all the tools working together. Too often, people think of their accounts in silos: "This is my 401(k), this is my IRA, this is my rental property." RIPT forces us to look at the integration.

Stocks and ETFs drive growth. Bonds add stability. Real estate hedges inflation. Annuities lock in guarantees. The right portfolio is less about finding the "perfect tool" and more about creating a **balanced toolbox** that can handle whatever the market throws at you.

Morningstar's 2025 analysis noted that balanced portfolios (often the classic 60/40 mix) are once again competitive after years of being declared "dead." But here's the nuance: not everyone needs 60/40.

Some need 70/20/10. Others need 50/30/20. The right allocation isn't about rules of thumb — it's about your blueprint.

Taxes: Keeping Uncle Sam Out of the Toolbox

Taxes are the sneakiest bolt-loosener in retirement. You can have the perfect toolbox, but if every time you pull out the drill Uncle Sam takes half your batteries, you're in trouble.

That's why tax planning is essential. Tools have to be placed in the right accounts:

- **Stocks and ETFs** often belong in taxable accounts where long-term gains get preferential rates.
- **Bonds** can sit inside IRAs, shielding their ordinary income from immediate taxation.
- **Annuities** can pair beautifully with Roth conversions, turning future taxable distributions into tax-free income.

Karen's RIPT alignment showed this clearly. Her annuity not only lowered risk and boosted income but also created an opportunity for tax-smart withdrawals. By pairing her new annuity with Roth conversions, we helped her lock in today's lower tax rates and reduce future exposure.

CLOSING THE SECTION:

RIPT is the organizing principle that prevents the chaos of retirement planning. Without it, tools get misused: too much stock risk, too little income, a portfolio out of balance, taxes ignored. With it, every hammer, screwdriver, wrench, and drill has its place.

That's the difference between building a retirement that creaks under pressure and one that lasts for decades. The tools matter. But the blueprint — RIPT — makes them work together.

YOUR TOOLBOX PLAYBOOK

By now, you've seen the toolbox in action: hammers for growth, screwdrivers for stability, wrenches for inflation protection, and drills for guaranteed income. You've seen how the RIPT framework organizes them. But how do you, the retiree or near-retiree, actually put it into practice? That's where the **Toolbox Playbook** comes in — a practical roadmap for building a retirement plan that lasts.

Step 1: Assess Your Needs

Every project begins with a blueprint. Start by asking: *What do I need this money to do for me?*

- Growth to outpace inflation? That's the hammer (stocks/ETFs).
- Stability to reduce sleepless nights? That's the screwdriver (bonds).

- A hedge against rising costs? That's the wrench (real estate).
- Guaranteed monthly paychecks? That's the drill (annuities).

Scenario: Imagine you're 60, planning to retire in five years. You've saved $1 million. If you only focus on growth, you might double your money — or cut it in half in the next market crash. If you only focus on safety, inflation could erode your purchasing power. Assessing your needs means balancing all four.

Step 2: Debunk the Myths Before You Choose

Before you pick up a tool, clear your head of the noise. "All annuities are bad." "Stocks always win." "Real estate is easy money." These myths distort judgment.

Self-check: List the assumptions you have about each tool. Then ask, "Is this belief based on facts, or on something I heard at a seminar, saw on TV, or read in a headline?" Clearing out myths is like sweeping the sawdust off the workbench before you start cutting wood.

Step 3: Diversify the Toolbox

A toolbox with only a hammer isn't useful. Neither is a retirement plan that bets everything on one investment.

- A 60/40 mix of stocks and bonds used to be the classic play. Today, it may be 50/30/20 with annuities and real estate included.
- BlackRock's 2025 analysis shows that diversified portfolios with alternatives (like REITs) often outperform traditional ones during volatility.

Scenario: Two neighbors retire with the same $1 million. One goes all-in on stocks. The other builds a mix: $500K in ETFs, $200K in bonds, $200K in a fixed-indexed annuity, $100K in REITs. When the market dips 20 percent, the all-stock neighbor loses $200K. The diversified neighbor? She loses less than half that, and her income keeps flowing. That's the power of multiple tools.

Step 4: Match the Tool to Your Risk Tolerance

Some people love the speed of the hammer; others panic at the first swing. Risk tolerance isn't about what looks good on paper — it's about what lets you sleep at night.

- High tolerance? More hammer and wrench (stocks, real estate).
- Low tolerance? More screwdriver and drill (bonds, annuities).

Self-check quiz:
- I've set up a free site for you to check your own risk score: www.mfgrisktest.com
- Take it as many times as you like, with or without a partner.

Step 5: Work With a Fiduciary Guide

Even the best toolbox is overwhelming without a skilled hand to guide you. That's where fiduciary advisors come in. Unlike brokers who may push certain tools because of commissions, fiduciaries are required to put your interests first. They help you decide not just *what tools you need*, but *how to use them together*.

At Main Financial Group, we often remind clients: our role isn't to sell you a tool — it's to help you build the house.

CLOSING THE PLAYBOOK:

The Toolbox Playbook isn't about perfection. It's about practicality. You don't need the fanciest drill or the most expensive wrench. You need the right mix, used in the right way, guided by a clear framework.

Assess your needs. Clear out the myths. Diversify your tools. Match them to your tolerance. Work with a fiduciary. Do that, and your retirement plan won't just be sturdy — it'll be built to last through storms, surprises, and everything in between.

CLOSING THE CHAPTER: BUILDING A STURDY FUTURE

Remember, Karen came into my office clutching her variable annuity statement like a broken power tool — angry, frustrated, and ready to throw it in the trash, and Sanj arrived with spreadsheets and formulas, convinced he could calculate his way through retirement but unsure if his plan would hold up. Both of them walked out with something far more valuable than a product. They walked out with a toolbox.

For Karen, the right drill — a fixed-indexed annuity — turned what felt like a financial prison into a source of freedom. She gained steady monthly income, zero annual fees, and the peace of mind that her hard-earned savings were finally working *for* her, not *against* her. For Sanj, the hammer of stocks was balanced with the screwdriver of bonds and the drill of an income rider. His growth goals were preserved, but his income floor was raised high enough that he could face retirement without fear.

That's the power of the right tools, used in the right way. Not one tool. Not one myth. Not one-size-fits-all. A toolbox.

When my dad fixed things around the house, he never bragged about owning the fanciest gadget. He bragged about solving the problem with the right tool. That's the mindset retirees need today. You don't need to chase the latest trend or gamble on Wall Street's flavor of the month. You need a hammer, a screwdriver, a wrench, and a drill — aligned by the RIPT framework, matched to your goals, and wielded with purpose.

As we move into Chapter 12, we'll shift gears from tools to leadership. Because every strong project — whether it's building a house or building a retirement — needs a CFO. Not the corporate kind in a corner office, but the personal kind: the Chief Financial Officer of your household. Someone has to oversee the toolbox, balance the budget, and make sure the blueprints are followed.

You've built your toolbox. Now it's time to step into the CFO role and put those tools to work.

CHAPTER TWELVE

Your Personal CFO:
Taking Control of Your Financial Future

Picture this: I'm sitting at a small marina café on Florida's Gulf Coast, the kind of place where the salt breeze clings to your skin and boat masts clang lightly in rhythm with the waves. The coffee in front of me is lukewarm — that's how you know I've been talking more than drinking. Across from me sits Roger, a 72-year-old retired engineer from Grand Rapids. His wife is off chatting with another couple about their next sailing leg to Key West, but Roger's attention is locked on me, the way a man looks when he's remembering a different version of himself.

You see, Roger wasn't always this relaxed, this sun-kissed, this free. Five years ago, when he first walked into my Brighton office, he looked like a man carrying an invisible backpack filled with bricks. He had worked for decades designing bridges — structures that had to endure storms, shifting soils, and heavy loads. Yet when it came to his retirement, he confessed he felt like a passenger on a ship without a compass.

"Jordan," he told me, his hands clasped so tightly his knuckles whitened, "I've engineered steel spans that carry semis across rivers. But this?" He waved his brokerage statement like it was a bad report card. "Retirement feels like foggy water. Markets crash, taxes change, grandkids need help with tuition. I don't know if I'll make it to the other side without sinking."

At that time, Roger had about $1.2 million spread across a patchwork of investments. His advisor had him in what I call a "set-it-and-forget-it" model: a cookie-cutter allocation heavy in stocks, light on protection, and completely blind to taxes. It was fine for the ride up, but when the storm of 2022 hit — with markets dropping 20 percent in a single year — Roger's portfolio sank by nearly $180,000. Add in the looming sunset of tax cuts in 2025, and the rising cost of his first grandchild's college tuition, and his so-called plan looked more like a leaky raft than a seaworthy vessel.

That's when Roger learned an important distinction: **in retirement, he was the owner, but he couldn't also be the CFO.**

THE OWNER VS. THE CFO

Think about how a business works. A CEO sets the vision — where the company is headed, what markets to pursue, what values to uphold. But every successful CEO relies on a CFO to chart the numbers, manage the risks, and anticipate what's coming around the corner. A CEO who tries to handle both jobs usually ends up either exhausted or blindsided.

Roger had been trying to play both roles. He thought being a diligent saver and keeping an eye on the markets was enough. But retirement is different. It's not just about growth anymore — it's about distribution, taxes, income stability, and planning for the "what ifs" of life. That's why he needed to stop trying to be his own CFO and instead hire one.

TAKE CONTROL OF YOUR FINANCIAL FUTURE

The Turning Point

When Roger and I sat down, I explained it this way:

"Roger, you're the captain of this ship. You get to decide the destination — how long you want to sail, what lifestyle you want to live, what kind of legacy you want to leave behind. But no captain crosses an ocean without a navigator and a CFO below deck watching the numbers. That's our role. We're here to handle the charts, monitor the storms, and make sure your ship doesn't run aground."

That clicked for him. He didn't have to be in the weeds of tax codes or rebalancing schedules. He didn't need to panic over every headline. He just needed to stay the owner — clear on his goals — and trust a CFO partner to handle the execution.

Building His CFO Team
We began by putting his retirement plan through the **RIPT framework** — Risk, Income, Portfolio, Taxes — not once, but every year. This wasn't a one-time setup; it was an ongoing CFO process.

- **Risk:** After the 2022 dip, Roger's true comfort level shifted. We adjusted his portfolio from aggressive growth to a balanced approach that fit his new risk tolerance.
- **Income:** Instead of crossing his fingers and hoping his stocks would produce enough, we secured guaranteed income through a fixed annuity with an income rider — about $3,000 per month, covering essentials like housing and food.
- **Portfolio:** We trimmed his high-flying winners, diversified into sectors less exposed to volatility, and reduced fees that were quietly eating away at returns.
- **Taxes:** Perhaps most importantly, we started Roth conversions. By steadily converting a portion of his IRA each year, Roger was able to reduce his lifetime tax bill by over $200,000.

The Result:
Fast forward to today at that marina in Florida. Roger doesn't look like a man carrying bricks anymore. He looks like an owner — someone in charge of his destiny. Every year when he docks in Florida, we meet for coffee, review the plan, and make adjustments. One year we raised his Roth conversions to save an extra $10,000 in taxes. Another year we added a long-term care rider to his annuity, protecting him against the possibility of needing expensive care down the road.

Roger sleeps well because he knows his ship has a CFO watching the numbers. He's not guessing. He's not white-knuckling through every headline. He's living.

Why This Matters
Roger's story isn't unique. I've met countless retirees who confuse ownership with control. They think that because they worked hard and built up savings, they should also be their own CFO. But the truth is, retirement is too complex and too important to manage alone. Tax laws shift, markets swing, medical costs inflate, and behavioral traps like panic-selling can destroy decades of progress in a moment of fear.

The owners who thrive in retirement are the ones who know when to hire a professional CFO. That doesn't mean giving up control; it means gaining clarity. It means having a partner who acts as a fiduciary — legally and ethically bound to put you first — while you focus on living the life you've envisioned.

As Roger told me later, "I didn't need someone to sell me products. I needed someone to help me run my financial life like a business. I'm the owner. You're my CFO. Together we make it work."

And that's the message of this chapter: you are the captain of your financial ship, the owner of your retirement destiny. But every owner needs a CFO — and that's where we come in.

THE CFO MINDSET: WHY EVERY OWNER NEEDS A FINANCIAL CO-PILOT

Every business that survives the test of time has a strong leadership duo: the visionary CEO who sets direction, and the pragmatic CFO who manages the numbers, anticipates risks, and makes sure resources align with the mission. One without the other almost always ends in trouble.

Retirement is no different. You are the CEO — the owner of your financial empire. You decide the goals: when you want to retire, what kind of lifestyle you want to maintain, whether you'll travel the world, help grandkids with college, or build a family legacy. But the CFO role? That requires specialized skills: watching the books, stress-testing the plan, anticipating taxes, and adjusting when storms appear. That's not your job — it's ours.

The Trap of Going It Alone

One of the most common mistakes I see among successful professionals — engineers, doctors, business owners — is the belief that they can serve as both CEO *and* CFO. After all, they've built careers on competence. If they can design systems, save lives, or run a company, surely they can also handle investments and taxes.

But just because you're skilled doesn't mean you should fly solo. I've seen too many intelligent people run aground trying to manage both roles.

Take Paul, a retired auto executive from Ann Arbor. Paul was brilliant in the boardroom — he could analyze spreadsheets and market trends like few others. But when it came to his retirement, he made the classic DIY error: he believed market timing was possible. In 2020, he pulled $600,000 out of equities during the pandemic crash. By the time he reinvested, he had missed most of the rebound. A Fidelity 2025 study shows that missing just the 10 best days in the market over 20 years cuts returns in half. Paul missed eight of them in a single year.

The problem wasn't that Paul lacked intelligence. It's that he didn't have a co-pilot. He was acting as CEO and CFO simultaneously, reacting emotionally instead of strategically. When we met, he admitted, "I thought I was steering the ship, but I was really just gripping the wheel in a storm without a compass."

The Cost of Inaction

The opposite problem is equally dangerous: doing nothing at all. Too many retirees embrace a "set-it-and-forget-it" mentality, assuming a plan created 10 years ago will carry them through the next 30. But life doesn't stand still, and neither should your financial plan.

Consider Lucy, a 67-year-old nurse from Novi. She had worked with a broker who placed her in a portfolio years earlier and barely touched it since. On paper, her investments had done well, but beneath the surface, her risks were badly mismatched. Nearly 80 percent of her assets were in equities at an age where volatility posed a serious threat. When markets dipped in 2022, she lost almost $200,000 — not catastrophic, but enough to force a change in retirement travel plans she had dreamed of for decades.

Had she had a CFO by her side, someone reviewing her plan annually, the red flags would have been spotted long before. Vanguard's 2025 report shows adaptive portfolios — those rebalanced regularly and adjusted for taxes — outperform static ones by 1–2 percent annually. Over a 20-year retirement, that difference is the line between running out of money and leaving a legacy.

The CFO Mindset in Practice

So what does the CFO mindset actually look like?

1. **Proactivity over passivity**

   Owners with a CFO mindset don't wait for crises; they anticipate them. They review their plan at least annually, often more. A 2025 Transamerica survey found that retirees who reviewed their financial plan yearly were 30 percent less stressed and 40 percent more confident about their future than those who didn't.

2. **Adaptation over rigidity**
   Markets shift, tax laws evolve, life events happen. Owners with a CFO mindset expect change and build flexibility into their plan. They don't cling to outdated strategies.

3. **Objectivity over emotion**
   Behavioral finance research proves what we've all seen firsthand: humans are wired to make poor investment decisions under stress. DALBAR's annual Quantitative Analysis of Investor Behavior consistently shows that the average investor underperforms the market, not because of bad investments, but because of bad decisions — selling low, chasing returns, freezing in fear. A CFO provides the discipline and guardrails to avoid these traps.

4. **Integration over silos**
   Most people think of risk, income, portfolio, and taxes as separate issues. A CFO connects them. Taxes influence income decisions. Risk tolerance affects portfolio allocation. Longevity planning changes tax strategies. It's all integrated — and without a CFO, owners often miss these connections.

When the Owner and CFO Work Together

Emily and Jake, a couple from Grosse Pointe, are a perfect example. Emily was a teacher planning to work until 65, while Jake, an engineer, wanted to retire at 62. Their timelines didn't match, and their old advisor had treated them as if they did. That mismatch could have cost them over $50,000 in lost Social Security benefits and forced premature withdrawals from Jake's IRA.

When they came to us, we reframed their roles. Emily and Jake remained the owners — their vision was clear: travel, support their grandchildren, and retire on staggered schedules. Our role was CFO: we created a two-track plan. Jake's assets were repositioned into annuities for income, while Emily's remained growth-oriented in ETFs. Every year we review and adjust, making sure both timelines stay in sync.

The result? Instead of tension and uncertainty, they now feel like true owners with a CFO team running the financial engine room.

Why Independence Matters

There's one more layer to the CFO mindset that owners must understand: independence. In business, a CFO who isn't accountable to the owner but instead to outside shareholders can create conflicts of interest. The same is true in financial services. Too many advisors are paid to sell products rather than serve as fiduciaries.

That's why independence matters. A true CFO for your retirement isn't beholden to Wall Street firms or insurance companies. They're beholden only to you. That's the standard we hold ourselves to — fiduciary duty. It's not about pushing products; it's about aligning every decision with your vision as the owner.

The Payoff of a Co-Pilot

When Roger, Paul, Lucy, Emily, and Jake stopped trying to be their own CFOs and embraced the role of owner, the shift was immediate. They no longer had to white-knuckle through market downturns or lose sleep over tax law changes. They had a partner — a financial co-pilot — to help them steer.

And that's the payoff: confidence. A BlackRock 2025 survey found that retirees with adaptive, CFO-style planning reported their money lasting five to ten years longer than those without it. More importantly, they reported higher satisfaction with their lifestyle — fewer regrets, more freedom.

As an owner, your job is to dream, to direct, to enjoy the fruits of your labor. Our job, as your CFO, is to make sure those dreams have the financial engine to carry them forward. Together, we make the voyage not just possible, but enjoyable.

Flexibility: The Characteristic of a Smart CFO

If there's one truth every retiree eventually learns, it's this: life doesn't unfold in straight lines. You plan for calm waters, but the storms always come. Sometimes it's a market dip that shaves six figures off your nest egg. Sometimes it's an unexpected illness, a grandchild's tuition, or even the joy — and expense — of relocating to chase the sunshine.

That's where flexibility becomes the defining trait of a smart CFO. It's not enough to build a plan once and hope it holds. The owners who thrive in retirement are the ones who pair their vision with a CFO who reviews, adapts, and retools the plan as the tides shift.

The Health Curveball: Jocelyn's Story

Jocelyn, a 66-year-old widow from Flint, thought her retirement plan was set in stone. With an $850,000 portfolio, she was leaning heavily on stocks for growth, convinced that staying aggressive was the best way to outpace inflation. Then came a diagnosis that changed everything: breast cancer.

Treatment was expensive. Fidelity's 2025 Health Care Cost Estimate pegs the average out-of-pocket costs for a 65-year-old retiree at $172,500 — and that figure is climbing 5 percent annually with medical inflation. For Jocelyn, that meant chemotherapy bills, travel for specialists, and extra living expenses during recovery.

Here's the problem: her costs spiked during a year when markets were wobbling. The S&P had 15 percent swings in the second quarter of 2025, fueled by tariff uncertainty and global market jitters. If Jocelyn had continued pulling money from her stock-heavy portfolio, she would have locked in losses just when she needed stability most.

That's when the CFO role made the difference. Together, we rebalanced her plan: shifting 30 percent of assets into annuities that provided $2,500 per month of guaranteed income during treatment, moving the rest into a 50/50 stock-bond mix for reduced volatility, and accelerating Roth conversions to lower her taxable income and avoid higher Medicare premiums (IRMAA surcharges that would have cost her an additional $3,000 annually).

The result? Jocelyn not only weathered her health storm, but she emerged with a plan still on track — flexible enough to protect her during one of the hardest years of her life.

The Family Curveball: Theo's Story

Health isn't the only curveball. Families have a way of introducing both joy and strain into a retirement plan. Theo, a 70-year-old retiree from Midland, experienced this when his granddaughter announced her engagement. Overcome with pride, Theo wanted to gift her $30,000 for the wedding. But his timing couldn't have been worse: markets were in one of those periodic slumps that make retirees hesitate.

Here's where a CFO steps in. Instead of selling stocks at a low point, we tapped Theo's cash buffer — an emergency fund we had established precisely for surprises like this. By keeping six months of expenses and a cushion for gifts or emergencies in a safe, liquid account,

Theo was able to give generously without sabotaging his long-term portfolio.

This is the essence of flexibility: planning not just for what you expect, but also for what you can't predict. Theo remained the owner, making the decision about his gift. Our role as CFO was to structure the resources so his generosity didn't derail his retirement.

The Relocation Curveball: Roger's Florida Move

Roger, the engineer-turned-sailor we met earlier, faced his own curveball when he and his wife decided to become snowbirds. Moving residency from Michigan to Florida saved them around $10,000 per year in state taxes, but it also triggered new considerations: establishing proof of residency, updating estate documents, and adjusting their portfolio to match their new cost-of-living profile.

As owners, Roger and his wife set the vision — more sunshine, less snow. As their CFO, we handled the mechanics: from ensuring his Roth conversions aligned with Florida residency to coordinating health insurance options across state lines. A 2025 NerdWallet report shows retirees often underestimate the ripple effects of relocation, from property taxes to eligibility for certain benefits. Without a CFO partner, those oversights can become costly surprises.

The Divorce Curveball: Janet's Story

Not every curveball is joyful. Janet, a 64-year-old teacher from Farmington, went through a divorce just two years before retirement. She suddenly found herself with half the assets she expected and double the uncertainty. Divorce in retirement is more common than many realize — "gray divorce" rates have doubled since 1990 according to Pew Research — and the financial consequences are profound.

Janet's ownership role didn't change: she still had a vision for retirement. But she needed a CFO partner to rebuild the numbers. Together, we created a new plan: reallocating her portfolio to balance growth and protection, delaying Social Security until age 67 to maximize benefits, and using a portion of her IRA to fund an annuity that would guarantee income for life. We also restructured her estate plan to reflect new beneficiaries and reduce taxes for her children.

Janet's takeaway? "I thought divorce meant my retirement dreams were gone. Instead, I learned I just needed a new CFO to help me redraw the map."

The Inheritance Curveball: James's Story

Sometimes the curveball looks like a windfall. James, a 69-year-old retired engineer, inherited $400,000 from his brother. On the surface, it felt like a blessing. But because the assets were in a traditional IRA, he was required under the SECURE Act to empty the account within 10 years, potentially pushing him into a higher tax bracket.

Without a CFO, James might have withdrawn too much too quickly, triggering a massive tax bill. Instead, we created a schedule of strategic withdrawals paired with Roth conversions, spreading the tax impact and saving him over $90,000 in unnecessary taxes. We also directed a portion of the funds into a charitable remainder trust, allowing James to support his church while creating a new income stream for himself.

For James, flexibility meant turning what could have been a tax headache into a lasting legacy.

Why Flexibility Matters More in Today's Landscape

All of these stories point to a larger truth: the financial landscape itself is a curveball factory. With Congress passing the 2025 "Big Beautiful Bill," some of the biggest retirement planning questions have shifted — but they haven't gone away. The top tax brackets remain lower for now, with an added senior deduction through 2028, while the estate tax exemption holds at historically high levels.

But other parts of the bill create new planning challenges: tighter Medicaid and SNAP requirements, a raised but temporary SALT cap, and new deductions that may phase out in just a few years.

For retirees and business owners, this can feel overwhelming. Yet with a CFO mindset — supported by a fiduciary partner — these changes become opportunities instead of roadblocks:

- **Still-low tax rates?** Continue Roth conversions before provisions sunset in 2028.
- **Interest rates remaining elevated?** Lock in stronger bond yields while adjusting equity exposure.
- **Medical costs still outpacing inflation?** Consider long-term care riders, HSAs, and other tax-advantaged strategies while benefits remain available.

One of the most important lessons of recent years is that adaptability pays. A 2025 BlackRock survey found that retirees with adaptive plans — those revisited and adjusted yearly — saw their money last five to ten years longer on average. That's the dividend of flexibility.

Ownership and Partnership

Flexibility doesn't mean handing over the wheel. You remain the captain, the owner of your retirement vision. You choose where you want to go, who you want to help, and how you want to live. But storms will come — that's guaranteed. Your role is to set the course. Our role, as your CFO, is to adjust the sails, chart the backup routes, and make sure the numbers work no matter what surprises arise.

Because in retirement, flexibility isn't just a nice-to-have. It's survival. And with the right CFO at your side, it's also freedom.

RIPT: THE DASHBOARD EVERY OWNER NEEDS

Every captain needs a dashboard. Think about a modern ship; it has a GPS, radar, fuel gauges, and wind sensors. Without them, even the most skilled sailor risks running aground. Retirement works the same way. You are the captain, charting the course. But you need a CFO by your side to monitor the dashboard, interpret the readings, and warn when adjustments are required.

At Main Financial Group, that dashboard is the **RIPT framework**: Risk, Income, Portfolio, and Taxes. Four dials, working together, that tell you if your retirement plan is on track or drifting off course. Let's walk through each one.

Risk: Driving at Your Speed

Risk isn't about guessing what the market will do next week. It's about aligning your investments with your personal capacity and tolerance — your financial speed limit.

When Roger's portfolio lost $180,000 in the 2022 dip, his confidence cratered. That's because his risk *tolerance* had shifted — he no longer had the stomach for aggressive growth — but his portfolio hadn't kept pace. As his CFO, we recalibrated, dropping his risk number from 65 to 40, shifting 20 percent of his assets into bonds, and creating guardrails that let him sleep at night.

We measure risk two ways:
- **Tolerance:** the emotional side. How much volatility can you live with without panicking? Tools like Nitrogen or Orion assign a number — 1 to 100 — that translates feelings into a measurable speedometer.
- **Capacity:** the mathematical side. How much risk can your plan *actually* afford based on your income needs, time horizon, and health? A 55-year-old surgeon with 15 working years ahead has more capacity than a 75-year-old widow relying on every dollar to cover living expenses.

When tolerance and capacity align, the ride is smooth. When they don't, disaster follows. A Fidelity study shows that mismatched risk levels reduce retirement outcomes by 15–20 percent over time.

As owner, your role is to be honest about your comfort level. Our role, as CFO, is to translate that into a portfolio speed you can safely maintain — neither crawling in the slow lane nor speeding into a crash.

Income: Paychecks in Retirement

Here's a secret every retiree eventually learns: investments don't pay the bills. *Income* does. You can have $4 million in assets, but if they're not structured to deliver reliable, tax-efficient paychecks, you're still financially insecure.

Social Security covers only 30–40 percent of most retirees' needs, averaging $2,005 per month in 2025 (SSA). The rest must come from your plan. That's where the CFO role matters most.

Emily and Jake, the Grosse Pointe couple with mismatched timelines, taught us this lesson. Jake wanted to retire at 62, Emily at 65. Without a CFO, they would have drawn too aggressively from Jake's IRA, risking depletion. Instead, we structured his assets into annuities that generated $3,000/month of guaranteed income, while Emily's stayed in growth ETFs until her retirement. Together, their plan smoothed the gap. Reliable income comes from multiple levers:

- **Annuities:** Modern fixed-indexed annuity accounts offer 4–6 percent yields, providing guaranteed "paychecks" for essentials.
- **Dividends and Bonds:** Equities and fixed income for growth and supplemental cash flow.
- **RMD Planning:** Required minimum distributions at age 73 must be coordinated so they don't cause tax surprises.
- **Spousal Coordination:** Couples who retire on different timelines can lose over $50,000 in Social Security benefits without careful planning (AARP 2025).

The CFO's job is to orchestrate these moving parts into a paycheck system. Your job, as owner, is to decide what lifestyle those paychecks need to fund.

Portfolio: Healthy or Bleeding?

Most owners see their portfolio as a statement of wealth — a number on a page. A CFO sees it as a living machine: is it efficient, diversified, and cost-effective, or is it quietly bleeding?

Remember Lucy, the nurse from Novi who stayed in an 80 percent equity portfolio well into her late 60s? Her broker hadn't reviewed fees, sector overlap, or rebalancing in years. When markets dipped, she lost $200,000 unnecessarily. Worse, she was paying over 1 percent in hidden fund fees — the equivalent of $108,000 lost over 30 years on a $100,000 account (Vanguard).

Here's how a CFO evaluates a portfolio:

- **Diversification:** Do you own 20 mutual funds that all hold the same stocks? Overlap magnifies risk.
- **Fee Audit:** Are you overpaying for funds when ETFs or managed accounts could deliver the same result for less?
- **Sector Balance:** Are you too heavy in tech or energy? Sector tilts create unnecessary volatility.
- **Rebalancing:** Are you trimming winners and buying laggards annually? Studies show rebalancing adds 1 percent per year to returns (Vanguard 2025).

When we ran these diagnostics for Lucy, we restructured her holdings into a balanced 60/40 portfolio, reduced her annual fees by 0.7 percent, and improved her long-term sustainability by a decade.

Owners often focus on the headline number of their portfolio. CFOs focus on the mechanics beneath. And that difference often determines whether the plan lasts 20 years or 30.

Taxes: The Silent Drain

If there's one dial on the RIPT dashboard that too many owners ignore, it's taxes. Yet taxes are often the biggest lifetime expense a retiree faces — sometimes larger than healthcare or housing combined.

Angela, a 68-year-old retiree from Dearborn, had an $800,000 IRA. Without planning, her RMDs would have pushed her into the 37 percent bracket post-2025, draining her account far faster than expected. By working together, we began converting $80,000 per year into a Roth, saving her over $200,000 in lifetime taxes.

The numbers don't lie:

- Up to 85 percent of Social Security benefits are taxable if your income exceeds $32,000 (married).
- The 2017 tax cuts expire after 2025, raising rates for many retirees.
- The estate exemption drops to $7 million post-2025 (Tax Foundation), exposing more families to estate taxes.
- Roth conversions during low-income years can save 20–30 percent in Qualified charitable distributions (QCDs) from IRAs after age 70½ allow donations to bypass income tax — a powerful tool for charitable owners.

The CFO's role is to anticipate these traps, run projections, and recommend moves at the right time. The owner's role is to define priorities: Do you want to maximize lifetime income, reduce taxes for heirs, or support charitable causes? With clarity on your vision, we can run the numbers to make it real.

The Dashboard in Action

When you put Risk, Income, Portfolio, and Taxes together, you get a true dashboard. One dial alone doesn't tell the whole story. But all four, working in concert, give you clarity.

Roger checks in with his dashboard every year over coffee in Florida. Emily and Jake review theirs every spring to sync their timelines. Angela tracks hers annually to maximize conversions before tax law changes.

As owners, they don't spend nights poring over spreadsheets. They don't need to. That's our job as CFO. They steer the ship — we watch the dials, alert them to changes, and adjust the course.

Because retirement isn't about guessing the future. It's about building a dashboard flexible enough to handle it.

THE BLIND SPOTS THAT SINK RETIREMENTS

Every shipwreck has one thing in common: the captain didn't see the danger until it was too late. Sometimes it's a hidden reef, sometimes a sudden squall, but the result is the same. In retirement, blind spots are the reefs that can sink even the strongest portfolios. Owners who try to steer alone often don't spot them in time. That's why every captain needs a CFO — a co-pilot who knows where to look, what to measure, and how to act before the hull cracks.

Let's look at four of the biggest blind spots.

Blind Spot #1: The Myth of Market Timing

The first and most dangerous blind spot is the temptation to time the market. On paper, it sounds simple: buy low, sell high. In practice, it's nearly impossible. A Fidelity 2025 study found that missing just the 10 best market days over 20 years cuts returns by half. And those "best days" almost always come right after the worst days — when fear is highest and most investors are bailing out.

I've mentioned Paul before, the retired auto executive from Ann Arbor. In 2020, during the pandemic crash, he pulled $600,000 out of equities. He thought he was being prudent. But by the time he reinvested, he had missed most of the rebound. His lifetime returns were permanently scarred.

As his CFO partner, our job wasn't to scold Paul. It was to build guardrails that kept him from repeating the mistake. We established automatic rebalancing, dollar-cost averaging for new contributions, and a cash buffer for unexpected expenses. Now Paul doesn't react to headlines. His plan hums along, immune to the market-timing trap.

THE TAKEAWAY:
Owners decide their destination. CFOs make sure the engine isn't sabotaged by emotional detours.

Blind Spot #2: The Tax Traps Lurking in Your Nest Egg

The second blind spot is taxes — the silent drain on retirement wealth. Unlike market volatility, tax erosion is predictable, yet many retirees underestimate it.

Take Required Minimum Distributions (RMDs). At age 73, the IRS requires you to withdraw a percentage of your IRA, whether you need the income or not. Those withdrawals count as taxable income, often pushing retirees into higher brackets and triggering taxes on up to 85 percent of Social Security benefits.

Angela, the 68-year-old from Dearborn, faced this exact problem. Her $800,000 IRA would have generated RMDs large enough to push her into the 37 percent bracket once tax cuts expire in 2026. Left unchecked, she would have paid over $200,000 in unnecessary taxes. Instead, by converting $80,000 per year to Roth while rates were low, we flattened her tax curve and freed her Social Security from taxation.

Here's the truth: most owners don't see tax traps until they're already caught. But a CFO monitors the tax dial on the dashboard constantly. That's how we help clients make proactive moves — Roth conversions, Qualified Charitable Distributions, bunching deductions — that save not just thousands in a single year, but hundreds of thousands over a lifetime.

Blind Spot #3: Longevity Risk — Outliving Your Money

One of the hardest truths to face in retirement is that the biggest risk isn't dying too soon — it's living too long. The Social Security Administration projects that one in ten retirees will live to age 95. That means a 30+ year retirement is not the exception, but a very real possibility.

For Catherine, a 64-year-old from Rochester, this was the blind spot she didn't want to face. With $900,000 saved, she assumed she was fine. But when we ran her plan, it showed her money depleting by age 85. That meant ten years of potential scarcity — or worse, dependence.

Together, we solved the gap. We layered in an annuity with a lifetime income rider, added a long-term care rider for health contingencies, and rebalanced her portfolio for greater efficiency. Those moves extended her plan by more than a decade.

This is the CFO's role: to run the numbers no owner wants to run. To ask, "What if you live to 95? What if healthcare costs rise by 5 percent annually? What if your spouse outlives you by 12 years?" These aren't comfortable questions. But they're necessary. Without them, longevity risk quietly sinks too many retirements.

Blind Spot #4: Behavioral Mistakes

Finally, perhaps the most common blind spot is human behavior itself. We like to think we're rational creatures, but when money meets emotion, reason often takes a back seat.

A DALBAR study shows the average investor consistently underperforms the very funds they invest in — not because the funds are bad, but because investors buy high and sell low. In downturns, fear drives panic-selling. In bull markets, greed fuels chasing returns.

Marla, a 70-year-old widow from Birmingham, was a case in point. After her husband's death, she panicked during a market wobble and wanted to sell everything. Had she done so, she would have locked in losses and jeopardized her income. Instead, as her CFO partner, we created guardrails: automatic rebalancing, quarterly reviews, and a structured income stream that gave her confidence to stay invested.

That's the beauty of having a CFO. Owners don't have to fight their instincts alone. We provide discipline, perspective, and structure — the antidote to emotional mistakes.

Seeing What Owners Can't

Market timing, tax traps, longevity risk, behavioral errors — these are the reefs beneath the surface. Owners can't always spot them, no matter how skilled or intelligent. That's not a failure; it's reality. Just as a CEO relies on a CFO to monitor financial health, retirees rely on us to catch blind spots before they become crises.

The good news? Every blind spot has a solution. With a dashboard like RIPT and a CFO who knows how to read it, you don't have to guess. You don't have to react blindly. You can steer with confidence, knowing the reefs are charted, the storm signals are watched, and the ship is equipped to last the journey.

Because retirement isn't just about having a plan. It's about avoiding the traps that sink plans. And that's what a true CFO does.

THE OWNER'S CHECKLIST FOR CHOOSING AND USING A CFO

Every successful business owner knows that a good CFO is not a luxury — it's a necessity. Without one, even profitable companies can crash from poor cash flow, hidden fees, or unexpected risks. Retirement is no different. You are the owner, the captain of your financial ship. But the question is: **who is your CFO, and are they doing the job?**

Too many retirees mistake a salesperson for a strategist. They think they have a CFO, but what they really have is someone selling products without looking at the whole picture. The difference is profound. A true CFO acts as an independent fiduciary, legally obligated to put your interests first. Their goal isn't commissions — it's your confidence.

So how can you tell the difference? Here's the checklist every owner should use.

1. Do They Review Your Plan Annually?

A CFO doesn't "set it and forget it." They review, adapt, and retool every year — because life changes every year. Fidelity's 2025 study shows 75 percent of successful retirees revisit their plan annually, adding both confidence and returns.

Ask yourself:
- Does my advisor schedule yearly reviews without me prompting them?
- Do they stress-test my plan for different market or tax scenarios?
- Have they adjusted my allocations as my life circumstances shifted?

If the answer is no, you don't have a CFO. You have a placeholder.

2. Do They Adapt to Changes or Ignore Them?

Markets shift, tax laws evolve, and life throws curveballs. A real CFO adapts in real time.

Take Roger's move to Florida. Without a CFO, he might have missed the residency rules that allowed him to save $10,000 per year in state taxes. Our job was to catch the change and adjust everything from his Roth conversion schedule to his estate planning documents.

Ask yourself:
- Has my advisor discussed the impact of the 2025 tax law sunsets?
- Do they proactively bring me strategies when the environment shifts, or do they wait for me to ask?
- Have they helped me prepare for life events like relocation, inheritance, or health costs?

If not, your dashboard is missing half its dials.

3. Do They Help You Avoid Market Timing and Emotional Mistakes?

A CFO's role is to provide discipline when emotions run high. That means putting systems in place: rebalancing, cash buffers, and structured withdrawals.

Ask yourself:
- Did my advisor panic during downturns, or did they calmly guide me through?
- Do they have a written plan for handling volatility?
- Have they ever explained the danger of missing the best market days?

If your "advisor" reacts with you instead of guiding you, they're not a CFO. They're a passenger.

4. Do They Integrate Taxes into Every Decision?

Here's the test: bring up Roth conversions. If your advisor says, "We don't do taxes," you don't have a CFO. Taxes aren't an afterthought — they're central. Vanguard and Fidelity both show tax-smart planning adds 1–2 percent annually to outcomes. That's the difference between outliving your money and leaving a legacy.

Ask yourself:
- Has my advisor created a multi-year tax strategy, not just an annual filing?
- Do they coordinate RMDs, Social Security, and investment

withdrawals to minimize taxes?
 · Do they explore strategies like Qualified Charitable Distributions or donor-advised funds?

If not, you're missing one of the most powerful tools in retirement planning.

5. Do They Plan for Longevity and Healthcare?

A CFO doesn't just look at today. They look 30 years down the line. That means planning for long lives, rising medical costs, and long-term care.

Ask yourself:
 · Has my advisor run scenarios showing my money lasting to age 95?
 · Have they discussed healthcare inflation and how to cover it?
 · Do I have a plan for long-term care costs without draining my portfolio?

If not, your retirement could run out before you do.

6. Do They Educate and Empower You as the Owner?

A CFO isn't there to drown you in jargon. They're there to give you clarity. The best ones explain the "why" behind every move, so you stay in control.

Ask yourself:
 · Do I leave meetings more confident, or more confused?
 · Has my advisor ever explained how my portfolio actually works?
 · Do I feel like I'm the owner — setting direction — or just a bystander?

If you don't feel empowered, you don't have a CFO.

7. Do They Operate as a Fiduciary?

Finally, the most important question: do they legally act in your best interest? Not every advisor does. Brokers can operate under a "suitability" standard — meaning they can sell you a product that's merely "suitable," not necessarily best. A fiduciary CFO, on the other hand, is obligated to put you first, always.

Ask yourself:

- Have they signed a fiduciary oath?
- Do they clearly explain how they're compensated?
- Do they avoid conflicts of interest by being independent?

If you can't answer yes, you don't have a CFO. You have a salesperson.

Using the Checklist

When Emily and Jake applied this checklist, they realized their old broker had failed almost every point. He never reviewed their plan, never discussed taxes, and never addressed their mismatched retirement timelines. They weren't surprised — they were frustrated. That's when they sought out a fiduciary CFO, and their retirement strategy transformed.

The checklist isn't just a way to evaluate advisors. It's a tool to empower you as the owner. It helps you demand the accountability you deserve, and it ensures you have the right co-pilot at your side.

Because in retirement, the stakes are too high for half-measures. You need a CFO who sees the blind spots, integrates the dials, and fights for your vision.

CAPTAIN OF THE SHIP, CFO AT THE HELM

Let's go back to the Florida marina, where Roger sits across from me with that relaxed grin only a retiree who's figured it out can wear. The same man who once walked into my Brighton office white-knuckled and anxious now spends his winters on the water and his summers up north. What changed? He didn't suddenly become a financial genius. He didn't memorize tax codes or start day-trading stocks. He made one decision that altered everything: he stopped trying to be both captain *and* CFO.

Roger embraced his true role — owner, captain, decision-maker. He set the course: retire on his terms, enjoy time with his wife, leave a legacy for his grandkids. Then he handed the financial engine room over to a team whose full-time job was to monitor the dials, adjust the sails, and steer around storms. That's what gave him freedom.

Why Owners Need a CFO

Here's the truth every retiree must face: no matter how smart, successful, or disciplined you've been, retirement is not the time to go it alone. You don't run a $1 million portfolio the way you ran a checking account in your 30s. You don't navigate complex tax laws with the same casual glance you give a W-2 form. Retirement is too nuanced, too high-stakes, and too dynamic.

That's why every owner needs a CFO. It's not about surrendering control — it's about securing confidence. You remain the captain, choosing the direction, setting the goals, and living the life you've envisioned. But your CFO — if they're a true fiduciary — becomes your co-pilot, your navigator, your strategist. They see what you can't, anticipate what's ahead, and make sure your ship not only stays afloat but thrives.

The Owner's Advantage

When you position yourself as the owner, a few things shift immediately:

- **You stop second-guessing.** You don't need to chase headlines or panic over downturns, because you know the financial engine room is monitored.
- **You focus on vision, not mechanics.** Owners decide what they want — travel, family, legacy — not how the cash flow, taxes, and portfolio all coordinate.
- **You reclaim your time.** Instead of spending retirement glued to screens or fretting over tax brackets, you spend it living.

Owners who pair themselves with the right CFO partner enjoy longer-lasting wealth, fewer regrets, and more freedom. A 2025 BlackRock study found that adaptive plans with ongoing oversight last five to ten years longer than static ones. That's not magic — that's management.

Full Circle

As Roger finished his coffee that morning, he leaned back, looked out at the sailboats gliding by, and said something that stuck with me: "I used to feel like I was on this boat alone, gripping the wheel in fog. Now I feel like the captain. I know where I'm going, and I've got the right team below deck keeping the ship steady. That's why I can finally enjoy the ride."

That's the heart of this chapter. You are the captain. You set the vision. But no captain crosses an ocean alone. With the right CFO at your helm, your retirement won't just be a journey — it will be the adventure you always imagined.

CLOSING THE CHAPTER: THE CAPTAIN'S CALL TO ACTION

Think about your own ship. Where are you headed? What kind of retirement do you want? If you're already retired, how confident are you that your plan will last as long as you will? Do you know how taxes, healthcare, or longevity risk will impact your voyage?

If you don't have clear answers, that's your signal. It doesn't mean you've failed. It means you need a CFO. Just as no successful business would operate without one, no retirement should be left to chance.

At Main Financial Group, that's what we do. We don't sell products. We don't offer cookie-cutter plans. We act as fiduciary CFOs, partnering with owners like you to turn vision into reality. We monitor the dashboard, we adapt to storms, and we make sure your financial empire runs like a well-oiled machine.

CONCLUSION
Your Moment is Now

This is your time. For years you've worked, saved, sacrificed, and built. You've endured market swings, paid your taxes, and shouldered the uncertainty of a system that was never designed with Main Street in mind. But now you stand at the threshold of choice. You can drift with the tide—hoping your plan holds up—or you can take the wheel, own your future, and become the architect of the retirement you deserve. That is the call of the Main Street Millionaire: to rise above confusion, claim clarity, and live with confidence.

The path is clear. Build income streams you can't outlive. Convert today's tax uncertainty into tomorrow's advantage. Protect your wealth from the silent dangers that rob others of their dreams. And above all, design a plan that reflects your story—not Wall Street's agenda. This isn't about chasing hot returns or following the herd. It's about creating a blueprint that turns your lifetime of hard work into freedom, security, and lasting impact.

So don't wait. Don't hand over control to chance, to markets, or to advisors who fail to see the whole picture. Step forward. Partner with those who understand that your legacy is more than numbers—it's family, freedom, and a future worth fighting for. This is your moment to act boldly, to secure not only your own peace of mind but also the inheritance of wisdom and stability you'll leave behind.

The Main Street Millionaire isn't just a book title—it's a mindset, a movement, a declaration. You have the tools. You have the knowledge. You have the power. Now is the time to claim it. Take control, live with purpose, and let your wealth serve the life you've always imagined. Your future starts today—make it one you own.

I wish you great success on your wealth journey,

- Jordan D. Main

BONUS CHAPTER

Top 10 Mistakes to Avoid in Building Wealth and Planning Retirement

Wealth is not built by perfection—it is built by recovering from mistakes. The path to financial security is never a straight line. It is a series of choices, some wise, some costly, and some whose true consequences only reveal themselves years later. The difference between those who retire with confidence and those who find themselves unprepared is not intelligence, discipline, or even luck. It is whether they recognize and avoid the errors that quietly erode wealth, year after year.

In more than two decades advising professionals, business owners, and retirees across Michigan and beyond, I've learned that financial failure rarely comes from one catastrophic event. It comes instead from patterns—common, almost predictable missteps, that accumulate over time. I've seen physicians who saved diligently but ignored taxes, engineers who designed intricate spreadsheets that collapsed under real-world volatility, and educators who relied too heavily on a pension that didn't keep pace with inflation. Different stories, same result: what should have been financial independence became financial strain.

The good news is that these mistakes are not mysteries. They are identifiable, preventable, and in many cases, reversible. Ten of them in particular account for the majority of retirement struggles I've encountered. Some are born from optimism—believing the market will always rise, or that Social Security will always be enough. Others are rooted in fear—selling out of investments at the wrong time, or avoiding tools like annuities because of misconceptions. And still others stem from neglect—failing to plan, failing to account for taxes, or failing to consider longevity.

This chapter is about shining a light on those ten mistakes. My purpose is not to point fingers at those who've made them, but to give you the clarity to avoid repeating them yourself. Because in wealth, as in life, it is often less about chasing perfection than it is about sidestepping preventable failure. Awareness is the first defense, and preparation is the ultimate cure.

Let's look together at the ten most common—and most costly—financial mistakes, and more importantly, how to turn them into lessons that strengthen your plan rather than weaken it.

Mistake #1: Not Having a Plan (It's Just a Wish)

One of the most dangerous assumptions in wealth-building is that saving money, on its own, is a plan. Too many hardworking professionals accumulate accounts, pay down debt, and hope that their financial future will "sort itself out." But hope is not a strategy, and wealth without direction is like a ship without a rudder—it may float, but it will drift aimlessly, often into treacherous waters.

I remember meeting Carl, a 65-year-old physician from Flint. Brilliant in the operating room, disciplined in his career, yet his finances told a different story. Over three decades he had amassed nearly $900,000 across various accounts—old 401(k)s, a brokerage here, a Roth IRA there—but he had no cohesive plan. His approach to retirement was simple: draw down as needed, and trust that the numbers would work themselves out. The problem? Numbers don't sort themselves out. They respond to sequence, to timing, to taxes, to markets—all of which demand foresight. When we ran projections, it was clear Carl risked depleting his savings by age 80, even while still in good health.

Carl's situation is far from unique. A recent study by Northwestern Mutual found that the average American believes they need $1.46 million to retire comfortably—yet fewer than half have a written plan to get there. Fidelity's 2025 Retirement Savings Assessment revealed that 43 percent of baby boomers still lack a structured roadmap, despite sitting at the very doorstep of retirement. The absence of a plan doesn't just create uncertainty; it destroys opportunity. Without tax coordination, retirees often withdraw in ways that add unnecessary liability. Without risk alignment, they hold portfolios mismatched to their tolerance or capacity. Without income mapping, they fail to turn their nest egg into reliable cash flow.

This is where the RIPT framework becomes invaluable. For Carl, we began by quantifying his **Risk tolerance**. He considered himself "moderate," but his scattered accounts reflected no clear alignment. By reallocating into a balanced portfolio—50 percent equities, 50 percent bonds—we gave him both growth and stability. Next came **Income**. Rather than haphazard withdrawals, we established a fixed-indexed annuity that guaranteed $2,500 per month for life, regardless of market conditions. That simple decision transformed uncertainty into predictability.

Then, for his **Portfolio**, we consolidated accounts into low-cost ETFs, bringing down his expense ratios to an efficient 0.14 percent. Finally, we addressed **Taxes**—Carl had the perfect window before Required Minimum Distributions to convert portions of his traditional IRA into a Roth. Over twenty years, those conversions were projected to save him over $120,000 in taxes, while also reducing the burden on his heirs.

Carl now plays golf with his grandchildren without wondering whether his next withdrawal might jeopardize his future. His story illustrates the principle beautifully: a goal without a plan is just a wish, but with a plan, that same goal becomes attainable.

The lesson is this: **retirement planning must be intentional**. A plan is not a thick binder of charts or a complicated spreadsheet. It is a clear, written document that connects your resources with your goals and adjusts as life unfolds. It forces you to ask the right questions: How much income will I need? How much risk can I accept? How will I protect against taxes and inflation? And how do I align my wealth with the life I want to live?

Too often, people avoid this exercise because it feels overwhelming. But the truth is, failing to plan is simply planning to fail. And failure in retirement isn't about losing status—it's about losing peace of mind, freedom, and the ability to live on your own terms.

Start with a plan. Write it down. Review it annually. Refine it as your life changes. Because wealth without a plan is little more than a wish, and wishes alone rarely fund a fulfilling retirement.

Mistake #2: Relying Too Much on Social Security (It's Not Enough)

For many Americans, Social Security is imagined as the bedrock of retirement—the dependable check that arrives each month, the reward for decades of payroll taxes. But while Social Security is an important piece of the puzzle, it was never designed to be the whole picture. To rely on it as your primary income is to mistake a safety net for a foundation. Safety nets can catch you, but they cannot carry you.

I recall meeting Hank, a retired factory worker from Detroit. He had spent forty years on the line, steady and disciplined, paying into Social Security every paycheck. When he came to see me at age 67, his question was simple: "Jordan, I've paid in all my life—surely it's enough to retire on, right?" His monthly benefit was $2,100. Respectable, yes, but his projected monthly expenses were closer to $4,800, even before accounting for health care and rising costs of living. In other words, his Social Security covered less than half of what he needed.

Hank's case is not unusual. When Social Security was created in 1935, the average life expectancy was just 64 years. The program assumed most people would not draw benefits for very long. There were 42 workers for every retiree, and the system could easily support itself. Fast forward to today: life expectancy has climbed to nearly 79 years, and the ratio of workers to retirees has plummeted to 2.8. That shift alone explains why Social Security is under such pressure. Without reform, projections from the Social Security Trustees Report show that by 2034, benefits could be cut by roughly 19 percent.

This overreliance on Social Security is more than a numbers problem; it's a mindset problem. People view the benefit as a pension, when in fact it's simply a supplement. Studies confirm this disconnect. A 2025 AARP survey revealed that 67 percent of Americans consider Social Security their most important retirement resource—yet barely half of younger adults expect the system to provide full benefits in their lifetimes. This mismatch between expectation and reality is dangerous.

So, what's the solution? First, recognize Social Security for what it is: a reliable baseline. It was designed to replace only about 40 percent of the average worker's pre-retirement income. If you plan to live solely on that, you are planning for scarcity. The fix is to treat Social Security as one instrument in a broader orchestra.

For Hank, we began by optimizing timing. By delaying his benefit until age 70, he could boost his monthly payment by nearly 8 percent per year of delay. That single decision increased his monthly check by almost $500 for the rest of his life. But timing alone wasn't enough. We layered in a personal pension through a fixed-indexed annuity, providing another $1,500 of guaranteed monthly income. Together, these sources gave him a stable foundation: Social Security as the "floor," the annuity as the "reinforcement." His other investments could then be used for growth and flexibility rather than survival.

In the RIPT framework, the logic is clear:
- **Risk:** A guaranteed annuity reduces the danger of market downturns eroding income.
- **Income:** Social Security is your base, not your ceiling.
- **Portfolio:** Diversification provides growth beyond the fixed government benefit.
- **Taxes:** Coordinating withdrawals helps minimize taxation of Social Security itself, which can reach up to 85 percent of benefits for those with higher provisional income. For Hank, shifting some assets into Roth accounts meant thousands saved in future taxes and a lighter tax bite on his Social Security.

The broader lesson? Social Security is like a hammer—vital for building, but useless without wood, nails, and blueprints. To rely on it alone is to guarantee frustration, because retirement today demands multiple income streams working together. The families who thrive are those who view Social Security as a starting point, not an endpoint.

Mistake #3: Ignoring Inflation (The Silent Thief)
Of all the forces that erode wealth, inflation is the most subtle. It does not arrive with the drama of a stock market crash or the shock of a sudden tax bill. Instead, it creeps quietly, year by year, stealing purchasing power in increments so small that they often go unnoticed— until the damage is undeniable. This is why inflation has earned the nickname "the silent thief."

I think of Gina, a 70-year-old retiree from Lansing. She lived on a fixed pension that, when she first received it, provided more than enough to cover her monthly needs. "Jordan," she said, her voice tinged with both disbelief and worry, "my $3,000 check used to fill the pantry, pay the bills, and still leave room for dinners out. Now I feel like I'm rationing just to make it last." The pension had not adjusted for inflation. What once felt abundant had, over twenty years, lost nearly half its purchasing power.

This is the cruel math of inflation. Even at a modest 3 percent annual rate, prices double in roughly 24 years. The cart of groceries that cost $100 when Gina retired now costs nearly $200. Gas, utilities, healthcare—all creep upward while her income remained frozen. The result is a standard of living that quietly erodes until a retiree finds themselves cutting back not because they want to, but because they have to.

History offers sobering reminders. In 1980, inflation peaked at 13.5 percent, a level that devastated retirees living on fixed incomes. More recently, in 2022, inflation reached 9.1 percent—the highest in four decades. Even though the Federal Reserve projects a more stable 2–3 percent moving forward, spikes can and do occur, often triggered by global events, energy shocks, or supply chain disruptions. Retirees who fail to account for this volatility find themselves unprepared for the storm.

And inflation is not just about higher grocery bills. It is magnified in retirement by two critical factors: healthcare and longevity. Healthcare costs have historically risen faster than general inflation, averaging 5–6 percent annually. Combine that with the fact that retirees are living longer than ever, and ignoring inflation is not just careless—it is perilous.

So, what can be done? Gina's solution began with shifting her mindset. Instead of treating her pension as her entire foundation, she began layering in investments designed to grow faster than inflation. We allocated part of her portfolio into equities, which historically provide average annual returns of 7 percent above inflation. We also added Treasury Inflation-Protected Securities (TIPS), which rise in value as inflation increases, ensuring her fixed-income side could keep pace. And because income must be stable, not just growing, we balanced these with an annuity that guaranteed a baseline of monthly income regardless of what inflation did.

This is the RIPT framework in action:
- **Risk:** The blend of stocks and fixed instruments prevents overexposure to volatility.
- **Income:** Stable guarantees ensure she can cover essentials regardless of rising prices.
- **Portfolio:** Equities and TIPS provide growth and protection.
- **Taxes:** Placing TIPS in a Roth shielded the inflation adjustments from being taxed as ordinary income. The result was not a promise that inflation would vanish—it never does—but confidence that her plan could withstand it.

The larger principle is this: failing to plan for inflation is failing to plan for reality. Inflation will always exist, and its compounding effect is more destructive than most realize. A retiree who ignores it will see their lifestyle slowly constrict, forced to do less with the same dollar. A retiree who anticipates it, however, can build a portfolio and income structure that not only keeps pace but grows stronger in the face of rising costs.

Inflation is not an abstract economic statistic. It is the reason your favorite restaurant raises prices, the reason your healthcare bill climbs, the reason a "comfortable" retirement can become uncomfortable over time. Those who prepare can outpace it. Those who do not will find themselves chasing a moving target they can never quite catch.

Mistake #4: Falling for Sequence of Returns Risk (Withdrawing in Down Markets)

Retirement is not only about how much you earn, but also about when you earn it. The same is true for losses. Two investors can average the same return over twenty years, yet end up with radically different outcomes depending on the sequence of those returns. This is the essence of sequence of returns risk—the danger that poor market performance early in retirement, when withdrawals begin, will permanently damage the longevity of a portfolio.

Consider Keith, a 66-year-old teacher from Flint. After decades in the classroom, he retired in 2021 with $600,000 in savings and the conventional wisdom that he could withdraw 4 percent per year— about $24,000—without worry. The problem was timing. Just one year into his retirement, the markets fell sharply, with the S&P 500 dropping nearly 20 percent in 2022. Keith, needing income, withdrew his $24,000 anyway. On paper, he had lost over $100,000 due to the downturn, but when you added the withdrawal, the damage deepened. Even when markets recovered the following year, his portfolio never fully rebounded, because he had sold assets at depressed prices to meet immediate needs.

This is the cruel reality of sequence risk: early losses magnify withdrawals, withdrawals magnify losses, and together they shorten the lifespan of a portfolio. Academic studies confirm what Keith experienced firsthand. According to Investopedia's 2025 analysis, sequence risk can cause retirees to outlive their money ten years earlier than those with identical returns but different timing. A CNBC survey in 2025 found that nearly 80 percent of retirees feared sequence of returns risk more than inflation—a remarkable admission given how dominant inflation concerns usually are.

The math explains why. In the decade before and after retirement—often called the "retirement red zone"—portfolios are uniquely fragile. A sharp decline at the beginning of retirement is far more damaging than the same decline later on, because withdrawals lock in the losses. It is like tripping on the first step down the stairs: the fall hurts more when you have the entire staircase left to descend.

Keith's solution came from restructuring his income sources. Instead of drawing directly from equities during volatile years, we created a guaranteed income buffer. His Social Security benefit was delayed until age 70, which increased it by 8 percent annually and provided a larger, inflation-adjusted base. To bridge the gap, we established a fixed-indexed annuity paying $1,500 per month, insulating him from market downturns. With these two income sources covering his essentials, Keith could leave his investment portfolio intact during bear markets, allowing it time to recover.

This illustrates the power of RIPT:
- **Risk:** Annuities shield against downside markets.
- **Income:** Guaranteed streams provide resilience.
- **Portfolio:** Equities remain invested for growth, not liquidation.
- **Taxes:** By tapping Roth accounts first during low-income years, Keith kept his tax bracket manageable and his Social Security taxation lower when it eventually kicked in.

The principle is straightforward but vital: it is not only about how much your investments earn on average, but when those earnings occur relative to your withdrawals. A retiree who ignores sequence risk may find themselves cutting back, returning to work, or worse—outliving their money. A retiree who plans for it, however, can weather downturns with dignity and maintain their lifestyle even when markets stumble.

In retirement, downturns are inevitable. The question is whether they derail your plan or merely become bumps in the road. With buffers in place, the answer is clear: downturns become survivable events, not catastrophic ones.

Mistake #5: FOMO – Chasing Trends (Buying High, Selling Low)

Human behavior is often the greatest threat to wealth. Markets rise and fall, but it is the investor's reaction that determines long-term success. Few behaviors are as destructive—or as common—as chasing trends out of fear of missing out, the infamous FOMO effect.

I think of Vince, a 52-year-old IT manager from Royal Oak. In 2021, everyone around him seemed to be making money in cryptocurrencies. Headlines buzzed, friends bragged, and Vince felt the pull of opportunity slipping away. Against his better judgment, he liquidated $150,000 of his retirement savings to "get in on the boom." For a brief moment, he felt brilliant—his balance shot up 20 percent in just a few months. But when the inevitable crash arrived, he panicked and sold, locking in a $90,000 loss. What began as a rush of optimism ended as regret.

The danger of FOMO is not limited to crypto. It appears in every generation of investors. In the late 1990s, it was tech stocks. In the mid-2000s, real estate. In the 2020s, it has been everything from meme stocks to artificial intelligence ETFs. The underlying pattern is the same: the crowd runs one way, and individuals, fearing exclusion, abandon discipline and run with it. What they rarely see is that by the time the crowd notices, the opportunity has already peaked.

Data backs this up. Morningstar's 2025 Investor Behavior Study found that investors who chase hot sectors underperform disciplined investors by an average of 2–3 percent annually. Fidelity's research confirmed that the majority of individual investors overestimate their risk tolerance during bull markets, leading them to buy high and sell low. Over a lifetime, this gap translates to hundreds of thousands of dollars lost—not to market volatility, but to human behavior.

So how do you break the cycle? For Vince, the solution was to return to fundamentals. We built a portfolio of diversified ETFs spanning all 11 market sectors, ensuring he had exposure to growth opportunities without overconcentration. We used dollar-cost averaging to automate contributions, removing the temptation to "time" purchases. We added dividend-paying funds that provided steady income, reducing his reliance on speculative growth. Slowly, discipline replaced impulse.

This too fits neatly into RIPT:
- **Risk:** Measured allocations align with true tolerance, not momentary emotion.
- **Income:** Dividends and steady returns replace the volatility of speculation.
- **Portfolio:** Diversification prevents overexposure to a single trend.
- **Taxes:** ETFs minimize unnecessary turnover and capital gains.

The deeper lesson is this: wealth is built not by chasing what is fashionable, but by owning what is durable. As Warren Buffett has famously advised, invest in businesses you would be comfortable holding forever. Chasing trends is like sprinting after a train—you may catch it, but you'll be exhausted, and often it's already leaving the station.

Discipline, not excitement, wins in the long run. The retirees who flourish are not the ones who rode the latest fads; they are the ones who built steady portfolios, avoided panic, and stayed focused on their plan. When the noise of markets grows loud, remember this: you do not need to catch every wave to reach your destination. You only need a vessel sturdy enough to carry you there.

Mistake #6: Trying to Time the Market (You're Not a Fortune Teller)

If FOMO is the temptation to jump in too late, market timing is its twin: the temptation to jump out too early. Both stem from the illusion that we can predict the future—that with enough news, charts, or gut instinct, we can anticipate when markets will rise or fall. But the truth is sobering: not even the most seasoned professionals consistently time markets correctly. For everyday investors, the attempt usually does more harm than good.

Maggie, a 60-year-old nurse from Dearborn, learned this the hard way. In early 2022, rattled by news of inflation, rising interest rates, and geopolitical turmoil, she sold nearly her entire $400,000 portfolio, convinced that worse was on the horizon. Her plan was to "sit on the sidelines until things looked better." The problem? By the time she felt comfortable reinvesting, the market had already rebounded. In trying to avoid losses, she created them—missing the recovery and leaving her portfolio permanently behind.

The data is conclusive. Fidelity's 2025 study showed that missing just the 10 best days in the market over the last 20 years cut investors' returns in half—from 7 percent annually down to 3.5 percent. Vanguard's analysis found that timers underperformed buy-and-hold investors by an average of 1.5 percent per year, primarily because they were out of the market during critical rebound periods. And according to a 2025 NerdWallet survey, nearly 70 percent of investors admitted they had tried to time the market at least once in the last five years—most with disappointing results.

Market timing is seductive because it offers the illusion of control. Headlines scream warnings, analysts issue predictions, and it feels responsible to "do something." But wealth is not built in spurts of clairvoyance—it is built in seasons of patience. The best days in the market often come clustered near the worst. To step aside during downturns is to risk missing the very recovery that drives long-term growth.

The solution lies not in predicting the unpredictable, but in designing a portfolio that can withstand it. For Maggie, that meant embracing diversification across all major sectors and geographies, rebalancing annually so that market volatility became a tool, not a threat. Instead of reacting emotionally, she built a system that automatically sold what was high and bought what was low. We also created an emergency cash reserve—so that if she needed funds during a downturn, she wouldn't be forced to liquidate investments at a loss.

RIPT provides the structure again:
- **Risk:** Allocations are set according to tolerance and capacity, not headlines.
- **Income:** Reserves and annuities provide stability during downturns.
- **Portfolio:** Broad diversification and disciplined rebalancing prevent guesswork.
- **Taxes:** A long-term approach minimizes unnecessary capital gains from jumping in and out.

The lesson is clear: markets cannot be consistently timed. Attempting to do so is like trying to forecast Michigan weather in March—sun one minute, snow the next, and no certainty until it's already passed.

Investors who succeed are not those who guess correctly, but those who stay invested, rebalance with discipline, and let compounding work in their favor.

Market timing is a fortune teller's game, and fortune tellers rarely retire wealthy. The real fortune lies in patience.

Mistake #7: Dismissing Annuities as "Bad" (They're Tools, Not Villains)

Few financial products are as misunderstood—or as maligned—as annuities. For many, the very word conjures images of high fees, hidden clauses, and aggressive sales pitches. And in fairness, some annuities deserve their poor reputation. Variable annuities, for example, often carry layers of fees that eat away at returns, leaving investors with disappointing results. But to dismiss all annuities as "bad" is to throw out an entire category of tools that, when used correctly, can provide exactly what retirees need most: guaranteed income for life.

I recall meeting Lyle, a 63-year-old from Midland, who came into my office skeptical. "Aren't annuities just for suckers?" he asked. His previous advisor had pushed a variable annuity that cost him nearly 3 percent annually in fees—money that went to commissions and riders he didn't fully understand. No wonder he was wary. But Lyle's real need was clear: he had $600,000 saved, and he wanted predictable income that would last as long as he did. A product with high fees and market exposure was the wrong fit, but that didn't mean all annuities were off the table.

We examined alternatives. A fixed-indexed annuity, for example, offered Lyle the chance to participate in market growth (through an index crediting strategy) while protecting him from losses in down years. More importantly, it came with the option of a guaranteed lifetime income rider, providing him $2,000 a month he could never outlive. For Lyle, this was transformative. Instead of fearing another market downturn, he could count on a paycheck every month—just as reliable as his Social Security check.

The larger point is this: annuities are not villains. They are instruments. Like any tool, their value depends on how they are designed and how they are used. Pensions and Social Security are, in essence, annuities—and no retiree dismisses those. Yet many overlook annuities in their private planning, clinging instead to portfolios that may be too exposed to market risk.

Studies confirm the rising recognition of annuities' value. According to LIMRA's 2025 report, fixed indexed annuities are now among the fastest-growing retirement products, with sales up more than 10 percent year over year. Why? Because they address the two needs retirees consistently voice: protection from downside risk and income they cannot outlive.

Through the RIPT lens, the role of annuities becomes even clearer:
- **Risk:** They provide a floor of protection against market downturns.
- **Income:** Annuities create guaranteed, predictable cash flow.
- **Portfolio:** By covering essential expenses with guaranteed income, the rest of the portfolio can be invested for growth without fear.
- **Taxes:** Certain annuities offer riders or strategies that provide tax efficiency, reducing the burden of withdrawals.

The lesson is not that everyone should buy an annuity. The lesson is that dismissing them out of hand is a mistake. Retirees who categorically reject annuities often end up drawing too heavily from volatile accounts, leaving themselves vulnerable to sequence risk, longevity risk, and income shortfalls. Retirees who use them wisely, however, find peace of mind in knowing that no matter what the market does, they will always have a check coming in.

In retirement, confidence matters as much as returns. Annuities, when chosen carefully, provide that confidence. They are not the enemy of a well-crafted plan; they are often one of its most dependable allies.

Mistake #8: Underestimating Longevity (Outliving Your Money)

When people think about retirement planning, they often picture a 25-year horizon: retire at 65, live comfortably until 90, and leave something behind for their heirs. But what if you live longer? What if your retirement lasts 30 or even 40 years? Suddenly, the math changes—and without preparation, what once looked like financial security begins to look like scarcity. This is the risk of longevity: not dying too soon, but living longer than your money lasts. What if you screw up and live too long?

Olga, a 71-year-old widow from Lansing, illustrated this reality vividly. She had worked for decades as a hospital administrator, saving diligently and building a $700,000 nest egg. When she came to see me, she was confident: "Jordan, I think I have more than enough to cover the rest of my life." On paper, her plan seemed reasonable. She budgeted $3,000 a month from Social Security and withdrawals, and she assumed she would live to around 85. But her mother had lived to 98, and her grandmother to 96. Genetics alone suggested her timeline might be much longer than she had planned.

When we ran the projections out to age 95, the cracks began to show. Her portfolio, largely invested in bonds yielding 2–3 percent, simply could not keep up with both withdrawals and inflation. Even worse, we factored in long-term care. Her mother had required three years of dementia care that cost over $200,000. Olga had not accounted for that possibility at all. By her late 80s, the probability of running out of money became alarmingly high.

This is not unique to Olga. A 2025 study by the Society of Actuaries found that a 65-year-old woman has a 50 percent chance of living to 90, a 25 percent chance of living to 95, and nearly a 10 percent chance of reaching 100. For couples, the odds are even higher that at least one spouse will live into their 90s. Meanwhile, healthcare costs continue to rise faster than inflation. Fidelity's 2025 Retiree Health Care Cost Estimate pegged the average lifetime healthcare expense for a couple retiring this year at $315,000—not including long-term care. Add those two forces together—longevity and healthcare inflation—and it is clear why outliving money is one of the most pressing fears retirees face.

The solution is not to guess at your lifespan, but to plan as though it will be long. For Olga, that meant reshaping her income strategy. We added a fixed-indexed annuity with a lifetime income rider, guaranteeing that no matter how long she lived, she would receive $40,000 a year for essentials. We also secured a long-term care rider, which provided a pool of benefits specifically for potential medical or custodial needs, reducing the risk of draining her core assets. We reallocated part of her portfolio into equities—about 30 percent—to provide the growth necessary to outpace inflation over decades. And we executed a series of Roth conversions to reduce the tax burden later in life, when Required Minimum Distributions would otherwise have pushed her into higher brackets.

Through RIPT, the alignment was clear:
- **Risk:** Hedged by guarantees and long-term care coverage.
- **Income:** Secured for life, not just 20 years.
- **Portfolio:** Positioned for growth, not merely preservation.
- **Taxes:** Minimized through proactive conversions.

The broader lesson? Longevity is not a risk to fear, but a reality to plan for. Those who underestimate it risk spending their final years in financial stress, cutting back at the very time they should be focusing on family, health, and dignity. Those who plan for it gain peace of mind, knowing their income will last as long as they do—whether that is 85, 95, or even 105.

Retirement is not a sprint; it is a marathon. The winners are not the fastest at the start, but those who conserve their resources to cross the finish line strong. Planning for longevity ensures that your retirement is not only long, but also fulfilling.

Mistake #9: Falling for Tax Traps (No Plan Means Paying More)

Many retirees assume that taxes fade away once the paychecks stop. After all, they've "paid their dues" during their working years. But the reality is sobering: Uncle Sam doesn't retire when you do. Withdrawals from retirement accounts, Required Minimum Distributions (RMDs), Social Security taxation, and Medicare surcharges can combine to create a hidden tax bomb that erodes wealth far faster than most expect. Without a strategy, retirees often pay tens or even hundreds of thousands more in lifetime taxes than necessary.

Tyson, a 69-year-old retired mechanic from Flint, learned this the hard way. All his working life he deferred taxes, contributing steadily to his 401(k) and later rolling it into an IRA. He assumed that in retirement his tax burden would be light—after all, his income would be lower than it was during his working years. But in his first year of withdrawals, he received an unpleasant surprise: a $15,000 tax bill. Not only were his IRA withdrawals taxed as ordinary income, but they also triggered taxation on 85 percent of his Social Security benefits. To make matters worse, his income pushed him over the threshold for Medicare's Income-Related Monthly Adjustment Amount (IRMAA), increasing his premiums by thousands of dollars annually.

Tyson's story is all too common. According to Kiplinger's 2025 Retirement Tax Report, nearly half of retirees are caught off guard by the taxation of Social Security benefits, which can be taxed up to 85 percent if provisional income exceeds just $32,000 for married couples—a threshold that hasn't been adjusted since 1983. Add to that the mandatory RMDs starting at age 73, and many retirees suddenly find themselves in higher tax brackets than during their working years.

The good news is that these tax traps can be defused with foresight. For Tyson, we implemented a Roth conversion strategy, moving portions of his traditional IRA into a Roth during his "gap years" between retirement and age 73. By paying taxes at today's lower rates, he avoided higher brackets later when RMDs and Social Security would have collided. We also used Qualified Charitable Distributions (QCDs), which allowed him to donate directly from his IRA without the withdrawals counting as taxable income. Together, these strategies saved him nearly $150,000 in projected lifetime taxes.

This is the power of integrating taxes into the RIPT framework:
- **Risk:** Planning reduces exposure to sudden tax spikes that can destabilize budgets.
- **Income:** Predictable, tax-efficient streams reduce surprises.
- **Portfolio:** Positioning tax-inefficient assets in tax-deferred accounts and growth-oriented assets in Roths amplifies efficiency.
- **Taxes:** Roth conversions, QCDs, and careful withdrawal sequencing minimize lifetime liability.

The principle is simple: taxes don't disappear in retirement—they often grow more complex. Those who assume otherwise walk into hidden traps that siphon away their savings year after year. Those who plan proactively turn taxes into one of their greatest advantages, using today's rates, laws, and opportunities to create future flexibility.

The difference between these two paths is not intelligence or effort—it is planning. As the old saying goes, "You can either pay the IRS with a plan, or pay the IRS without one. But you will pay." The choice is whether you pay more than you need to.

Retirement is challenging enough without hidden tax surprises. Avoiding these traps requires looking ahead, not backward—anticipating how your income sources, withdrawals, and healthcare costs intersect under the tax code. Those who take the time to do so keep more of what they've earned, and in doing so, buy themselves not just wealth, but peace of mind.

Mistake #10: Poor Estate Planning (Leaving a Tax Bomb for Heirs)

The final mistake is often the most overlooked. Many retirees carefully plan for their own needs but neglect to consider what happens after they're gone. The result? A lifetime of disciplined saving can turn into a massive tax liability for the very people they wanted to bless. This is the tragedy of poor estate planning: a legacy intended as a gift becomes a burden instead.

Nina, a 74-year-old from Midland, had built a $600,000 IRA over the course of her career. Her plan was simple: leave it to her two children. "They'll be fine," she told me, sliding her account statement across the desk. But under the SECURE Act's 10-year rule, her children would be required to liquidate the inherited IRA within a decade, paying ordinary income taxes on every dollar. For high earners, this meant as much as 37 percent in federal taxes, plus state taxes on top. When we ran the numbers, Nina's $600,000 gift would likely shrink to closer to $360,000—a loss of nearly a quarter million dollars to the IRS.

This is not an isolated case. Cerulli Associates projects that $124 trillion will transfer between generations by 2048, but without proper planning, 30–40 percent of that wealth could be lost to taxes. What feels like financial security to one generation can quickly become a tax bomb for the next.

The solution is not complicated, but it does require foresight. For Nina, we implemented a combination of Roth conversions and life insurance. By converting portions of her IRA each year, she paid taxes at today's historically low rates, creating tax-free accounts her children could inherit without the 10-year liquidation requirement. To further protect her legacy, we used a permanent life insurance policy structured for efficiency, turning taxable dollars into a tax-free death benefit. Together, these strategies nearly doubled the value her heirs would receive, transforming $600,000 of taxable assets into more than $1.2 million of tax-free wealth.

Through RIPT, the impact is clear:
- **Risk:** Planning reduces the risk of leaving heirs with a financial burden instead of a blessing.
- **Income:** Life insurance provides guaranteed, tax-free liquidity.
- **Portfolio:** Assets are structured for efficient transfer.
- **Taxes:** Roth conversions eliminate forced taxable withdrawals for heirs.

The broader lesson is this: estate planning is not just about documents or trusts—it is about intentionality. It asks the question, "Will my wealth continue to serve my family after I'm gone, or will it be siphoned away by taxes and poor planning?" Too often, people leave that answer to chance. But chance is not a plan, and the cost of inaction can be staggering.

A legacy should provide peace, not paperwork. It should empower the next generation, not entangle them in confusion and unnecessary tax bills. With planning, it can. Without planning, it almost certainly will not.

CLOSING THE CHAPTER: WRAPPING UP: LEARN FROM THESE MISTAKES, DON'T REPEAT THEM

From Carl's lack of a plan to Nina's unintended tax bomb, these ten mistakes represent the most common ways wealth is lost in retirement. They are predictable, preventable, and—if addressed early—reversible. The key is not perfection, but awareness and preparation.

The RIPT framework—**Risk, Income, Portfolio, Taxes**—offers a way to evaluate each decision in the light of long-term security. By running every choice through those four lenses, you ensure that no piece of your financial life is ignored, and no blind spot becomes a costly mistake.

Remember, the goal of retirement is not simply to die with money in the bank. The goal is to live with confidence, generosity, and freedom. To know that your income is secure, your risks are managed, your portfolio is aligned, your taxes are minimized, and your legacy is preserved.

Mistakes will happen—we are human. But by learning from the missteps of others, you can avoid paying the same tuition yourself.

Let this chapter be your roadmap to sidestep the potholes, disarm the traps, and keep your wealth intact for the people and purposes you care about most.

Because in the end, retirement success is not about luck—it's about planning. And the best time to start planning wisely is always now.

APPENDIX

Your Bonus Toolbox for Building Wealth and Planning Retirement

Think of this appendix like the extra drawer in your toolbox—the one your dad or granddad always had tucked away in the garage. You'd open it up and find not just the hammer and screwdriver you expected, but a measuring tape, a level, maybe even a gadget you didn't know you needed until something broke. That's what this section is meant to be: a set of practical, roll-up-your-sleeves tools you can use to take the lessons from the book and make them real in your own financial life.

Throughout the main chapters, we've told stories, shared strategies, and walked through the thinking of doctors, engineers, teachers, and business owners just like you. But reading is one thing—**application is another**. If you want results, you need to get hands-on. These worksheets, calculators, and quick guides are your opportunity to do just that.

I often say financial planning is like driving on Michigan roads: potholes appear when you least expect them. If you don't patch them early, you'll be paying for a new set of tires—or worse, a new suspension. With these tools, you can spot cracks before they widen, take corrective action, and keep your retirement vehicle running smoothly for the long haul.

So grab a pencil, pour yourself a cup of coffee (or something stronger, if you're staring at your tax return), and let's get to work.

1. RIPT Self-Assessment: Your Financial Dashboard

Every strong financial plan rests on four pillars: **Risk, Income, Portfolio, and Taxes**—what we call the RIPT framework. Think of it like the dashboard of your car. If one gauge is flashing red while the others look fine, you're not going to make it far down the road. This self-assessment lets you step back and ask: *Where am I strong, and where am I exposed?*

Step 1: Rate Yourself Honestly

On a scale of 1 to 10 (1 = "needs major work," 10 = "rock solid"), rate each pillar. Don't sugarcoat—this isn't a grade to show anyone else. Be as candid as a mechanic inspecting his own brakes.

- **Risk:** How comfortable are you with market ups and downs? If the S&P drops 20 percent, do you shrug and say, "That's investing," or do you lose sleep and swear off CNBC?
    - *Story Example:* Alex, a retired auto worker, scored himself a 9—until he lived through March 2020. When his account dropped $150,000 in two weeks, his real score was closer to a 4. The worksheet helped him reset, rebalance, and sleep again.
- **Income:** Do you have a reliable retirement paycheck, or are you cobbling it together year by year? Social Security may cover 30–40 percent, but what about the rest? Do you know exactly where the shortfall is coming from?
    - *Case Study:* Mandy, a retired teacher, discovered her pension plus Social Security covered only 52 percent of her needs. Using this assessment, she clearly saw how she needed a guaranteed source of another $2,000/month. That realization led to adding an annuity account that filled the gap.
- **Portfolio:** Is your money working efficiently, or is it bleeding fees like an old roof leaking after every storm? ETFs, mutual funds, stocks, bonds—all have different costs and roles. Do you know what you're paying?
    - *Tip:* If you can't answer this within 60 seconds, you probably don't know.
- **Taxes:** Are you managing taxes or letting them manage you? This pillar trips up more smart people than any other. The IRS already has a claim on part of your savings—the question is, how much?
    - *Real-Life Example:* Roger (our marina friend from Chapter 12) scored himself a 5 here, then used this exercise to realize his future RMDs would shove him into a higher bracket. That knowledge let him start Roth conversions earlier.

Step 2: Record Your Action Steps

After you rate yourself, don't stop. Write down *one action step* for each area that scored below a 7. Examples:

- **Risk:** Calculate your Nitrogen Risk Number and align your portfolio to it.
- **Income:** Compare your guaranteed vs. variable income streams and explore how to cover gaps.
- **Portfolio:** List your holdings and note their expense ratios; flag anything over 0.50 percent.
- **Taxes:** Run a projection of RMDs and explore converting $25k/year into Roth.

Step 3: Review Annually

Plans age quickly—tax laws change, markets move, life throws curveballs. Make this self-assessment an annual tradition. It's like changing the oil: cheap, easy, and vital for long-term performance.

2. Compound Interest Calculator: Watch Time Work Its Magic

Albert Einstein supposedly called compound interest the "eighth wonder of the world." Whether or not he really said it, the truth remains: time is the greatest multiplier in finance. The earlier you start, the lighter the lift.

Imagine two engineers:

- Travis, age 30, puts $200/month into a simple investment account earning 7 percent after inflation.
- Christina, his colleague, waits until she's 40 to start, investing the exact same $200/month.

By the time they're both 65, Travis ends up with roughly $250,000, while Christina has only $120,000. Same monthly contribution, but the difference—$130,000—is the price of waiting. That's a cabin up north or college tuition for a grandchild.

Step-by-Step Exercise:

1. Plug your own numbers into the formula or an online calculator:
   Future Value = P * (((1 + r)^n - 1) / r)
   - P = monthly contribution
   - r = annual return ÷ 12
   - n = number of years × 12
2. Create a table for yourself:
   - Start Age | Monthly Contribution | Years to Grow | Ending Value
   - Compare starting now vs. five or ten years later.
3. Adjust: If the projection falls short, don't despair. Add $50–$100/month and rerun the numbers. Small changes create massive differences when compounded.

Pro Tip: Automate your savings so it never relies on willpower. The less you "feel" the contribution, the more consistent you'll be.
Pitfall: Don't stop contributions during downturns. Bear markets are like a clearance sale—your dollars buy more shares at lower prices.

3. Inflation Impact Tracker: Spot the Silent Thief

Inflation is retirement's invisible enemy. You don't notice it year to year, but over decades it eats like rust through steel.

Take Beth, a retired nurse in Livonia. She budgeted $500/month for groceries when she stopped working in 2010. By 2025, that same basket cost her $820. Multiply that across healthcare, housing, and utilities, and suddenly her "comfortable" retirement felt squeezed.

Step-by-Step Exercise:

1. List your current annual expenses (groceries, healthcare, housing, leisure).
2. Apply a 3.2 percent annual inflation rate—close to the long-term U.S. average.
3. Project 10, 20, and 30 years forward.

For example:

Year	Starting Value	Buying Power at 3.2 percent
0	$100,000	$100,000
10	$100,000	$74,000
20	$100,000	$55,000

What feels abundant today shrinks by half in 20 years.

Action Step: If projections show your buying power falling below 60 percent, consider shifting part of your portfolio into equities or inflation-protected securities like TIPS.
Pro Tip: Healthcare inflation often runs hotter than general inflation. Plan for 5–6 percent increases in medical costs, not 3 percent.
Pitfall: Believing that "bonds are always safe." Safe from volatility, perhaps, but not from erosion by inflation.

4. Social Security Optimization Checklist: One Tool, Not the Box

Remember, Social Security is important, but it's not your whole retirement plan. On average, it covers only 30–40 percent of retirement income needs. Yet too many retirees treat it as the foundation rather than one of several beams.

Consider Nick and Isabelle, both born in 1960. Nick filed at 62, locking in $1,500/month. Isabelle waited until 70, receiving $2,640/month. Over their lifetimes, Isabelle will collect more than $200,000 extra just by waiting. That's the power of an 8 percent per year delay credit.

Your Checklist:
- **Full Retirement Age (FRA):** Know yours. For anyone born 1960 or later, it's 67.
- **Delay Strategy:** Each year you delay beyond FRA adds 8 percent to your benefit, up to age 70.
- **Spousal/Survivor Benefits:** Don't overlook them. A surviving spouse can receive 100 percent of the higher earner's benefit.
- **Taxes:** Up to 85 percent of your benefit may be taxable depending on your provisional income.

Step-by-Step Exercise:
1. Go to ssa.gov/myaccount and print your statement.
2. Write down your FRA benefit.
3. Calculate the difference between filing at 62, FRA, and 70.
4. Compare the break-even age (usually around 78–80). If you expect longevity, waiting often pays.

Pro Tip: Coordinating spousal benefits is one of the most overlooked strategies. Run the numbers for both, not just individually.

Pitfall: Filing early out of fear. Once you file, there's no do-over (beyond a one-time 12-month withdrawal option).

5. Legacy Tax Bomb Calculator: Passing Wealth, Not Burdens

The SECURE Act changed the rules of inheritance. If your kids inherit an IRA, they must drain it within 10 years. That's not a gift—it's a tax time bomb.

Take Dorothy, a widow in Midland with a $500,000 IRA. Her sons, both engineers in the 32 percent bracket, would owe about $160,000 in taxes over a decade. That's a third of her husband's life savings lost to the IRS.

We have a place for you:
1. Go to www.maintaxbill.com
2. Following the on-screen instructions
   a. It will need your age
   b. How much you have in your 401k and/or IRA account
   c. What tax bracket you want to use
   d. What rate of return you anticipate your account will do over time

Action Step: If the tax hit exceeds 20 percent, explore partial Roth conversions. A $500,000 IRA converted strategically could save heirs six figures.

Pro Tip: Consider pairing Roth conversions with life insurance (second-to-die policies). This can pass wealth tax-free while covering the cost of taxes you pay now.

Pitfall: Ignoring estate planning until it's too late. Without proactive planning, the IRS—not your heirs—becomes your biggest beneficiary.

6. Expanded Quick-Reference Glossary: Your Jargon Buster

Here's where we go deeper. Instead of a short list, let's make this a true "financial dictionary" for readers.

- **RIPT Framework:** Risk, Income, Portfolio, Taxes—the four dials on your financial dashboard.
- **Sequence of Returns Risk:** The danger of poor market performance early in retirement. Imagine climbing a ladder in the rain—the first few rungs are where you're most likely to slip.
- **Roth Conversion:** Paying tax now to avoid bigger taxes later. Like prepaying for gas when you know prices are going up.
- **Fixed-indexed annuity:** A contract that protects your principal while giving upside linked to a market index. Think of it as a seatbelt: you may not hit top speed, but you won't crash either.
- **Required Minimum Distributions (RMDs):** Forced withdrawals from IRAs after age 73 (as of 2025). Miss them and the penalty can be 25 percent—one of the harshest in the tax code.
- **Monte Carlo Simulation:** A computer model that runs thousands of "what if" market scenarios to test the durability of your plan. Engineers love this one.

MONTE CARLO SIMULATION

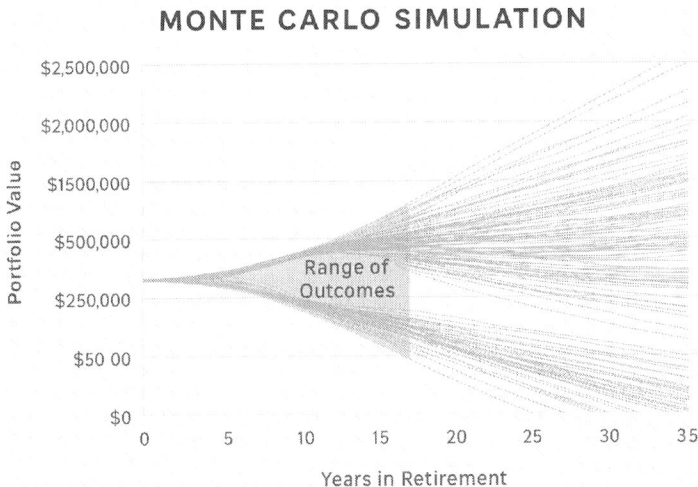

Source: Author's own calculations.

- **Liquidity Risk:** The danger of not being able to access cash when you need it. You don't want all your money tied up in assets you can't touch
- **Tax Diversification:** Spreading savings across taxable, tax-deferred, and tax-free accounts. The financial equivalent of not putting all your eggs in one basket.
- **FOMO (Fear of Missing Out):** The psychological trap of chasing trends. In investing, it often ends in buying high and selling low.

CLOSING THOUGHT

This appendix isn't just filler—it's your take-home kit. Like a set of blueprints, it shows you where to measure, where to cut, and where to reinforce. If even one of these tools helps you uncover a blind spot or avoid a mistake, it will have paid for itself many times over.

Your future self—and your family—will thank you.

REFERENCES

Hey, folks—Jordan here, like that teacher who always cited sources so you knew the homework wasn't pulled from thin air. This book's backed by real research, no smoke and mirrors. Here's the list, organized by chapter for easy digging—URLs where available, because transparency's key, like a fiduciary laying out fees (Chapter Nine). We've cited 'em inline, but this pulls it all together. Dig in if you want; it's your plan, after all.

Introduction & General
- BlackRock. (2025). Read on Retirement Survey. Retrieved from https://www.blackrock.com/us/individual/insights/retirement/read-on-retirement-survey
- Bureau of Labor Statistics (BLS). (2025). Consumer Price Index Historical Data, 1920-2025. Retrieved from https://www.bls.gov/cpi/

Chapter One: The Education Edge
- National Financial Educators Council. (2023, updated 2025). Financial Literacy Statistics. Retrieved from https://financialeducatorscouncil.org/financial-literacy-statistics/
- Morningstar. (2025). Advisor Fee Disclosure Report. Retrieved from https://www.morningstar.com/
- SEC. (2022, updated 2025). Investor Bulletin: Fees Impact. Retrieved from https://www.sec.gov/investor/pubs/feeimpact

Chapter Two: Climbing the Money Mountain
- Vanguard. (2025). Compound Interest Calculator. Retrieved from https://investor.vanguard.com/calculators
- Investment Company Institute. (2025). ETF Expense Ratios Report. Retrieved from https://www.ici.org/
- Fidelity. (2025). Market Timing Study. Retrieved from https://www.fidelity.com/

Chapter Three: Getting Down Safely

- Investopedia. (2025). Sequence of Returns Risk Guide. Retrieved from https://www.investopedia.com/terms/s/sequence-risk.asp
- Fidelity. (2025). Retiree Health Care Cost Estimate. Retrieved from https://www.fidelity.com/viewpoints/retirement/retiree-medical-expenses
- Transamerica. (2025). Retirement Survey. Retrieved from https://www.transamericacenter.org/

Chapter Four: Driving at Your Speed

- Morningstar. (2025). Risk Tolerance Study. Retrieved from https://www.morningstar.com/
- Julius Baer. (2025). Risk Levels Report. Retrieved from https://www.juliusbaer.com/

Chapter Five: Outsmarting Uncle Sam

- IRS. (2025). Tax Brackets and Rates. Retrieved from https://www.irs.gov/taxtopics/tc551
- Vanguard. (2025). Tax-Efficient Strategies. Retrieved from https://investor.vanguard.com/
- Tax Foundation. (2025). TCJA Sunset Analysis. Retrieved from https://taxfoundation.org/

Chapter Six: Beating the Inflation Monster

- Bureau of Labor Statistics (BLS). (2025). CPI Historical Data. Retrieved from https://www.bls.gov/cpi/
- Treasury.gov. (2025). TIPS Yields. Retrieved from https://home.treasury.gov/policy-issues/financing-the-government/interest-rate-statistics

Chapter Seven: Social Security Smarts

- Social Security Administration (SSA). (2025). Trustees Report. Retrieved from https://www.ssa.gov/oact/TR/2025/
- AARP. (2025). Social Security Survey. Retrieved from https://www.aarp.org/retirement/social-security/

Chapter Eight: The Great Wealth Transfer

- Cerulli Associates. (2025). Wealth Transfer Report. Retrieved from https://www.cerulli.com/
- Kiplinger. (2025). Inherited IRA Tax Guide. Retrieved from https://www.kiplinger.com/

Chapter Nine: The Second Opinion That Saves

- Fidelity. (2025). Second Opinion Benefits Study. Retrieved from https://www.fidelity.com/
- Rethinking65.com. (2025). Annuity Fee Analysis. Retrieved from https://rethinking65.com/

Chapter Ten: The LIST of Dangers

- Genworth. (2025). Cost of Care Survey. Retrieved from https://www.genworth.com/aging-and-you/finances/cost-of-care.html
- World Economic Forum. (2025). Longevity Risks Report. Retrieved from https://www.weforum.org/

Chapter Eleven: Tools in the Toolbox

- LIMRA. (2025). Annuity Sales Report. Retrieved from https://www.limra.com/
- Morningstar. (2025). Variable Annuity Fee Study. Retrieved from https://www.morningstar.com/

Bonus Chapter: Top 10 Mistakes

- Northwestern Mutual. (2025). Planning & Progress Study. Retrieved from https://www.northwesternmutual.com/
- CoinDesk. (2025). Crypto Volatility Retrospective. Retrieved from https://www.coindesk.com/

This wraps our references—dig in if you want more; it's all there for transparency. Thanks for the ride; here's to your well-rounded plan turning retirement into the bestseller it deserves.

ABOUT THE AUTHOR

JORDAN D. MAIN is an investment advisor representative, RFC® , and President of Main Financial Group Wealth Management, a full-service financial firm serving residents of Michigan and beyond. His mission is simple: to provide the education, tools, and personalized strategies you need to build a secure retirement. Raised in a family of teachers, Jordan has always believed in the power of education—a value that drives every aspect of his work. He has spent the last 30 years earning multiple licenses and certifications in the fields of Investments, Insurance, Accounting and Taxation. His approach to planning blends rigorous financial expertise with genuine community values to help hardworking individuals pursue the futures they envision.

After earning his bachelor's degree from Michigan State University, Jordan launched his career in accounting, collaborating with stockbrokers and financial advisors. Seeing significant shortcomings in the industry, he shifted toward financial advising—focusing on effective tax strategies to help clients retain more of their hard-earned money. Today, his Series 65 license enables him to serve as a fiduciary, guiding clients with transparency and diligence in the allocation of their portfolios. His firm, Main Financial Group, stands as a testament to his unwavering commitment to everyday Americans, combining Wall Street insights with Main Street integrity for a well-rounded plan in retirement.

A proud Spartan, Jordan lives in Brighton with his wife, Emily, and their daughter, Anniston. His son Jacob follows in his father's footsteps at Michigan State University.

CONTACT INFO:
Main Financial Group
mfgwm.com
248-347-MAIN (6246)

DISCLOSURES

The stories and characters in this book are inspired by real clients and real-life scenarios. To protect confidentiality, identifying details have been changed, and in some cases, multiple experiences have been combined into a single narrative to highlight the lessons in each chapter. These examples are intended as educational tools and should not be taken as specific recommendations for any individual situation. Readers should always consult their own tax, legal, and financial professionals before taking action.

Investment advisory services are offered through Foundations Investment Advisers, LLC, an SEC-registered investment adviser. The content provided is intended for informational and educational purposes only. The views, statements, and opinions expressed herein are those of the author and not necessarily those of Foundations and its affiliates. Foundations deems reliable any statistical data or information obtained from or prepared by third party sources cited in this book but in no way guarantees its accuracy or completeness. Any past performance is no guarantee of future results. Advisory services are only offered to clients or prospective clients where Foundations and its advisors are properly licensed or exempted.

A Roth conversion may not be suitable for your situation. The primary goal in converting retirement assets into a Roth IRA is to reduce the future tax liability on the distributions you take in retirement, or on the distributions of your beneficiaries. The information provided is to help you determine whether or not a Roth IRA conversion may be appropriate for your particular circumstances. Please review your retirement savings, tax, and legacy planning strategies with your legal/tax advisor to be sure a Roth IRA conversion fits into your planning strategies.

This book is not endorsed or affiliated with the Social Security Administration, any federal Medicare program, nor any U.S. government agency. If applicable, we do not offer every plan available in your area. Any information we provide is limited to those plans we do offer in your area. Please contact Medicare.gov or 1-800-MEDICARE to get information on all of your options.

Although great effort has been expended to ensure that only the most meaningful resources are referenced in these pages, the author does not endorse, guarantee, or warranty the accuracy, reliability, or thoroughness of any referenced information, product, or service. The views expressed herein are exclusively those of the author and do not represent the views of any other person or any organization with which the author is or may be associated.

.